FRONT RUNNERS

FRONT RUNNERS

The First Athletic Track Champions

Warren Roe

The Book Guild Ltd
Sussex, England

Picture Credits

The author and publishers wish to thank the following for permission to reproduce the images on the pages listed:

Reproduced by permission of the British Library.
12, 14, 17, 20, 25, 29, 31, 32, 39, 41, 46, 50, 54, 56, 58, 59, 63, 66, 71, 74, 78, 81, 82, 84, 86, 90, 96, 100, 103, 106, 108, 110, 113, 118, 120, 129, 130, 136, 141.

Reproduced by permission of Hackney Archives Department, London Borough of Hackney.
80, 89, 92, 95, 101, 114, 115, 145, 149, 150, 151, 154, 162.

Reproduced by permission of Tower Hamlets Borough Local History Library and Archives.
80.

Reproduced by permission of Wandsworth Museum, London Borough of Wandsworth.
67.

Reproduced from Ordnance Survey Maps 1873 and 1890.
11, 167.

First published in Great Britain in 2002 by
The Book Guild Ltd
25 High Street
Lewes, East Sussex
BN7 2LU

Typesetting in Times by
Acorn Bookwork, Salisbury, Wiltshire

Printed in Great Britain by
Bookcraft (Bath) Ltd, Avon

A catalogue record for this book is available from
The British Library.

ISBN 1 85776 655 5

CONTENTS

ILLUSTRATIONS

BIOGRAPHIES

BIOGRAPHIES

FOREWORD FROM SEBASTIAN COE

In my experience, publications dealing with the history of athletics in the nineteenth century are not particularly evident in public libraries or on private bookshelves. *Front Runners* should go some way to changing this. It is informative and interesting and will be of value not only to athletics enthusiasts, but also to social and sporting historians, as well as local archivists.

The book sheds light on a period prior to Baron Pierre de Coubertin's resurrection of an amateur Olympic Games. It illuminates an age of crowd pulling professional athletics events, which could be seen as the forerunner of today's IAAF Grand Prix circuit. The tensions arising from the opposing codes were not to be eased for a century or more.

Athletes past and present will find the performances described of particular interest, bearing in mind the understanding of diet, the knowledge of medical factors, physiology and the general standards of health that prevailed in the mid-nineteenth century. Athletes who have run on cinder tracks will have some understanding of what the runners encountered. The description of the race over ten miles, in July 1863, between Lang and Mills may raise a smile of recognition among a few 'vets'.

Those interested in history will be drawn to the exploits of Deerfoot, more particularly the historical context. His appearance at Hackney Wick in front of 9000 spectators, took place little more than half a century after Lewis and Clark's 'expedition of discovery', in the middle of the Civil War, three years prior to a fellow Seneca Indian witnessing Lee's surrender to Grant – was Deerfoot a pioneer?

The preview of this event in *The Sporting Life* and the wording of the handbill, with references to 'the Crowcatcher', the 'Redoubtable Indian', 'Paleface' and 'Good Men and True', evoke an atmosphere not always evident from primary sources.

I have enjoyed this book immensely.

INTRODUCTION

In the early Victorian period, beyond the few universities and public schools, athletics was an entirely professional sport. The runners and walkers who participated in professional matches were known as 'pedestrians' and the sport as 'pedestrianism'.

Walter Rye, an early secretary of London Athletic Club whose members trained at Bow and Brompton, described the difficulties for pedestrians competing on running tracks in London during these years in the following words:

LONDON RUNNING TRACKS IN THE 1860s

From Walter Rye's 'The Champion Sports. A prophecy', written in 1868.
Published in *Rubbish and Nonsense* in 1887

A broken paling, a grass grown pathway,
A dressing room ravaged, a grand stand gone,
I saw in a dream, and I knew it was Brompton,
And for a lost running ground cried out forlorn.

Ah, woe on the spread of bricks and mortar;
We soon shall have never a training place left.
The 'Old Cope' has vanished, and Garrett Lane's built on,
And now, beloved Brompton, of you we are bereft.

There's no place to run at, for Bow is too stinking,
A mile round the 'Wick' is seven laps and a bit.
No more may we hope to produce a good runner,
How the deuces can a Londoner hope to get fit?

In 1991 Tony Ward wrote a book entitled *Athletics, The Golden Decade*. However, there was a decade some 120 years earlier, the 1860s, when British athletes were leading the world and breaking records with equal frequency. They were the 'pedestrians' – and despite the sad state of the running tracks in London during the 1860s described so vividly by Walter Rye, many magnificent performances were accomplished. Possibly the greatest was by John White over six miles, a British record that was not to be beaten for 73 years! Even the great Olympic runner Paavo Nurmi could not better the time until 1921.

When research for this book first began it was my intention that it be a history of one of the most famous running tracks; the Metropolitan Running Ground at the White Lion public house, Hackney Wick. However, it soon became apparent that to do justice to the subject, it would not be possible to write about Hackney Wick in isolation. In order to present a more complete picture, other pedestrian achievements of this decade of major record breaking by middle and long distance pedestrians on the running path would have to be included; hence the content of this present book. The concentration is on middle and long distance running because this was the mainstay at the 'Wick' (which remains the theme of the book) and these were the events that attracted the crowds. The Hackney Wick grounds were not suitable for sprinting and when sprint races were staged they were rarely well supported.

Over a period of ten years virtually every top middle and long distance pedestrian of the era competed at Hackney Wick, producing a series of races that included a number of British (World) Records. In this book the many records that were set are generally referred to as British Records, although they were effectively World Records with only Britain, Ireland, North America and Australia having organised track running at this time. The NUTS *Statistical History of UK Track & Field Athletics* edited by Andrew Huxtable has been used as the definitive work for these records although *Sporting Life* has been used as the primary source and this sometimes differs from the NUTS book by the odd ¼ or ½ second. *Sporting Life* also includes a number of performances unrecorded or unaccepted by Huxtable. If the times are reported by both *Sporting Life* and *Bell's Life* and cast no doubt as to authenticity I have included them.

The story follows the history of the various championship cups and belts at distances from one to ten miles, at Hackney Wick and other running venues.

Commencing in 1861 times were taken on a very accurate Benson's Marking Chronometer first bought by *Sporting Life* in October 1861. In their editorial dated 12 October, they praised the work of Mr Benson, a noted watch manufacturer of Ludgate Hill.

> 'Amid all the pompous announcements of what newspaper proprietors are going to do on the repeal of the paper duty, the public have become somewhat confused, and judging from the tone of letters from a number of correspondents, an idea seems to have been entertained that the *Sporting Life*, a glass of ale, and a sandwich would be obtainable for a penny. We did not even make our journal four times the usual size, but simply bought ourselves something. An immense sum has been spent in new type, and now we have bought ourselves a watch, such has never before been manufactured, and more perfect than ever left the workman's hands. The timing of races involves many disputes, and, upon the fluctuation of a moment, thousands

may be said to depend. Impressed with the necessity of recording unimpeachably the duration of matches or races, whether on the turf, on the river, or pedestrian running ground; we have purchased, at a cost of fifty guineas, a watch of such beautiful, and even marvellous perfection, that it might almost be described as a perpetual reporter, chronicling undeviatingly and dotting down on its face as fast as the holder may wish, the precise instant at which any succession of moments require noting. For the first time in the history of horology, a watch has been invented, which by a simultaneous and imperceptible action, the second hand being charged with a black fluid, writes down the instant at which an event is commenced and completed without stoppage or interruption of the ordinary working.

For so beautiful an invention as this, Mr Benson deserves the thanks of all lovers of sport, and for the future, by the instrumentality, all great races and matches will be timed by it, and our paper will be regarded as the scrupulous authority on all questions of time, while no practical sporting man should be without this novel and valuable companion.'

From January 1862 the watch was generally available and Mr Benson's advertisement read:

BENSON'S WATCHES AND CLOCKS
'Perfection of mechanism.' – *Morning Post*

To the sporting public and all interested in pursuits who require the time (exact to one-tenth of a second), to be marked which elapses between two or any number of events, Mr. Benson wishes to introduce his new 'Chronograph' watch, as manufactured for the *Sporting Life* (see *Sporting Life*, Oct. 12). This is so called from the fact of the long second-hand dotting the dial at the will of the holder, without stopping the watch. Thus a watch can be observed, and the time at which the competitors come in, be accurately marked down, without the attention being once distracted from the race. Its advantage over the old style stopwatch is at once evident.

BENSON'S CHRONOGRAPH WATCH – 'No practical sporting man should be without this novel and valuable companion.' – *Sporting Life*

Silver ...... £42 Gold ...... £52.10s.
James W. Benson, 33 and 34, Ludgate Hill, or 46 and 47, Cornhill, E.C.
Established 1749.

By the 1860s running tracks were firmly established, primarily at public houses but also at cricket and pleasure grounds, and with accurate stopwatches professional records that are recognised today were being established. With today's professional athletics there seems to be no reason why the professional records of the past should not stand shoulder to shoulder with their amateur counterparts.

The history of athletics in the United Kingdom, in the eyes of many people, started with the public schools and universities and the contribution of the pedestrians throughout the nineteenth century is sadly all too often overlooked. In this small volume it is intended to rectify some of these omissions and acknowledge the athletic standards and major contribution that the sportsmen mentioned achieved, to place the United Kingdom in the forefront of world athletics development.

Many of the early amateur middle distance champions were either trained or advised by pedestrians of the day. Walter Chinnery of the London Athletic Club (L.A.C.), who was the Amateur Athletic Club ('A.A.C.', forerunner of the Amateur Athletic Association) one and four miles champion in 1868 and 1869, took advice from Edward Mills. James Gibb, also of the London Athletic Club, the A.A.C. four miles champion in 1875, 1877 and 1878 was guided by John White, as was Sid Thomas the UK three and six mile record holder in the 1890s. John White, one of the greatest pedestrians of all time eventually went on to coach at Cambridge University and was officially employed by the L.A.C. with whom he travelled with the 1895 team that met New York Athletic Club in New York.

Another London Athletic Club member, Walter Slade, the A.A.C. one mile champion from 1873 to 1877, was trained by Bob Rogers, the one mile pedestrian champion of London, who was the first trainer at the L.A.C., and frequently acted as their starter. The celebrated William Lang was the trainer behind the success of James Edgar from the Isle of Man who won the A.A.C. one mile championship in 1872. Nat Perry, possibly the most famous of all nineteenth-century trainers, was an ex-pedestrian employed as groundsman at Stamford Bridge, where among others, he trained the L.A.C. athlete James Cowie to the A.A.A. 100 yards championship in the years from 1883 to 1885 and the 440 yards in 1883 and 1884.

Other pedestrians involved in training amateurs during these years included Harry Andrews who lived in Fulham and trained runners at the nearby Star Grounds and Beaufort House Grounds. John Brighton coached amateurs at the Middlesex Running Ground in Islington and later at the Tufnell Park Grounds.

Another who bridged the gap between professional and amateur athletes was John MacDonald. MacDonald, an accomplished amateur miler, was a solicitor in Cambridge who frequently ran at professional grounds. He ran at Sheffield against Deerfoot in November 1861 and was influential in bringing him to run at Cambridge the following month. Any prize money he won in professional races he donated to amateur events in Cambridge. It was because of his racing against professionals that he was in full touch with the training of pedestrians such as Westhall, Lang, Mills and White, which allowed him to train non-university athletes in Cambridge.

There were undoubtedly many others but this gives some insight into the contribution of these pedestrians in setting high standards themselves and being of the utmost assistance to the new amateur sport.

There are a number of reports from *Sporting Life* that are quoted verbatim. This is in an endeavour to bring more colour to the narrative, although sometimes showing the seedier side of pedestrianism as expressed in the following report dated September 1863:

> On the 7th of September last, two men, Ambrose Davis and Charles Thompson, both of Billingsgate, appeared at the Bow Running Grounds, to run one mile, for £10 aside. The match was entered into in the usual way, and the articles and stakes were deposited in our hands. On the day mentioned above, both men appeared to run, but it was evident that Thompson could not win, so a plan was determined upon to deprive Davis of his money. The 'game' was to refuse to agree to any referee who was likely to give an impartial decision in case of a dispute, and endeavour to make a draw of it, but Davis, rather than not run, agreed to a man as referee who was a partisan of Thompson's. The men started, and Davis, in endeavouring to pass Thompson, was deliberately run against by the latter, for the purpose of throwing him down. In this, however, Thompson did not succeed, but he himself fell. The interested referee then rushed up, and, without any appeal, awarded the race, in his fashion, to Thompson. Davis, in the meantime, ran the distance. The manifest unfairness of Thompson's conduct was observed by many persons on the ground, including our reporter and the proprietor and manager of the grounds, and Davis waited upon us a day or two afterwards, and requested us not to give up the stakes. Subsequently, we heard the evidence brought before us, and as a means of settlement proposed that the men should run over again. To this Thompson's principal backer refused to agree, and demanded payment of the money. As we did not think it proper to be parties to such a disgraceful business, we declined to comply with the request, but ordered the men, on our own responsibility, to meet again and run on the following Monday. This we considered fair to both parties. Thompson did not show, and Davis ran over the course by himself, and we paid him the stakes. Thompson, upon this, commenced an action against us,

which was heard yesterday in the Lord Mayor's Court, and Thompson was non-suited. We have contested the matter on principle, although perhaps it has cost us more than the whole value of the stakes; we are determined in every case to carry out what is fair and just. It seems to be the impression among a certain class that they only have to 'square' a referee to get the stakes; but the proceedings yesterday will, we hope, serve as a warning to those who are not particular how they gain their ends.

Fortunately it is possible to say that this was an infrequent happening and in the main the top pedestrians, their managers and the proprietors of the running grounds were men of principle.

On occasions the reliability and objectivity of correspondents was also brought into question as expressed in the letter published in *Sporting Life* in January 1861 – no different from the present day!

Sir,

Knowing, that you are ever willing to assist 'right' against 'might,' I have taken the liberty to forward you the enclosed lines. I have latterly seen in the columns of your valuable paper a letter from Beddow, the guardsman complaining of an attempt made in the columns of Bells Life to defame his character, and I have since seen a letter from the correspondent of that paper, attempting to defend himself in the attack. Now, sir, in the first place, it is well known in Manchester, that there are certain 'cliques' that can have anything they require to suit their nefarious ends. In proof of which you will find in Bells Life of Jan 6, in the description of Beddow and Lang's race, the following rich bit: – 'We have seen sufficient of Lang to note him down as an excellent pedestrian – though now and then a defeated one – but his attempt (and one of his latest) against Sanderson, of Whitworth, near Rochdale, must not be taken into account, inasmuch as Lang himself, to prevent the backer being tricked, openly admitted that he made no effort to win.' Now, sir, I am positive there has been no one that knows it was a complete 'sell,' Lang giving up when it was 'York' to a 'China orange' on him. The cause of which was that it was 5 to 4 on him against the field. Lang's principal backer at the time staking the odds to a good sum, and placing it in the hands of the 'major domo,' known as Legs, near the 'Sun,' this sum being actually paid over before the race, so that the worthies might victimise the public with it on the ground. In the same paragraph you will find the following, speaking of Beddow and Cox: – 'As to his engagement at Salford we will not here refer, because the least said about it the better, he then permitting Cox, of Coventry to triumph.' I think, sir, you will agree with me, and so will a number of your readers, that there is a great difference in the style of these sentences, and show that there is a leaning to one side. It is also well known that the 'correspondent' does not attend one half the races himself, but goes from hearsay, and should he put in an appearance he is in such a state of 'beer' that it accounts for the immense number of 'fogs' you will, find chronicled in his description of the races. I know that he was not present at all at the race between Cox and Beddow, about which he has so much to say. There is also another thing that I would call to your attention to, which is, that if you have an advertisement you must pay double to him for it to what you can get it inserted if you send it direct to yourself in London. In conclusion, I would say to him, as the servant of a mighty organ – 'Do justice to all, show favour to none, for the day of reckoning is nigh at hand.'

I remain, Yours truly,
Albert Smith.

Again I think this was in general an unusual occurrence, and I hope this book does 'do justice' to the spirited pedestrians of the nineteenth century and the records that in some cases were to remain unbeaten well into the next century.

Warren Roe

SPORTING LIFE, SATURDAY, 9 MAY 1863

HACKNEY WICK.
THE LAST RACE OF DEERFOOT IN ENGLAND
THE ENGLISH CHAMPIONS

On Monday next, May 11, at the above famous grounds, adjoining the Victoria Park Station, the last race of the Seneca Indian in England will take place, on which occasion he will contend against the very *elite* of English Champions, as the following list will sufficiently demonstrate, namely. – Lang (Crowcatcher), The Ten Miles Champion; Mills (Young England), Six Miles Champion; J. White (the Gateshead Clipper); Brighton (the Milkboy), Four Miles Champion; Stapleton, One Mile Champion; the indomitable Sam Barker; the unwearying Harry Andrews; and the speedy Welshman, W. Richards. The genuineness of the affair is best understood by the fact that the prize to be contended is open to all, free, and the fine trophy, one of the most splendid belts ever yet produced, will be the property of the victor the moment he first passes the goal. Money prizes will also be awarded to the fourth in the race, an incentive for the gallant fleetfoots to persevere, so that the most exciting race of any period will be the result. The whole of the above first-rates have arrived in the neighbourhood, and surely but truly have been trying to the uttermost to get fit. The order is to get first and keep first, and when all so strive the result is foreknown. For this once, and this once only, Deerfoot has trained. He has run over eleven miles and a half in the hour, ten miles in 51 min. 26 sec. (the fastest on record), and at twelve miles was only defeated by the Crowcatcher by a bare yard. Of Lang's pretensions, no comment is necessary; whether his *rider* will pull him double, and only let him out if needed, will be seen; he must be near if meant. Mills's chance, if fit, his friends would consider treason to doubt. The Norwich Milkboy is much fancied by his friends, but the Gateshead Clipper has come with a rush in the market, and in the betting is within a shade of the Indian himself. Like the *Gow Chrom*, 'he does battle for his own hand,' and wary must Indian and Englishman be of John White. Stapleton, although One Mile Champion, it is thought may prove another Lang at the distance (ten miles), and hence his position in the betting. Of Sam Barker, it can only be said that they who oppose him must not linger on the road; he is backed heavily for 'place,' and it would not surprise us if he is near, or not before third. A prize out of the four is a *moral* for Old Harry Andrews, and the speedy Welshman will make the pace a cracker for the 'stable.' Large sums depend upon the issue, and 'making a book' at Carthage, the 'back of breweries,' and even at the 'Corner,' has been brisk, the following being the latest odds, which we now quote: –

2 to 1 agst Deerfoot	5 to 2 agst Mills
2 to 1 agst Lang	6 to 1 agst Stapleton
5 to 2 agst White	8 to 1 agst any other

33 to 15 each against Lang or Deerfoot, and at a short point above that price the Indian for choice.

PLACE BETTING

3 to 1 agst Barker	5 to 1 agst Andrews

An even 'tenner' was taken that both Richards and Stapleton go the distance, and £5 that the Welshman is one of the first four. The start will take place at six o'clock precisely on Monday next. Special trains will run, as usual, and many are expected from Manchester, Sheffield etc. Mr Baum has made an immense preparation, and an early attendance is respectfully requested ...

1

1857–1859, Early Years at Hackney Wick

An uncertain start

In the early Victorian period athletics was an entirely professional sport beyond the few universities and public schools. The runners and walkers who participated in these professional matches were known as pedestrians and the sport as pedestrianism. It was a sport organised predominantly from public houses and among the most famous in London were the Spotted Dog in the Strand managed by Thomas Wilson and the Proud Peacock in Covent Garden managed by Jesse Smith. Matches were generally made between two men as a result of a challenge for a monetary stake. 'Articles of Agreement' would be signed with the publican frequently acting as stakeholder and referee. The events were held mainly on the turnpike roads where reasonably accurate measurement was available between the milestones.

However, the police gradually pushed pedestrians off the public highways where they frequently attracted large and disorderly crowds, and during the late 1840s and 1850s dozens of running paths attached to public houses, pleasure gardens and cricket grounds were established in the metropolis and major industrial cities. Many of the tracks were unfortunately short-lived, closing for a variety of reasons, and by the late 1850s many had disappeared.

Noted London grounds which closed during this period included the track around John Garratt's cricket ground at Copenhagen House in Islington in 1853, following storm damage, the Flora Tea Gardens in Bayswater in 1853, after an Old Bailey trial concerning a conspiracy to fix races, and the Royal Oak Grounds, Barking Road near Canning Town in 1855. All these venues had hosted famous races in their heyday. Among the many which had closed in the late 1840s were the Beehive Ground in Walworth, the Rosemary Branch Ground in Peckham and, for a time, Lord's cricket ground in St. John's Wood, although the last two sites continued as cricket grounds.

Virtually the only track remaining by 1857 was Robert Sadler's famous, or should it be infamous, New Surrey Pedestrian Ground opened in 1853 next to the Wellington Inn in Garratt Lane, Wandsworth. Infamous in that there were a number of notable 'barneys' there; probably the most well known when William Jackson was matched to run against a Tonnawanda American Indian only for the disgusted spectators to find it was an impudent 'sell' organised solely for a rich harvest of gate money and that the Indian was in fact a Piccadilly crossing sweeper! This ground had a squarish path with sharp corners measuring 307 yards in length until transformed to a 440-yard oval in 1859.

Fortunately the decline began to reverse in December 1857 when James Baum, the proprietor of the White Lion in Wick Lane, created a new venue at Hackney Wick. In the one acre grounds of the public house, his father John Baum, who had been landlord from about 1825 until his son took over, had already developed a reputation for managing a sporting establishment with among other things the promotion of pugilist contests and horse racing. The boxing ring was specially set up on land just to the north of the pub, while the unpretentious 'Victoria Park Races' managed by John Baum in the 1840s with James acting as steward, were held in the nearby Victoria Park.

James Baum was a bachelor, born in 1823 in Holborn, where his father was proprietor of the Kings Head public house in Fetter Lane. As well as being landlord of the White Lion James undertook property development in the area and among his many developments were two sets of cottages in Wick Lane known as Baum's Cottages and Deerfoot Cottages, named after the famous American Indian runner who would help make pedestrianism at Hackney Wick so popular. The gravel running path James constructed in the gardens of the White Lion – a pear shaped oval of 260 yards (6.75 laps to the mile) – was very much dictated by the shape and features at the ground. Its first meeting opened with little publicity soon after Christmas in 1857.

The path did not provide an ideal view for spectators as much of the course was lined on both sides by trees and at the early meetings crowds tended to congregate in the middle of the ground or on the railway embankment that bordered the slightly uphill first straight. At the top of the course there was an awkward pavilion turn which the local pedestrians soon learned to negotiate to their advantage before returning to the start and the much tighter turn where the White Lion was situated. At this time the area surrounding Hackney Wick was still fairly rural with Hackney Marshes to the north, and market gardens and Victoria Park, first used in 1846, to the south. Hackney Wick station, as it was then known, on the North London Railway opened in 1856, overlooked the running grounds and gave easy access from Fenchurch Street and Camden Town for just sixpence return.

The following years saw the opening of other important tracks competing with Hackney Wick, among them Old Ford Road, Bow in 1859, John Roberts' West London Cricket and Running ground at Thistle Grove, West Brompton in 1860 and Charles Wilson's Prince of Wales Olympic Ground at Bow in 1863.

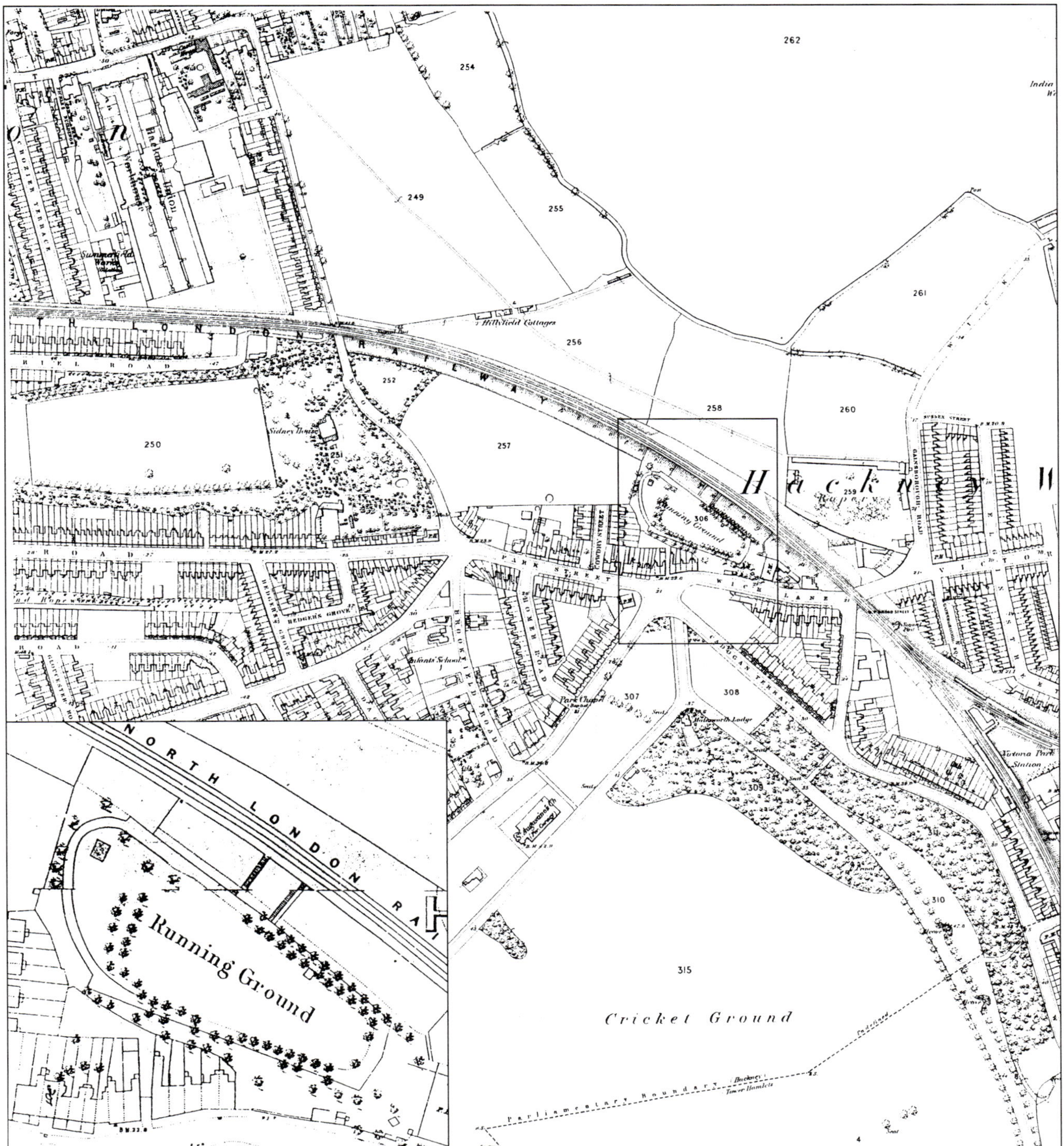

Map of the White Lion running ground, Hackney Wick

MR. BAUM, the well-known Proprietor of the Hackney Wick Grounds.

James Baum, proprietor of the White Lion and Hackney Wick running grounds

James Baum employed Frank Diamond, a 25-year-old pedestrian sprinter and one-time walker from Whitechapel, to manage the grounds and within a few weeks he was drawing crowds of 500 or more to handicap meetings.

The opening meeting, announced without much fanfare, took place on 28 December 1857, attracting 37 pedestrians competing in four heats and final of a quarter-mile handicap for a silver cup valued at fourteen guineas. The winner, Bill Price from Mile End, who soon afterwards became manager of the ground, elected to take the monetary value of the cup that was competed for again two weeks later. The meeting, like all major events at the ground, was held on a Monday, starting at half-past two in the afternoon with the final race inevitably run in the dark!

Mondays were the most popular day for pedestrianism in London with Saturday being a working day for the majority and Sunday a 'day of rest'.

Between the heats and final of the quarter-mile there was a four-mile walking handicap in which the major attraction was Charles Westhall, by then nearing the end of his career as probably the most versatile professional athlete of the century. He recorded first class running performances from 150 yards to the mile, walking records from 7 to 21 miles and even ran 440 yards hurdles against a horse on 26 February 1850 and lost! Virtually all his last races, in 1857 and 1858, were at Hackney Wick where he won two four-mile walk handicaps before completing his famous 21-mile walk in 2h.59m.01s. at Newmarket on 20 February 1858. In 1859 he walked the two final races of his career at the 'Wick'; in the first completing one mile in 8¼ minutes to win a bet for half a dozen bottles of wine, in the second, on 3 August, when ill-prepared, failing to walk seven miles in one hour.

As the early part of 1858 progressed, the sporting press became quite critical of Baum and Diamond. At a very poor meeting in early March the proceedings were disrupted by a 'ruffian' who ran in front of the competitors and caused them all to fall and the sporting newspaper, *Bell's Life in London*, reported:

> As the proprietor appears to be all but a novice to the business, he will do well to see that none but bone fides matches are allowed to come off, for if he does not, he will soon lose the support and confidence of the public. The whole matters relative to the ground are under the management of Diamond, the pedestrian.

However, Frank Diamond's time as manager was not to last long. Matters came to a head in May, after a race between Bolton and the Hoxton Baker. These men contested a mile race for £10.

> The betting was pretty brisk at evens, and at slight odds on the Baker. The men got off well, and ran the whole distance with slight alternate leads. Bolton, at the termination of the race passing the mark first by a couple of yards, but in consequence of a suspicion of foul play, the referee withheld his decision. It was subsequently discovered that the Baker was no other than Bull of Walworth, who ran Levett for the championship at the Rosemary Branch, Peckham, about five years back, but was beaten. He has been a noted runner in London for some time having beaten Griffiths, Williams, Bond, Thompson and many others. The 'barney' affair was so clear that the referee very properly refused to give any decision, and recommended all bets to be off, which was accordingly done. It should be remembered the Baker admitted to the referee he had been drinking and

Charles Westhall, one mile record holder and famous walker

CHARLES WESTHALL (1823–1868)

Charles Hall, 'the London Clipper', who assumed the name Westhall, was born at 251 Tottenham Court Road, London on 6 March 1823. In due course he became a student of medicine, where his extraordinarily well-developed physical powers led into athletic exercise, and it was not long before he was carried away by the excitement of the 'path' far beyond the bounds of the hospital and lecture room. His first public appearance as a pedestrian was on 24 October 1842, when he beat Mr W. McKay in a six-mile walking match at Acton Bottom in a time of 50 minutes. His great talent was soon perceived, and in December of the same year he received £25 forfeit from R. Graves, in a match to run ten miles for £200 a side. From that time his career was a wonderful success. In walking, long distance running and sprinting, he was able to hold his own on occasion against the best men of his time at their own distances. At various times he beat the walker William Spooner and the sprinters George Seward and Harry Reed. Possibly his most notable early success was his 150 yards in 15 seconds, the best on record, at the Belle Vue Grounds, Manchester on 14 February 1851. He established the first British record at one mile at the old Copenhagen Ground, Islington, where he ran 4m.28s. on 26 July 1852, on a course so muddy that his feet sank below shoe-level. Later that year he won the first one-mile champions' belt in 4m.35¾s. at Hyde Park, Sheffield. He was also a fine hurdle-jumper, and would often get over astonishingly long distances at a leap; but it was his walking on which his fame truly rested. His first, though not his greatest, feat came at Slough on 13 June 1857, when on a blazing hot day he undertook to walk seven and a half miles within the hour and beat the time by 1m.35s. The following year was his greatest triumph when on 20 February, for a wager of £120, he walked 21 miles in under three hours on the carefully measured mile between Toll-Gate and the Duke's Stand on Newmarket Heath. It was accomplished on a bitterly cold day; there was a hard frost and a biting wind from which the only shelter was one of Sam Roger's horse-vans. His times were at 7 miles 56m.; 14 miles 1h.55m.50s.; and 21 miles 2h.59m.01s. The final track races of his career all took place at Hackney Wick between 1857 and 1859 when his walking career ended, although he was sometimes to be found at the 'Wick' acting as referee or starter. He acquired billiard-rooms in Holborn, shortly after retirement and became associated with the sporting press, first with the *Sporting Life* and then *Bell's Life in London* where he was the most highly respected of pedestrian commentators as well as editing the boxing column for some time. In 1868 he was presented with a magnificent gold chronometer and a purse of sovereigns at a public dinner in his honour at the Clarence Hotel, Charing Cross in London. He died aged 46 at his home at 10 Stafford Terrace, Britannia Road, Fulham, on 12 October 1868, leaving a widow and large family.

> smoking till the time of running; that he had no training; and that he only knew the gentleman who put down the money for him by sight. A gentleman in the room where the meeting was held said that the Baker had admitted to him that he received £1 to sell the race. The Baker although in the house, refused to come forward and deny this before the referee. Such conduct as this is very disgraceful, and we recommend Mr Baum, if he has any regard for the character of his grounds to guard against a repetition of it.

Soon after this Frank Diamond was replaced by Bill Price, who was to make the re-named 'New Metropolitan Ground Hackney Wick' into one of the most popular pedestrian venues in the country. Later in the year Diamond was managing the Aston Cross Ground in Birmingham. But again there were problems, this time over handicapping and prize money, and his reign there seems to have been quite short.

Another episode involving Frank Diamond at Hackney Wick occurred in October 1859 when the *Sporting Life* reported:

> During the running, the proceedings were marred by three ruffians – F. Diamond, and Faber and son, of Billingsgate, and whose conduct was such as would not be tolerated even in that nice locality; indeed so badly did these fellows behave, that the public took them in hand and administered summary chastisement, and drove them from the ground. Diamond was at the opening of the grounds, the M.C., but, through gross mismanagement, was dismissed from his office. Since then he has started a rival ground, and no doubt came with the express purpose of creating a disturbance, knowing that the proprietor (Mr. Baum) was confined to his room by illness.

The impression is that proceedings at Hackney were pretty sordid, but in fact James Baum was a very principled gentleman and determined that meetings at his ground would be above reproach.

Bank holiday meetings

From the very early days James Baum made his bank holiday meetings special by providing wrestling, sometimes boxing, alongside the pedestrian events, and ending the evening with music and fireworks. The main event for the first such meeting – Easter 1858 – was announced as 'The Great All England 500 yards Handicap' with a first prize of £10. Forty athletes accepted their handicaps, and Cumberland and Westmorland wrestling augmented the running programme.

Greatly encouraged by the success of this meeting a 'Great Metropolitan Half Mile Handicap' was announced for the two-day Whitsun

Wrestling at Hackney Wick

meeting. Invitations were sent out to as far afield as Salford, Liverpool, Manchester, Bradford, Sheffield, Norwich and Yarmouth. The entry was 10 shillings, paid in four weekly instalments of 2s 6d and provided there were at least 30 entrants the first prize was to be £25. The response was so great that there were nine heats on the Monday and three semi-finals and a final on the Tuesday. The winner, Harry Nobbs of Norwich, returned home with £30 first prize while second-placed Sam Barker, destined to become one of the best pedestrians of the era, won £4.

Again on both days wrestling, this time Devon and Cornwall style, supplemented the running and the prize money attracted many of the 'crack' wrestlers from the south-west of England. As for musical entertainment, this was provided by the Eastern Counties Railway Company Band and several hundred couples danced on the wooden stage. The meeting attracted around 3,000 persons, the biggest crowd so far at the ground.

The year ended with a repeat of what was to become a traditional and very successful Christmas meeting held over two days commencing on Boxing Day.

Benefit meetings

Benefits for notable pedestrians, wrestlers and pugilists, whose management of their financial affairs was often poor, soon become popular at the ground as they frequently attracted some of the best sportsmen of the day to compete and spectate. One of the first for a pedestrian was on Monday 13 February 1860, a meeting for William Jackson (nee Howitt), 'The American Deer', a name acquired through living in America as a youth, long before his two successful tours of the United States and Canada in the 1840s and 1850s.

At the time of his benefit Jackson had been competing for 22 years and with his career thought to be reaching an end, it was felt the time was right to enable his admirers to raise something to start him in a new line to get a living for himself and his family. Little did they know that due to a business failure, his main source of income would remain running for many years to come even though he was already a veteran even by today's standards.

The meeting was well publicised with entries being taken at three of London's major sporting houses; Mr Thomas Wilson's Spotted Dog public house in the Strand, James Pudney's Coach and Horses public house in Back Church Lane, Commercial Road, Mile End and James Baum's White Lion at Hackney Wick. Tickets were also available at public houses all over London. The events scheduled were heats and final of a 500 yards handicap for a silver cup, a ten miles handicap for a first

WILLIAM JACKSON (1821–?)

William Jackson, who adopted the surname for family reasons, was born William Howitt in Norwich on 2 February 1821 and became known as the 'American Deer' before venturing across the Atlantic in the 1840s. He was one of the smallest pedestrians of the time, only 5ft. 2in. in height and weighing just 7st. 2lb. His exploits included two tours of America, from 1845 to 1846 and from 1849 to 1851. He commenced his racing career at Birmingham in 1837 (where he worked as a cabinet-maker and French polisher) and came to prominence by running 11 miles 40 yards in an hour on the Hatfield Road, Gannick Corner, Barnet on 6 January 1845. William Jackson first raced in America over five miles on the Beacon Course at Hoboken, New Jersey on 3 July 1845 against Billy Barlow, winning convincingly in 27m.39s. Two days later he again won easily over ten miles in 56m.29s., before a rare defeat in September by Barlow over two miles in 9m.44½s., considered a new record time for the distance. Due to these successes he could find no other opponents and with the sprinter, George Seward, who had accompanied him to America, he set out for Canada. Here he had two wins at ten miles over Gildersleeve, an American born of Suffolk farming stock, before returning to America in an endeavour to generate interest in further matches. Eventually one was made with Gildersleeve; Jackson giving away 600 yards over 15 miles and losing by one yard, many thinking that Jackson had thrown the race. His last race was in June 1846 when he attempted to run 11 miles in one hour, losing by just 20 seconds. He returned to England in August. In 1847 he set a new ten miles record of 53m.10s. at the Rosemary Branch Ground in Peckham. However, by 1849 he had returned to America for a tour which lasted until the summer of 1851 and included a whole series of wins against American Indians. Back in England in 1852 he continued his record-breaking ways at the Copenhagen Grounds, Islington, in March running 11 miles in the hour (a feat he had first achieved on the Hatfield Road in January 1845), then on 31 May, setting a new ten mile record of 52m.00s. He won the 'Champion of the World' silver cup races, the best of one, five and ten miles in January 1853, at the Royal Oak Race Grounds, Barking Road, Canning Town. Around this time he set up as a market gardener and began to race less. Unfortunately, his premises were burned down without being insured and he had to return to running to earn a living. Although past his best he formed one of the troupe put together by George Martin to tour England in 1862 with Deerfoot, but it ended acrimoniously with Jackson taking Martin to court over the conduct of races and non-payment of wages. Jackson continued to race with less success throughout the early 1860s. Little was heard of him after that until he was reported winning a ten-mile race for veterans at Chelsea on 28 November 1892. He was still alive in 1896, aged 75, living in Woodford, Essex.

William Jackson, 'The American Deer,' ten miles record holder

prize of ten pounds and a two-mile walking handicap. In spite of the weather the meeting drew a good crowd, estimated at nearly 3,000, with a strong body of police present to keep the course clear – a necessity at all popular meetings if the athletes were to be allowed to run unhindered. On this occasion, however, the number of spectators was so great that it was amazing the pedestrians could find sufficient space to run.

Jackson, waited on by the famous pugilist champion Tom Sayers, ran in the ten miles handicap off half a minute but after 54 of the 68 laps was compelled to cry a 'go', the traditional way to concede. James Pudney won the race off scratch from Sam Barker. Joseph Jenn won the walk, although doubt was cast on whether it was fair heel and toe as all the competitors finished! As for the final of the 500 yards, this had to be postponed until the following Monday, 20 February, because it was too dark. It was eventually won by the well-known sprinter George Beddow of the Grenadier Guards. The evening was a financial success for Jackson, who received £23 4s. made up of £53 taken at the gate, less prize money and expenses, including costs of printing, policing, etc.

JOSEPH JENN (1834–1879)

Joseph Jenn was born in Somerstown, London, in 1834. He started as a runner, winning his first race at the Royal Oak Grounds, Barking Road, in 1853 over 880 yards. His first success as a walker came in 1855 when he won a silver watch in a novice walking race over four miles at Garratt Lane, Wandsworth. He first walked at Hackney Wick in a five miles race in March 1858 and had many successful races there up to 1861 when he went into semi-retirement. He won his last race at the 'Wick' in 1866 and died at Camden Town on 1 October 1879 aged 45.

GEORGE BEDDOW (1837–?)

George Beddow, born on 20 November 1837, was a sergeant in the Grenadier Guards. His first race in 1857 was against a fellow sergeant over 170 yards at Garratt Lane, Wandsworth. He ran regularly at Hackney Wick in 1860 winning his first race, a 500 yards handicap, at Jackson's benefit. Being a sprinter he began to race at the northern venues in 1861. One of his best races was in beating Nevin for the 400 yards championship at Salford Borough Grounds on 28 June 1862 in 46½s. His last race was at Wigan in 1867; the same year he became proprietor of the Manor Arms Hotel at nearby Golborne.

Another successful benefit meeting in 1860 took place in July for Abraham Cann the champion wrestler from Devon. Many top Devon wrestlers competed and around £70 was raised for this 65-year-old ex Champion of England.

The 'Wick' attracts the leading pedestrians from the north

The first time that James Baum was able to attract one of the leading pedestrians from the north of England was in September 1858 when a four-mile handicap race for £25 aside was arranged between the well-known local man James Pudney and James Rowan from Gateshead, both ten-mile champions in the 1850s.

The two contestants had met once before, at Newcastle, when Rowan with a start of 100 yards proved an easy winner. This time Rowan was given 50 yards start. The course, prepared earlier in the day by repeated rolling with a heavy roller, was in admirable condition. The race was due to start at six o'clock with Pudney, the elder of the two, favourite at 6 to 4. The two athletes had prepared well for the race, Pudney at Garratt Lane, Wandsworth under the guidance of George Clarke of Yarmouth and Rowan at John Levett's racecourse in Newcastle. The race, unfortunately, was not the spectacle expected, with Pudney having closed the gap before the two-mile mark and Rowan giving up complaining of a bad foot before three miles. The race time of 21m.10s. was of little significance with Pudney finishing at his ease. Rowan, although he was to become one of the greatest pedestrians of his day, was to prove an unreliable competitor on many occasions when appearing in the metropolis. The locals, however, were delighted to have their man beat Rowan, who was highly regarded and heavily backed by his supporters who had travelled from the north. They danced the night away to music from the Eastern Counties Railway Band and there was a fireworks display to complete their day.

The successful early years at Hackney Wick proved instrumental in reviving pedestrianism in London. With the continued enthusiasm of James Baum and Bill Price the running ground was destined to become one of the best supported in England, hosting some of the country's finest races.

2

1859–1860, The Introduction of Challenge Cups and Belts

Ten miles champion cup

The most significant event at Hackney Wick in 1859 was James Baum's introduction of a Ten Miles Champion Cup, contested for a whole decade and providing some of the most exciting pedestrianism of the era.

During the latter part of 1858 and the first half of 1859 James Baum was successful in attracting many of the top London distance men to Hackney Wick including as well as those previously mentioned, Harry Andrews of Holborn, Toddy Ray of Limehouse and Charles Cooke of Marylebone. It was then he decided it was the right time to introduce a Champion Challenge Cup to be competed for on the Grounds. James Baum commissioned a cup from J. Street and had it engraved: 'The Ten Mile Champion Cup, given by Mr J. C. Baum, Metropolitan Running Grounds, Victoria Park, Hackney, 11th July, 1859'. It was valued at thirty guineas, with money prizes of £5, £3, £1.10s. and 10s. also offered for the first four men. The conditions applying to the Championship Cup were:

> The winner of the cup to hold himself in readiness to run any one who may challenge him through the columns of *Bell's Life*, at six weeks notice, for £25 a side. In case of a match being made, the holder of the cup to hand it over to Mr Baum by 12 o'clock on the day of the race. The winner of the cup not to be allowed to take it away until he has deposited the sum of £15, and given a guarantee for its production in the event of a match being made before the expiration of eighteen months. It must state in the articles for the both to start by the first report of a pistol, and the referee to name a man to fire the pistol. If a referee were not chosen in the articles, the proprietor of the ground to be referee. If a match be made for the cup towards the expiration of eighteen months, and there is only time for one match to take place, a third or fourth person may claim to run in a sweepstake, on the same conditions, providing the challenge to do so in *Bell's Life* of the week following the match is made. No man is allowed to have his name engraved on the cup until he has held it against all comers for the space eighteen months, after which

EARLY HISTORY OF THE TEN MILES CHAMPIONSHIP
James Baum's cup was not the first championship trophy at this distance. John Garratt introduced a ten miles championship on an enclosed running track on 8 December 1851, when he donated a 4½ft. long challenge belt to be competed for at his Copenhagen Grounds (Old Cope), Islington. The terms and conditions of the belt were that to become the outright holder, the winner had to defend it for one year, accepting all challenges within one month for the not inconsiderable sum of £50 a side. This first race was designated a walk and the entrants included all the top walkers of the time including Westhall, Spooner, 'Old' Smith, Newman and Hotine. Spooner won in 1h.22m.05s. from Westhall and Smith. A ten-mile running championship for a similar challenge belt, again donated by John Garratt at the same venue, followed on 12 January 1852 and was won by George Frost, from a field of eighteen runners, in a time of 54m.09s. John Levett then relieved Frost of his title on 22 March, with a new record winning time of 52m.35s. He lost the belt to William Jackson on 31 May, in yet another record of 52m.00s. but regained it once again on 11 October, in 51m.45s; a British record that was to last for 33 years. With the closure of the Copenhagen Grounds in 1853 John Garratt transferred his interest in the belt to Mr Beswick, proprietor of the Royal Oak Grounds in Barking Road, Canning Town. Two challenges for the belt were held at this venue; the first on 25 March, when George Frost beat Levett, the second when Levett was beaten by Jackson on 4 July. The two best distance runners of the time, Jackson and Levett, could never agree terms for a further contest. In 1854 Hannah Heathcote put up a ten-mile belt at Hyde Park Grounds, Sheffield, won by James Pudney from John Levett on 6 March 1854 and the following week Pudney won the 'Old Cope' belt defeating William Jackson at Westhill Park, Halifax. Pudney successfully defended the Hyde Park belt against John Levett on 5 June 1854 in 54m.15s. and remained unchallenged to become outright holder of both belts. On 15 June 1857 Pudney beat Levett at Wandsworth in a so-called championship, even though the belt was not at stake, in a time of 53m.18s.

> time it shall become his own private property. In the case of the Metropolitan Grounds being done away with for public improvements, Mr Baum will have the right to name another ground for the belt to be run for.

These conditions were the basis for other challenge trophies introduced in the years that followed.

The entries for the 68 lap race on 11 July 1859 were, Pudney, Rowan,

The first Ten Miles Running Championship, Copenhagen House, Islington in January 1852

Jackson, Cooke, Ray, Barker, Andrews, Trainer, Cummings of Liverpool, Bunn of Norwich, Harry Baines of Marylebone, Job Smith of Manchester, Paddy Burns of Preston and W. Jones of Islington. All were to run in colours announced on the day. A crowd of 4,000 assembled for the event but were disappointed to find that of the northern entries only Rowan appeared and even he withdrew at the last minute, although known to be on the ground and backed to win. Pudney was ill, Jackson injured and Cummings and Burns failed to appear. It was left to the six London pedestrians to race for the title which was won by Cooke nearly four laps ahead of Barker, Ray and Andrews.

Although the number of starters had been disappointing there was glowing praise for the event from the *Sporting Life*, which reported:

> The prizes were all paid over in the evening, the rich and vintage champagne flowing in the cup at the sole expense of the worthy proprietor, for the gratification of all the pedestrians who had joined in the struggle. We cannot close our remarks without referring to the able and efficient exertions of Inspector Bywater and Sergeant Bussaine in keeping a clear passage, amongst such a crowded assemblage, for the men to run. As to the arrangements of Mr. Baum, the veritable lion of the day, they were perfect in the extreme; and the hearty and willing assistance rendered on the part of all connected with this popular establishment renders the proprietor's task far more easy, and only sustains the fame in which he is universally viewed as a generous and spirited caterer for public diversions of all kinds. Dancing to Froggitt's popular band, and fireworks concluded the gala festivities of the day.

Maybe the reporter was writing under the pleasing effect of the generous supply of champagne. But in any case the competition for the Cup became firmly established with two challengers appearing before the end of the year.

James Rowan became the first challenger in a race on 17 October 1859. Articles for the match with the necessary £25 a side were drawn up at Mr J. S. James's William the Fourth public house, in Exeter Street, Lisson Grove, Marylebone where Cooke had deposited the Cup. Charles Cooke had first come to notice in 1855 when he won a ten-mile handicap at Garratt Lane, Wandsworth. However, it was not until he became holder of the Champion Cup that it could be claimed he had truly made his mark.

The race was set for three o'clock, but it was four o'clock before the 3,000 spectators, arriving mainly by train, were settled in the ground. For once Rowan, who had spent some time in London staying at Mr Wilson's Spotted Dog in the Strand and training at Wandsworth, showed his true qualities at Hackney and as he went through five miles in 26m.40s., Cooke, nearly a lap behind, realised he had no chance and pulled out on the 36th lap. Rowan after running two more laps put on his flannels and walked the remainder of the distance. As usual the main participants retired to the White Lion to celebrate, where it was soon rumoured that Jackson would be the next challenger for the Cup at Mr Baum's Boxing Day meeting. Jackson made an offer to Pudney to enter into a sweepstake with them, with the winner to receive all the stakes, but Pudney was not in the form to make him competitive and declined.

James Rowan prepared well for the Boxing Day race under the 'watchful eye of Hogg on the banks of the Tyne' before a final week spent training at Robert Sadler's Duke of Wellington Inn, Garratt Lane, Wandsworth. He deposited the Cup in the hands of Thomas Wilson at the Spotted Dog in the Strand, where Rowan's friends also stayed. Meanwhile Jackson trained under the once renowned Charlie Jenkinson, 'The London Stag', at George Conquest's Spelthorne Inn, Sunbury Common.

On the day of the race only one or two thousand spectators assembled, in gloomy weather, on the heavy rain-sodden ground. Rowan looked in bloom of youth, compared with the 39-year-old Jackson, and was the firm favourite to retain his title. Dressed in his usual orange with black drawers he was keen to show his superiority over the older man and led

THOMAS WILSON (1814–1866)

Thomas Wilson, a native of Brigstock in Northamptonshire, was born on 17 January 1814. He became proprietor of the Spotted Dog public house in the Strand, opposite the offices of *Bell's Life in London*, where members of all sports and pastimes gathered for nearly 20 years. As a young man he entered service, first at the seat of Lord Lyvden, followed by a term with Mr Holforde, an eminent millionaire living near Regents Park, London, and finally with the Duke of Cambridge with whom he travelled to Europe and became conversant in a number of European languages. On his retirement he acquired the Spotted Dog and put all his energies into improving many national pastimes, more especially pedestrianism. In conjunction with John Garratt he promoted champion contests for numerous belts and cups. Many matches were arranged under his auspices and many a forfeit was saved by an appeal to his good offices. Jem Mace in particular was always thankful for the help given by Thomas Wilson in the early days of his pugilistic career. Wilson often worked closely with Bill Price and James Baum with whom he was also associated in connection with the Licensed Victuallers' School and Asylum. He died on 23 February 1866 and is buried in Highgate Cemetery.

throughout to win easily by 140 yards in 58m.23s. James Rowan who celebrated vigorously in the evening (putting on eight pounds in weight!) began to win the respect of the knowledgeable London crowd and it looked as if he was a man who could defend the Cup for the full 18 months and make it his own.

His next challenger, on 23 April 1860, was the experienced and by now reportedly fitter James Pudney from Mile End whose long and successful career caused him to be favourite in a race where the stakes had been raised to £50 a side. The challenge had attracted a good number of experienced followers of the sport including many pugilistic celebrities as well as

JAMES PUDNEY (1830–1897)
James Andrew Pudney, known as Jem, was born on 13 May 1830 in Lambeth. He first appeared in public as a runner on 13 August 1849 when he won a silver snuff-box in a one-mile race at the Lord Gough public house, Plaistow Lane and was soon spotted as a pedestrian with potential by Bill Price, (who remained his mentor throughout his career). Bill took him in hand and in 1850 and 1851 Pudney won a number of matches on the roads around Ilford for stakes of £5. During Easter Week 1851 Bill Price matched him to run ten miles in under an hour at Hove Cricket Ground, which he did with one minute to spare. In 1852 at the Copenhagen Grounds, Islington, he beat the celebrated Lancashire runner Byrom and set a new British Record at two miles of 9m.38s. In 1853 he brought his ten-mile time down to 53m.30s. in beating C. Cooke at the Royal Oak, Barking, then beat Jackson over four miles in 20m.6s. for £50 a side at Slough. In 1854 at Hyde Park, Sheffield, he beat Levett and three others to win the ten miles Champions Belt given by Mrs Heathcote. The following week at West Hill Park, Halifax he beat Jackson for the 'Old Cope' Ten Mile Belt, originally put up by John Garrett in 1852, to become unofficial Ten Miles Champion of England. He defended the belt against Levett at Sheffield and continued to beat the best throughout the late 1850s. His victories included one at ten miles against Levett at Wandsworth in 1857 in a very fast 53m.18s. In 1861, by now a veteran of 31, he won the new Ten Miles Champions Cup at Hackney Wick, although he did not feel up to defending it. That same year he also briefly held the Six Miles Champion Belt. His last race was an 80 yards for veterans at Hackney Wick where, with a six-yard start, he won a silver cup. James Pudney purchased the Three Horse Shoes public house in Osborne Street, Whitechapel, in 1854 and moved to the Coach and Horses in Back Church Lane, Commercial Road, Whitechapel, in late 1855 where he maintained a sporting house of some note until 1878. He finally took on the Prince of Wales in Leyton Green, Leyton, and died at Leyton on 27 April 1897.

James Pudney, Ten Miles Champion

pedestrians. Of the former, Jem Ward, Nat Langham and Jem Mace, all Champions of England, were to be seen, together with Jem Tyler, Bill Duncan, Dan Collins and Young Hartley. Amongst the leading pedestrians were George Martin, William Lang, Bob Bunn, John Smith, John Brighton and William Jackson.

Both men trained hard for the race; James Pudney under Bill Price who had been his trainer and manager since the age of 19 at the start of his career. James Rowan, whose reputation for being a 'thirsty soul' had now followed him to London, had on this occasion forgone his customary libations, and paid strict attention to training. Many of his friends had come all the way from the north and backed him freely, taking odds at 6 and 7 to 4, to the extent of £200 on the ground.

The course, again in a heavy condition because of rain, had been carefully roped off for the occasion with a large body of police in attendance. The start was delayed due to heavy rain, but eventually got under way at five o'clock. Pudney went through the first mile in 4m.51s. – fast considering the conditions – but then the lead continually changed as the two runners tried to exert their claim to the title. On the 25th lap Rowan broke away and two laps later Pudney retired complaining of a bad stitch. The spectators were not amused, particularly when it became known that his training had included no runs above four or five miles. With his opponent gone Rowan put on his coat and boots and walked around the course until having nearly completed the distance, Bill Price conceded on behalf of Pudney.

It is now that the title of 'Champion' enters cloudier times. In August 1860 Rowan was challenged by his fellow 'Gateshead Clipper' John 'Jack' White, the four and six miles champion. For the race Rowan again stayed at Robert Sadler's Wellington Inn in Garratt Lane while White, who was trained, backed and managed by the famed George Martin, did not travel down until the day before the race scheduled for 17 September. With a large crowd expected, a stand accommodating up to 2,000 at one shilling a head had been erected along the railway embankment. However, the immense crowd was once again to be severely disappointed, Rowan failed to appear, and without any explanation forfeited the cup to White, the crowd no doubt believing his drinking had got the better of him.

Further intriguing developments in the history of the cup were to follow in 1861 along with the arrival of Deerfoot from America. In the meantime, capitalising on the interest generated in his Ten Miles Champion Cup, James Baum was encouraged to present a new trophy in the form of a Six Miles Champion Belt to be contested on the same basis as the Cup.

Six Miles Champion Belt

The splendid fifty guineas belt manufactured by W. Preston of Clerkenwell, was composed of a broad dark-green velvet band, bearing gold and silver medallions and gold fringe trimming, tassels, and embroidery, with a large ornamental buckle attached. The principal shield bore the inscription 'Six Mile Champion's Belt given by Mr. J. C. Baum, White Lion Race Grounds, Hackney Wick, June 11, 1860'. This was surmounted by a pedestal crowned with a lion in frosted silver. All the ornaments were in frosted and burnished gold and silver, and represented two pedestrians on each panel. This magnificent trophy was displayed at the Spotted Dog and Coach and Horses on the Saturday and Sunday before the race.

James Baum went out of his way to attract the very best pedestrians to his event, offering to pay the railway fare to the ground from anywhere in the country, and also arranging a 'Great Metropolitan Five Mile Handicap' for the following week with a first prize of £20. Bill Price's handicaps for the five mile event give an indication of the ranking of some of the top long distance runners at this time: John Brighton of

John Brighton, 'The Milkboy,' holder of the Four Miles Champion Belt

Norwich (scratch); Paddy Burns of Preston (40y.); Job Smith of Manchester (200y.); John White of Gateshead (320y.); Bunn (360y.); Harry Andrews of Holborn (450y.); W. Jones of Islington (500y.); O'Connor of Northampton (500y.); Toddy Ray of Limehouse (500y.); S. Shepherd of Bethnal Green (500y.); M. Newman (500y.); J. Wilson of London (520y.); Teddy Mills of Bethnal Green, who was to make an important impact in the coming years, (520y.); Sam Barker of Billingsgate (800y.); William Jackson (820y.).

For the six miles championship race, Brighton, Lang of Middlesbrough, making his first competitive appearance at Hackney Wick, Smith, Barker, O'Connor, Jones, Ray and Mills lined up in front of a crowd numbering between two and three thousand. From the outset the race was between Brighton (recent winner of the 'Four Miles Champion Belt' given by John Roberts for his opening meeting on 28 May, at the pleasant well-roped 440 yard circuit on the West London Cricket Ground, Thistle Grove, Old Brompton) Lang and Smith. The lead changed constantly until five miles when Lang pulled up and Smith was dropped, leaving Brighton to win by five yards in the time of 21m.30s. from Smith, with Ray and Jones third and fourth, two laps behind. Afterwards John Brighton proudly exhibited both the six and four mile belts at Robert Bunn's Star and Crown public house on Orford Hill in his home city of Norwich.

W. Jones, pedestrian and one time manager of the Brompton Grounds

In the five mile handicap a week later Jack White, the 'Gateshead Clipper', made an impressive first appearance at Hackney Wick. Running with a peculiar bounding action, up on his toes, he was the winner by 12 yards from Barker, Jackson, Smith and Jones, with Ray last. Attempts were made to prove that Bill Price had made a mistake in the position of the

JOHN WHITE (1838–1910)

John 'Jack' White, known as the 'Gateshead Clipper', born at Gateshead on 1 March 1838, was another very small pedestrian 5ft. 2½in. in height and weighing 7st. 6lb. He first appeared in pedestrian matches in 1857, losing his opening half-mile race against James Rowan at Newcastle. The same year he ran second to Rowan in a ten mile handicap, receiving a 200 yard start, and came to the notice of George Martin, who took him in hand. After some careful handling, he won a 1,000 yard handicap at Hyde Park, Sheffield in 1860, and ran at Hackney Wick for the first time, winning a five mile handicap, afterwards defeating W. Jones of Islington over four miles. In Manchester he ran second to Siah Albison for the One Mile Champion Belt and by the end of 1860 was champion over four, six and ten miles holding the two Champion Belts and the Cup. That year at Brompton he also equalled James Pudney's two mile record of 9m.38s. In July 1861 George Martin took White (who at Manchester had recently reduced his two mile record to 9m.20s.), along with Charles Mower and John Nevin, across the Atlantic to compete against the best America could offer at the Fashion Pleasure Race Course at Long Island, New York. The visit was very lucrative with White remaining unbeaten including wins over Deerfoot, who Martin subsequently brought back to England. John White continued his good form into 1862 when he recorded a new British Record for three miles of 14m.50s. in a race with Teddy Mills for the Six Miles Belt on 15 December, and the following year on 11 May 1863 he again created new British Records at Hackney Wick in a race for a Ten Miles Champion Belt with times of 14m.36s. at three miles and 29m.50s. at six miles. The latter mark remained the World Record until beaten by the famous Paavo Nurmi in 1921 and was not beaten by a British athlete until 1936! This is possibly the longest period of time any record has been held. He held the Ten Miles Champion Cup briefly in 1864. White continued to race at a high level until the end of the decade; his last recorded race was on 7 April 1870 when he was beaten by Teddy Golder over five miles at the Star Grounds, Fulham. He was now living in Fulham where he trained pedestrians at the nearby Star Grounds and Lillie Bridge Grounds. He became a member of the ground staff at Lillie Bridge coaching athletes from London Athletic Club in the 1870s and 1880s and accompanying the L.A.C. team to New York for their match against the New York Athletic Club in 1895. He was also coach to Cambridge University Athletic Club. He was living at 58 Stanley Road, Fulham when he died on 21 November 1910.

men, and that White had, in fact, never passed Jones. The plea, however, was absurd and there was no doubt that Price had acted properly and impartially.

Jack White, now backed by George Martin, was determined to prove himself the best long distance pedestrian on the running paths by winning the four, six and ten mile champion trophies. First, however, White made a re-match with Jones at West Brompton where on 6 August, giving him 200 yards over five miles, he showed running form not seen since the early days of Jackson and Sheppard, emerging an easy winner with Jones dropping out at four miles. The same month he raced Brighton for the Six Miles Belt and proved by far the superior runner, leading by a hundred yards after five miles, at which point Brighton gave up exhausted and suffering from a bad cold. White's mile times were 4m.45s; 9m.47s; 15m.00s; 20m.04s; 25m.14s; ending with a very respectable 30m.57s. Finally, a week later on 27 August, at West Brompton, wearing a blue body dress and long drawers he relieved Brighton of the Four Miles Belt winning in a fast 20m.1½s. and passing 3 miles in an unrecognised British record of 14m.47s. He acquired the Ten Miles Cup the following month when Rowan failed to show, and for the time being could rightly be called the 'Distance Champion of England'. Some years later White recalled 'Bill Lang would beat me at a mile but I could lick all the other beggars from 4 miles up to ten when I was fit.'

One Mile Champion Belt

A new One Mile Champion Belt was put up by Thomas 'Tommy' Hayes in August 1860 at the Copenhagen Grounds in Manchester. Between his hectic schedule of races in London, John White appeared as one of the favourites alongside William Lang, Siah Albison the celebrated half-miler, Job Smith and Charles Mower. Albison, trained by his mentor Joe Etchells of the Weaver's Arms public house, Failsworth, was joint favourite with White and in a humdinger of a race Albison won by four yards in 4m.24½s., just 1½ seconds outside Horspool's fastest ever time recorded in 1858.

However, the battle for the One Mile Champion Belt in 1860 was not yet over for the year as Albison had to face the challenge of William Lang who had been suffering from a damaged ankle in the previous race for the Belt. The match was set for 27 October, and as a result of Albison's previous fast time and the form of Lang, now trained by Alfred Grinrod of Oldham (holder of the recently introduced 400 yards Champion Belt at Salford Borough Gardens), the crowd of 3,000 had great expectations that on this occasion the mile record time set by Tom Horspool on the same ground on 12 July 1858 could well be beaten. They were not to be

EARLY HISTORY OF THE ONE MILE CHAMPIONSHIP
As with the Ten Mile track championship, the One Mile was first introduced in the 1850s. Samuel Heathcote was the originator when he donated a magnificent championship belt seven feet long, incorporating 43 ounces of sterling silver, at his Hyde Park cricket ground in Sheffield on 23 August 1852. Valued at £50 it had to be defended by the holder within six weeks of receiving a challenge. The first winner was Charles Westhall from a field of ten in a time of 4m.35¾s. During 1853 the belt changed hands four times, won in turn by Robert Chadwick, James Sherdon and John Syddall and Thomas Horspool. Shortly after winning the belt, Horspool sold it back to Samuel Heathcote's widow, Hannah, who was now running the Sheffield grounds. She put the belt up for a two mile championship won by Syddall, who in turn sold it to George Cooke of the New Copenhagen Grounds at Shepherds Bush, where it was once again put up as the One Mile Championship trophy. In 1856 it was first won by Syddall, then by John Seville and finally, on 10 November, by Thomas Horspool. He defended it against Seville in Manchester on 28 September 1857, equalling Westhall's 1852 record of 4m.28s. to become the outright holder and on 12 July 1858 set a new British record of 4m.23s. at the same venue.

let down as the *Sporting Life* reports:

> No time was lost after the winning post was fixed in the men getting off, which they did at the third attempt. Lang as soon as he had fairly settled on his pins, went away a 'cracker' in his old style of running. There was no mistake about it, he was again in his old form. After about 300 yards Lang was winning by fully ten yards, and as he past the stand first time round he was at least 15 yards in front of Albison. (The path at the Copenhagen Grounds was a circuitous route measuring 604 yards 2 feet.) Both men were running beautifully, and no diminution whatever in the race or alteration in the respective places of the men took place as they passed the stand for the second time round. Going down the back stretch Albison lengthened his stride. Gaining gradually on his man, inch by inch, the favourite was within half a yard of Lang, when the canal turn was reached. The excitement was now intense, for Lang again shot ahead, and despite all Albison's efforts he held a lead of about a yard until the straight was reached. Here Albison gained a momentary advantage, which was again wrested from him in the next few yards. The pace was now tremendous, and the excitement awful. Not a soul stirred or spoke. On the two came, every muscle stretched, every

THOMAS HORSPOOL (1830–?)
Thomas Horspool, born at Carrington, Lancashire on 22 May 1830, spent most of his early life in Nottinghamshire apprenticed to a glove-knitter. His running career commenced in 1851 and many of his races were at Hyde Park, Sheffield where he won the One Mile Belt from John Syddall in 1853. He was victorious once again in 1856 at Shepherds Bush, London and then in 1857 at the Copenhagen Ground, Manchester. On July 12, 1858 he beat Job Smith, who had ten yards start in one mile for £100 in a British Record time of 4m.23s. John Levett said: '*Thomas Horspool of Basford, once champion one mile runner, ran one mile at Copenhagen Grounds, Manchester in 4min.23sec. Defeated by the great H.A. (Henry Reed) in a half mile race for the belt and £50 at Halifax, by 1 yd. after an accident at the bottom turn, about 150 yards from the finish. The edge of the race track, which was raised ground, gave way to his foot, just as Tom, as he tells me was going to tell the Great H.A. to write home to his friends. This unprecedented half-mile race was run in 1min.58sec. Any man to have beaten either that day would have known they had been running when the race was concluded. Tom has done some brilliant performances, but so recently that I have no occasion to enumerate them here. He is a well-behaved fellow, now mine host of the New Inn, Hyson Green near Nottingham.*' He later became proprietor of the Mansfield Arms public house in Nottingham from which he had his One Mile Belt stolen on 31 January 1865.

sinew exerted. It was plainly a case of 'do or die' with both. There was not a foot between them as they passed the stand. Albison just had his breast in front, and that was all. About eight yards had to be run ere the tape was reached. Spurt after spurt was made by each; but there they remained in their old positions, neither being able to gain one single inch. Nature was fast telling her tale upon both; and the countenance of each betrayed the mighty struggle within. At last Albison's immense stride gradually gave him the advantage, and struggling manfully on, he obtained Mr Hayes hat by a yard. The time, four minutes twenty two and a quarter seconds.
A new British Record.

There was another challenge to come before 1860 drew to a close. George Martin had persuaded Charles Mower to join his stable alongside Jack White and immediately backed him against Albison. Again there was another fast race but Albison failed to repeat the performances produced during the previous six months and, on heavy ground, Mower won in a time of 4m.24s.

In 1861 George Martin was to take his runners to compete in America –

SIAH ALBISON (1840–?)

Siah Albison, born at Bow Lee, near Middleton, Lancashire on 26 April 1840, was a weaver by trade. He was one of the tallest pedestrians of his time, standing 5ft. 11in. and weighing 11st. He began his running career, at the age of 16, as a quarter-miler, at which distance he showed considerable speed, and by 1859 had become well known at the Copenhagen Grounds, Manchester, where he ran his last race ten years later in 1869. His first great performance, under his mentor Joseph Etchells of the Weaver's Arms, was winning the One Mile Champion Belt at the Copenhagen Grounds, Manchester in 1860 and after only one defeat in eight races he became the outright holder in October 1862. In his first defence of the title he defeated Lang to break the British record with a time of 4m.22¼s. He held the One and a Quarter Mile Cup at Sheffield for 12 months, recording a time of 5m.33½s. before James Sanderson took it from him in 1863. Albison made a rare visit to London on 6 June 1864 when Edward Mills beat him in a one-mile race at Hackney Wick. He recorded fast times at 440 yards, being narrowly beaten by John Nuttall of Barnsley in the latter's record-breaking run of 51.0s. at the Copenhagen Grounds, Manchester on 19 December 1859. His best time for the half mile was 1m.59¾s. against Lang also at the Copenhagen Grounds, Manchester in December, 1861. He became proprietor of the Britannia Inn, Newton Heath.

a visit that would result in the transformation of pedestrianism in England in the years that followed.

3

1861, The Arrival of Deerfoot

John Garratt's benefit – pedestrian camaraderie

At the beginning of 1861 London's pedestrian fraternity led by James Baum agreed that John Garratt, former landlord of the once famed 'Old Cope' (Copenhagen Grounds, Islington), who had fallen on hard times, should receive a benefit. The organising committee included the proprietors of all the pedestrian sporting houses and grounds in London: Robert Sadler of Garratt Lane, John Roberts of West London Cricket Ground, James Baum of Hackney Wick, Thomas Wilson of the Spotted Dog in the Strand, James Pudney of the Coach and Horses, Fred Chandler of the Red Lion, Blackman Street, Borough, Bill Price, Mr Burnman, Mr Sillman and Bill Preston.

JOHN GARRATT (18??–1871)
John Garratt established a sports ground at Copenhagen House, Islington in 1835. In 1850 he enclosed it and laid out a sprint ground for races up to 200 yards. By March 1851 a running path had been added with three laps to the mile. It was here that Garratt inaugurated the first properly organised championship, a ten-mile walk for a belt on 8 December 1851. This was followed by a ten-mile running championship on 12 January 1852. Here, also, Charles Westhall, ran the first sub-4½ minute mile (4m.28s.) on 26 July 1852 to establish the inaugural British one mile track record. The 'Old Cope' closed in March 1853 and became the Metropolitan Cattle Market; it is now the Business Design Centre. Garratt took over the Garrett Lane, Wandsworth, ground from Robert Sadler in 1861, changed its name to the Copenhagen Running Grounds, and set to work improving the establishment. By January 1862 he had railed the course and added a shower bath and dressing rooms. A number of spectacular events were held there, including the appearance of 'Deerfoot' in 1862. Unfortunately John Garratt's health deteriorated in 1863 and the ground was sold to George Woody who managed it for a short while until 1864 when it was abandoned due to objections from the local residents. It was built over in 1868. Garratt continued in the licensing trade and died on his premises, The Denmark public house in Old Brompton, in November 1871.

Thomas Wilson, proprietor of the Spotted Dog in the Strand

They agreed on a programme comprising a ten miles running handicap 'open to all', first prize £8, a three miles walking handicap for a silver cup and a 300 yard handicap, also for a silver cup; the last race being for the 'old 'uns'. A whole host of pedestrians, including Pudney, Jackson, Levett, Mills, Cooke, White the four, six and ten miles champion, Henry Reed the past half-mile champion, Charles Mower the one mile champion and George Beddow the Army champion, promised to run. Walkers included Charlie Westhall, still the only man to have walked 21 miles in three hours, William Spooner, the champion at 20 miles, and Seel from Staleybridge, the two mile walking champion. Tom Sayers the pugilistic heavyweight champion and Jem Mace the middle weight champion and aspiring champion of the world promised to attend and display their cups, etc., while Jack White and Charles Mower were to bring their pedestrian cups and belts.

The feelings of everyone involved in the benefit event were summed up in a letter to the *Sporting Life* from James Pudney.

> As one ready to give my best aid to Mr Garratt on 11 February. As the once Champion runner, I will bring my belt and other trophies, don my guernsey and running shoes on that day, and 'pull foot' the best I can to serve one who is so deserving, and who was always ready to support others. No one has more claim on pedestrians than Mr Garratt. I ran at the 'Old Cope' for the first Champions belt ever contended for; it was my fortune afterwards to reach the top of the tree, and myself as well as others have to thank Mr Garratt for the position we have held. Let us now do our best to repay his kindness.

Race day attracted 3,500 spectators including some 1,000 who had bought tickets in advance. The 300 yards handicap was won by Harry Reed off 20 yards and the three miles walking handicap by the much-travelled pedestrian Professor J. Thomas (The Salopian). The 10 miles

JOHN LEVETT (1826–?)
John Levett was born at Battersea, Surrey on 1 June 1826. His first recorded race was a win over one mile on Wandsworth Common in January 1848. Most of his early races were on the turnpike roads. Then when enclosed running paths became popular he ran at the Rosemary Branch Grounds in Peckham and the Flora Grounds in Bayswater. In 1851 he ventured away from the London area for the first time and recorded a number of wins over ten miles at the Hyde Park Grounds in Sheffield. In 1852 he won the first Ten Miles Champion Belt by defeating George Frost in a British record of 52m.35s. at the Copenhagen House Grounds in Islington. He raced Jackson twice for the belt and on the second occasion won in record time of 51m.45s. that lasted 33 years until beaten by William Cummings in 1885. In 1854 he also ran a new one hour record of 11 miles 350 yards at Liverpool. It was not until the appearance of James Pudney in 1854 that he finally found a runner who was regularly his superior. His career was also somewhat curtailed by an achilles tendon injury. In 1860 John Levett moved to Ireland where he had handicap wins at ten miles over Jackson, Pudney and Deerfoot and for a time managed the Rotunda Gardens Ground. Although he was present at John Garratt's benefit, his only racing appearance at Hackney Wick was in September 1861 when, well past his best, he ran in a ten miles handicap against John Brighton and Sam Barker. In 1862 he tried his hand at writing and produced a moderately good farce which the lessee of the Queen's Royal Theatre, Dublin, produced for his benefit. Mr Levett played the principal character with success. He also published a book, *How to Train.*

handicap was won by Sam Barker starting off two minutes in his colours of red with a white stripe from Pudney (all white), Mower (crimson) and White (white, blue spot) all off scratch; Mills (red) 2 mins; Jackson (white, black cap) 2½ mins; Cooke (black) 3 mins; Ray (blue, pink body) and Martin (green) 3½ mins; Taylor (white, pink body) 4½ mins; Quinton (yellow) 6 mins. The wearing of colours was one of a number of similarities between pedestrianism, pugilism and the turf, which also included betting and publication of race cards, challenges for the champion cups and belts, signing of articles and placing of stake moneys for matches.

Although many of the contestants, in particular Mower who ran just eight laps, dropped out after showing their prowess for the benefit of the spectators, they all sat down after the event to a knife and fork tea in the large room at Mr Baum's White Lion. Fred Chandler chaired the proceedings and John Garratt's health was duly and musically honoured. At the prizegiving Messrs Reed and Thomas gave the value of their cups

John Levett, Ten Miles Champion

for Mr Garratt's benefit and Sam Barker half his £8 prize, as did the placed men. Fortunately John Garratt's situation had improved greatly by the end of the year when he succeeded Sadler as the proprietor of the Garratt Lane Grounds in Wandsworth.

Another major benefit meeting was in June for Bill Price who had been a popular figure amongst pedestrians and the public for many years before becoming the successful manager of the grounds at Hackney Wick. He was known for his extremely good handicapping skill and was one of the best promoters of the sport. It speaks volumes for the respect in which he was held that upwards of 2,000 persons were on the ground during the afternoon. Pedestrians came from all parts to run for him and for the first time there was the

HENRY ALLEN REED (1825–1874)

Henry Allen Reed (Harry or H.A. to his friends) was born in March 1825 at High Wycombe in Buckinghamshire. His first race was at Stepney in 1847 when he won a 100 yards race and a silver snuff-box. Later that year he beat George Martin over 120 yards for £10 a side. By the following year he began to make a big impression recording 53½s. for 440 yards on Wandsworth Common on 24 July, then reducing his time to 48½s. in beating George Seward for £100 a side at Harlington Corner. Possibly his greatest race came on 11 April 1854 when against Thomas Horspool he became the first runner to beat two minutes for the half-mile on the track, winning in a time of 1m.58s. at Westhill Park Grounds, Halifax. He retired in 1858, having recorded wins over Seward, Sherdon, Westhall and Chadwick, all top pedestrians of the day. He made a brief comeback when Hackney Wick opened, winning a 300 yards handicap on 11 February 1861 and losing a 100 yards the following March. On his retirement he followed a career as a sports journalist for both *Bell's Life in London* and *Sporting Life*, and would often be seen at Hackney Wick officiating in a variety of capacities. He died a resident of Hanwell Asylum in 1874.

added attraction of pole-leaping, causing much excitement and amusement; six entered, and a keen contest was won by T. Robinson of Carlisle clearing 7ft. 6in.

White loses his titles but sets a new record

It was never going to be easy for John White to defend his three championship titles at four, six and ten miles. His loss of form in December 1860, when he was beaten over ten miles at Hackney Wick by Sam Barker, was put down to a serious illness which did not allow him to compete again until the end of February.

In the interim he had to forfeit his Four Miles Belt to the challenge of James Rowan and his Ten Miles Cup to that of James Pudney. The eventual fate of the Ten Miles Cup became most acrimonious as a Mr Morrow, one of Rowan's backers, considered the cup should be returned to Rowan as neither White nor Pudney had run for the cup and held it only through forfeit.

Further light, or perhaps confusion, was thrown on the affair when in reply to Mr Morrow, the following letter from William Price appeared in the correspondence column of *Sporting Life* on 20 March:

> I beg to remind him of a transaction which transpired between me and him, and to show the public how honourable a man Mr Morrow is. Some months back, when Rowan and White were matched for the Ten Miles Champions Cup, hearing that Rowan would have difficulty in making up the stake, £25, I wrote to him and offered to stand £5 in his stake, which he could have any time he applied for it. I received a letter from Mr Morrow, accepting my offer, and stating that I was to remit the £5 to him; but I waited until I saw Rowan in London, the day the last deposit was staked, when he told me to give the £5 to Mr Morrow. I also received a telegraph message, on the Sunday previous to the day the race was to take place, stating he would see me at James Pudney's in the evening. Immediately I saw him I gave him the £5, and asked him how his man Rowan was; he told me he was never better in his life, and thought he was sure to win the next day, and that I could bet any money on him. Now, this honest Mr Morrow knew at the time he was taking my money that Rowan had broken down and never intended running, or appearing on the ground the next day. Now I think, in common justice (which are his own words) to Mr Baum and the public, after receiving my £5 (which I think I was entitled to forfeit, as we cannot help accidents) he might have told me the truth, so that we could have advertised in the morning papers that no race would take place, and not have dis-

> appointed the public and got the journals into disrepute. For the future I hope that Mr Morrow will not be so ready to condemn others before he improves himself, for I am certain that both the holder and giver of the cup are far more honourable in their dealings than Mr Morrow, for both Pudney and Mr Baum have given up the ten mile cup to Rowan; and Pudney has also staked to run for the six mile belt, so that their remarks on their honesty are quite uncalled for. I also wish to remind him that I will match a man against Rowan for the ten miles championship cup, according to the conditions; so that Rowan need not take the cup in the un-English way Rowan did – without a race for it. – I remain, yours respectfully, W. Price, Manager of Hackney Wick.

With the whole matter ending most distastefully, James Baum decided to present a new cup for competition and allow Rowan to retain the old trophy.

John White, meanwhile, was determined to defend his Six Miles Belt against Pudney on 25 February but showed none of his old form and was soundly beaten.

It was another month before he felt well enough to sign articles for another match and this time he was no doubt pleased to be back in his adopted home of Manchester. This next race was to be over two miles at the Copenhagen Grounds on 20 April against James Sanderson who was given 20 yards.

The followers of the sport were eager to discover whether White had regained his form and the correspondent from the *Sporting Life* vividly describes the scene.

> On arriving at the front of the 'hostelrie', we found it to resemble an immense cab-stand, down each side of the road being lined with a great number of coaches, cabs, omnibuses, carts, and in fact vehicles of every description, that had already delivered their living freight within the enclosure; whilst the tops of houses, walls of adjacent property, hedges, mounds and trees were completely studded with anxious spectators, whose means were 'seedy', consequently they were content, provided they only got a bird's eye view of the impending contest. After waiting patiently at the lodge and biding our time, we at length got within the enclosure, when we found the grandstand tolerably well filled whilst there were some ten or twelve trustworthy men elevated in the pulpits, on tubs, and other rostrums, as the stakeholders for bets ... On the articles being signed for the present match Sanderson betook himself to quarters in his own neighbourhood, whilst White stayed with his backer, Mr George Hardy, mine host of the Rising Sun, Shudehill, Manchester, and took his breathings

> regularly with Billy Lang, who also belongs to the same formidable stable; but during the last few days he had been placed under the vigilant eye of the adept, Billy Fish, of Royton: and judging from the beautiful condition and glow of health in which each man seemed when stripped and ready for action, reflects the great credit on all parties connected therewith ... White was the first to make his appearance on the course, and was soon followed by a person bearing the name Sanderson on his back covered with a rug. At length all the usual preliminaries having been arranged, the men agreeing to finish at the top of the straight run, no time was lost, the ground being measured out, each man being cautioned with regard to jostling each other, they at once toed their respective marks, and being asked if they were ready, and answering in the affirmative, bang went the pistol and off went both men pretty evenly together.

The race was close throughout, the first mile covered in 4m.28s., and only eight or ten yards separated them at the finish with White the winner in a new British Record of 9m.20s.

Alongside White's return to form the up and coming runner in 1861 was undoubtedly Edward Mills. Edward 'Teddy' Mills soon to be nicknamed 'Young England' was trained by Bill Price at Hackney Wick and in time was to become holder of the British one mile record. Mills made his first public appearance at Hackney in January 1860 and was immediately taken in by Price, with whom he took up residence.

Mills' season began in January with wins over Howard of Brighton at Tunbridge Wells, and at Hackney, Percy of Gateshead and Whitmore of Leicester over 3 miles, and Jones of Islington over ten. Then he beat Manchester's Patrick Stapleton at one mile at the Snape Inn, Audenshaw, and Gateshead's Rowan in a ten mile race at Newcastle. He also took part in a number of open handicap meetings. His first defeat of the year came as late as 10 June, in the race for the new Ten Miles Champion Cup won by Pudney. In August, in a four miles race against Brighton at Hackney Wick, he was spiked and pulled up lame after a fast first two miles in 9m.44s. Previous to this race he had become holder of the Six-Miles Champion Belt by default when James Rowan could find no backer. Rowan had won the belt in April by completely outclassing Pudney, passing 3 miles in 14m.52s. to equal the British Record.

Visit to America

In the middle of the year there were some momentous events in the history of pedestrianism. George Martin who had the sprinter John Nevin, 400 yards 'Champion of England', in his stable along with

JAMES ROWAN (1836–1864)

James Rowan was born at Oakwellgate, Gateshead on 9 October 1836. As a boy, he commenced work as a 'sparks' at Hawkes, Crawshay & Co., Gateshead. Although diminutive in stature (as a young man he was 5ft. 4in. and only 7st. 7lb.) he soon realised he had a talent for running and began his pedestrian career by competing in matches on the local turnpike roads and on the old Newcastle racecourse. His first recorded races were in 1854 at the age of 17 when he beat various local pedestrians in matches up to 1¾ miles on the racecourse, with the stakes gradually rising to £25 a side. At the end of the year he raced two miles against time on the Newcastle racecourse in 9m.20s. and by 1855 he was running in Sheffield for £50 a side. At the age of 19 he travelled to Ayrshire for what was to be his biggest challenge to date. Lord Elgie of Ayr offered a prize of £50 for a ten-mile handicap that attracted pedestrians from far afield, among them Cooke from London, Bunn from Norwich, John Levett and William Jackson. Rowan was given a handicap of 220 yards and won easily. By 1859 he had taken the scalps of William Cummings, James Pudney, John White and Paddy Burns of Preston. Rowan's first appearance in London was in 1858 when he lost to Pudney over four miles. The following year he accepted an entry for the inaugural Ten Miles Cup at Hackney Wick won by Cooke, but although on the ground he did his reputation no good by withdrawing with no explanation. However in October Rowan challenged and beat Cooke, then defended against Jackson and Pudney before forfeiting to White the following September when he again failed to appear with no explanation. He briefly held the Six Miles Belt in 1861, equalling the English Record for three miles of 14m.52s. en route, but failed to defend the title through lack of backers. His last race was at Hackney Wick on 7 April 1862, when beaten by Richards, who had 100 yards start over three miles. Little was heard of Rowan after this and no doubt his drinking was his downfall. James Baum held a benefit for Rowan in November 1864 when he was in ill health, but he died on 6 December 1864. A correspondent who knew Rowan well afterwards wrote: '*When once he started he was a keen trainer, but out of training he lived a fast life and this was what really broke up a sound constitution and cut short his career. I was the last to see him out alive. In a trap we drove through Low Fell and up Peggy's Bank Wrekenton and Sheriff Hill. One question has been asked me many times and that is whether White or Rowan was supreme. I am bound to answer "Rowan" for he was the best sprinter that I ever knew and as a long distance runner no one could beat him.*'

George Martin with his athletes Charles Mower and John Nevin

Charles Mower and Jack White, who had recently set a new British Record in Manchester at two miles departed for America to run his athletes in the Fashion Pleasure Race Course Meeting at Long Island on 1 July 1861.

The English runners were unknown in America and Martin could see the opportunity for easily won prizes and wagers. However, it was to be a lucrative venture for Martin in more ways than one because of his meeting with Deerfoot. In the 440 yards race at Long Island, for a purse of 250 dollars, added to a sweepstake of 25 dollars each, Nevin won by six yards in a time of 52¼ seconds from J. Thomas of Newark. In the one mile race, also for a purse of 250 dollars added to a sweepstake of 25 dollars each, White and Mower had as their opponents Louis Bennett, Deerfoot, a Seneca Indian from the Cattaraugus Reservation, G. Adams of New York and Hobson of Trenton. The result was dead heat between White and Mower, 20 yards ahead of Bennett in the time of 4m.39¼s. By some extraordinary process of pedestrian logic, the judge allowed the lot to run in the second and deciding heat, but only White and the Indian started; when '*the "Tonnawanda Boy" was again made an exhibition of by "John Bull"*' winning by some 80 yards in 4m.55¼s. The *New York Clipper* commented on the appearance of the pair after the race:

> The applause that followed this achievement of the game little hero was deafening as he retired with his friends, exhibiting no more fatigue than if he had only walked over the distance he had run. The Indian's bellows seemed to be severely taxed, and he puffed like a locomotive, while the big veins swelled out and palpitated on his bronzed forehead. But he has every amount of pluck.

As the crowd were about to leave it was announced that a purse of 50 dollars had been raised for Johnny Grindell, a runner and volunteer in the Union Army who had been there to watch, to challenge White and Bennett to a race over ten miles. In this race, White, after stopping twice for refreshment, won by 100 yards from Grindell in 58m.40s., the Indian having been obliged to be removed from the course with a broken toe. The Americans swore that White ran like 'Flora Temple' (an American racehorse).

Deerfoot in London

Although Deerfoot had lost, George Martin saw the possibilities of using the Indian for some grand promotions in England and arranged his passage across the Atlantic. A short letter in *Sporting Life* on 7 August, announced his imminent arrival.

> Sir,
>
> Red Jacket, better known as Deerfoot, the Seneca Indian, of Cattaraugus, who intends to visit England for the purpose of testing his ability for speed and endurance against the English pedestrians, will sail for England on the 27th instant, by the steamship City of Washington, and will call at your office as soon as convenient after his arrival. He has recommendations to Mr J. McDonald, the trainer

of Heenan. It is his intention to run for the champions' belts from one mile to ten, and will be prepared to make the races about the 15th August.

I remain, yours respectfully, Wm. Miller, for RED JACKET
New York, July 19th, 1861.

Edward Mills was the first to take up the challenge:

Sir,

Seeing a letter in your last Wednesday's edition from Red Jacket, alias Deerfoot, the Seneca Indian, who intends visiting England to compete with our pedestrians, I beg to inform him I will make a match for £25 or £50 aside, to run him from one mile to five; or if he wishes to contend for the champions belt, I will run him for his own sum and the six miles belt, which Rowan has forfeited to me; and as his first visit will be to your office, if he will leave a deposit at the same time, I will cover it, and send articles as soon as possible, so that he can ensure a match as soon as he wishes.

I remain yours respectfully, Edward Mills,
Hackney Wick. August 9th.

That same day Deerfoot called at the offices of *Sporting Life* with the information that he had left a deposit in the hands of *Bell's Life*, in accordance with the conditions of the articles, to run the holders of the Six Miles Champion Belt and the Ten Miles Champion Cup. He was described as:

A fine specimen of the sons of the forest, standing 5 feet 11½ inches in height, and to all appearance weighing about 11 stone [compared with the average English pedestrians height of under 5 feet 6 inches and weighing only seven or eight stone]. His countenance is definitely Indian, of a deep copper colour, sharp ... features, straight black hair, piercing black eyes, and walks with an easy gliding step and looks altogether like going [pedestrians were often described in terms more akin to a race horse]. He, when he called upon us was dressed in full Indian costume – buffalo robe, etc. We should advise our clippers to look well to their laurels, as he means business and nothing else.

Deerfoot's first race in England was in reply to Mills' offer to contend for the Six Miles Champion Belt for £25 aside and a share of the gate money. This latter arrangement was often entered into when it was undoubtedly the pulling power of the top pedestrians which brought in a large crowd. Deerfoot took his first look at Hackney Wick one week before the big race, during a ten mile handicap between John Brighton, John Levett and Sam Barker, and expressed his astonishment at the smallness of the track, as in America he was used to tracks up to a mile round.

Deerfoot meets Mills at Hackney Wick

Jack MacDonald became Deerfoot's business manager and arranged as much publicity as possible with personal appearances and the circulation of unsubstantiated stories about his lifestyle to create interest before the big race to be held on 9 September. The race was set for six o'clock. However, as early as three o'clock large crowds thronged Fenchurch Street Station, where the arrangements at the booking office were quite inadequate for the occasion. The crowd, estimated at some 4,000, was still arriving after the start and the police had their work cut out keeping a path for the runners. MacDonald paraded Deerfoot around the ground, wearing a wolfskin cape, before dropping the garment from his shoulders to reveal an imposing figure 'stripped to the buff' with a slight red apron round his waist and a band round his head with one eagle feather. Mills by contrast was dressed in long-sleeved vest, tights and scarlet shorts. The race was run in a way not normally seen on English tracks as Deerfoot wearing English running shoes for the first time, urged on by Harry Reed, continually made surges that disturbed Mills' rhythm.

Mills, however, was not to be denied and, although because of injury (the spiking he received in the match against Brighton was later discovered to be a broken toe) his preparation had not been as good as he would have wished, he still came home 20 yards ahead in 32m.31½s. to retain his title. The crowd were delighted with the performance of the Indian and it was obvious to the pedestrian connoisseur that with a little more training and loss of weight he was going to be a contender to be reckoned with.

Deerfoot's next race at Hackney was to be two weeks later for the Ten Miles Champion Cup that had been surrendered by the holder James Pudney due to his lack of competitiveness. Before then, however, there was a four miles race in Manchester against Jack White, his adversary from New York, to be settled. In the race for £25 a side, Deerfoot was given a 50 yards start that White gradually made up before Deerfoot sprinted away at the end to win by ten yards. For the race to be this close was seen as something of a surprise as White was far from being in good shape, having recently forfeited a challenge for the One Mile Belt and pulled out before halfway in a five miles handicap at the Victoria Running Ground in Newcastle. It would not be long before the public began to question the honesty of some of Deerfoot's races particularly when a share of the gate money was the main financial incentive to those competing.

Deerfoot, the renowned Indian pedestrian and one hour record holder

According to the *Sporting Life*'s editorial of 25 September:

> in recent years at grounds of the less scrupulous proprietors many "barneys" were "got up" upon the disgraceful principle of "gate money," and gate money only, that the detection led to disgust, the grounds were visited almost exclusively by roughs, who hustled and bullied the few decent people, and were not at all particular in whose pocket they found their hands. Mr. Baum, at Hackney Wick, has done much to amend this state of things; and any person of respectability who wishes to witness a pedestrian encounter, can do so with perfect safety and convenience ...

The race for the Ten Miles Champion Cup at Hackney the following week on 23 September, was to be an altogether different affair with Deerfoot and three of England's top pedestrians competing; Mills (now trained by William Richards, a Welshman based in Millwall and later joint holder of the English one mile record), Brighton, again the holder of the Four Miles Belt (trained by Alfred Milner), and White (now trained by John Nevin as George Martin his backer had found his conduct too difficult to handle). The three runners added a sweepstake of £10 each to the £20 offered by Mr Baum with the winner receiving £50 and the Cup. In order to keep the anticipated large crowd to a manageable size the price of entry was increased to an unprecedented one shilling.

The 3,000 to 4,000 spectators watched spellbound as White and Mills took on the Indian, but at three miles White succumbed. Mills tried everything possible to get away from Deerfoot but each time he gained a few yards his opponent came back and took the lead. At six miles Mills was beginning to show the strain of these continual surges and at eight and a half miles had run himself out and had to be helped off the track by his friends. Deerfoot went on to finish alone in 54m.20s. There was now no doubt that Deerfoot was something special.

The popularity of Deerfoot brought many who had not previously witnessed pedestrianism to Hackney and the following letter in the *Sporting Life* under the heading 'Revival of Pedestrianism' is interesting for its description of Hackney Wick by someone not used to the relatively seedy environment of professional running.

> Sir,
>
> Referring to some remarks recently made by you upon the subject of one of the most manly of our pastimes, and what should be one of our leading national sports – viz., foot racing, I am led to address you to uphold not only that which you so ably advance, but if possible, to pave the way to a regulation of this truly noble recreation. The other day I attended for the first time in my life, a pedes-

LOUIS BENNETT 'DEERFOOT' (1830–1896)
Deerfoot (real name Louis Bennett) was born on the Cattaraugus Reservation in Erie County, New York, around 1830. Deerfoot's first recorded races, many against Albert Smith, the Indian champion of the Tonawandas, were in Buffalo commencing in 1854 and by 1856 he had run a respectable 56m.19s. for ten miles. In June 1861 George Martin arrived in New York with John White, Charles Mower and John Nevin with the object of making some easy money by pitting his outstanding but relatively unknown runners against the best in America. A series of races with White and Mower matched against Deerfoot and Smith was won by the English pedestrians with ease. But Martin realised that Deerfoot was an outstanding runner and saw the possibilities of promoting him in England to their mutual advantage. Deerfoot arrived in London from New York on 7 August 1862 and challenges were immediately issued to the holders of the Ten Miles Cup and Six Miles Belt. Tired from his journey, Deerfoot made an inauspicious start but was soon beating the best that England could offer. He outran Mills, Brighton and White in October to win the Ten Miles Cup, but failed against Mills for the Six Miles Belt and was beaten by him on Boxing Day over eight miles. By the end of the year he had run 16 races and beaten many of the other top runners including John Levett in Dublin, William Jackson, Sam Barker and W. Jones. Early in 1862 Martin devised a scheme whereby a portable track would be transported around the country with Deerfoot running at a different venue each day against Jackson, Mower, Brighton and Andrews. The races were basically exhibitions with Deerfoot winning each time. By September he had completed over 100 appearances. Unfortunately the tour was poorly financed and by the end Deerfoot's stature was somewhat stained. Deerfoot quickly recovered, however, and was soon showing his true colours by attacking various long distance records. During his final months in England he established a world record at 10 miles (51m.26s.) and three times broke the one hour record, culminating in 11 miles 970 yards. By the time he left England in May 1863 he had raised the standard of English pedestrianism several-fold. On his return to America he ran several more races, including a five miles win over Richards on 19 June 1869 at the Fair Grounds, Cleveland for a stake of $2,000. Generally, however, he had no notable success and retired to his native reservation at Cattaraugus in New York where he died on 18 January 1896.

trian race – the late one between Deerfoot, White and Mills for the so called ten mile championship, at a place known as the White Lion, Hackney Wick. In my simplicity I expected to see something after the model of a public racecourse on a reduced scale. Judge of my surprise then, upon reaching this much talked-of place, to find the remains of what was once, I presume, a public tea garden, in the last state of decay. A ragged, uneven, dingy grass plot in the centre (which was permitted knock 'em-downs, to the annoyance and danger of the major portion of the public), encompassed by a wretched dirty walk (about five feet wide), bordered on either side by faded willow trees, here and there a frowsy shrub, broken posts and rails, and tumble-down tables, forming altogether the debris, or rather, I should say, the wreck of a place, as uninviting to the eye, as inconvenient to the person, and about the last, I should say, in which a race of the kind I saw should have been held. Round, and round, and round went the pedestrians – it takes six times round to make a mile, I believe – until it made me giddy to look at them, added to which, the public were allowed to congregate on the said path (course I cannot call it), so that the competitors had the appearance of forcing their way through a disorderly mob, while dodging between broken posts, decayed willow stumps, and other obstructions. Racing indeed; call it scrambling and scuffling along amid interruption, if you will. It is the first foot race to which I and my companions ever went; and if this be the best racecourse that London affords for this manly sport, it will be the last. Now, Mr Editor, having had my grumble, let us see if this state of things can be remedied. Since this child of the prairie – this Deerfoot is exciting so much attention, and causing thousands to attend foot races who never saw a man run before, cannot something be done towards establishing a metropolitan racecourse where these manly and healthy exercises can be encouraged and take place to advantage? I suggest the ground be secured ...

Yours very truly.

The editor under the initials S.L. commented:

Mr Baum is certainly labouring under the disadvantage of a small ground, and, from the fact of the great sewer having turned the old brook which ran through them, they naturally look in an unfinished state; but we know that Mr Baum has, at great expense, secured land to enlarge the race-ground, and he promises that next spring it shall be second to none; nevertheless, however small the ground and bad the accommodation maybe pedestrians will run where the advertised money is given, and where straightforward hands on the part of the management has always been the order of the day. This conduct accounts for the extraordinary number of entries for the different handicaps as well as the overflowing crowds to witness them.

Mills and Deerfoot now went their separate ways, running weekly in handicaps all over the country, although Deerfoot had one more match in

London, at Brompton, on 14 October when he easily beat William Jackson, the America Deer.

The accompanying illustration of the race from the *Illustrated Times* is graphically described in the *Sporting Life*.

> Mr. Roberts' intention was to have charged spectators outside the barrier, one shilling; and those within, half-a-crown; but after a rich harvest had been made from the last-mentioned source, the barrier was thrown open, and the mob admitted indiscriminately, to the annoyance of those who deluded themselves with an idea that they had paid for an exclusive position. The scene prior to the race was peculiarly imposing, and the dense mob of heads on the raised embankment could be compared with nothing but the Grand Stand at Epsom on Derby Day. Every elevated position from which a view of the race could be secured was taken possession of; while, notwithstanding numerous skirmishes with the police and others, some hundreds contrived to climb over the fences and into the grounds, without 'parting'. The windows of the many handsome villas overlooking the grounds were filled with ladies and gentlemen, while men wedged themselves in the branches of trees, or stormed the very insecure outhouses in the grounds, the rafters of which cracked and bent to the occasional alarm and nervousness of those inside.

The race between Deerfoot and William Jackson at Brompton in October 1861

It was not until 11 November that Mills returned to Hackney, this time to defend his Six Miles Champion Belt against the challenge of Brighton. Mills was now in terrific form and destroyed Brighton with an opening mile of 4m.44s. and by four miles the race was won.

Meanwhile James Baum and the manager, Bill Price, set about improving matters at the Hackney Wick Running Grounds, knowing full well that when Deerfoot next appeared for his match against Sam Barker they would probably have to cater for up to 10,000 spectators. The fence round the ground was set back some yards and the entire course railed in. The railway embankment was enclosed to form an immense grandstand and all the boxes on which spectators stood on the left-hand side of the ground were removed. The centre ground was also railed in to keep the spectators out, thus enabling everyone to have a view of the whole race from start to finish. To accommodate the many ladies who expressed a wish to attend, the pedestrians were to run in guernseys and long drawers and reserved seats were made available in a comfortable enclosed area for an extra charge.

Two weeks later, on 25 November, Deerfoot returned to Hackney to defend his ten miles championship against Sam Barker. Since Deerfoot had last appeared at Hackney there had been a deluge of correspondence in the sporting press about his ability – and match fixing. It seemed many of his opponents were just cashing in on his popularity without preparing properly. This time, however, with a genuine match in prospect, an expected crowd of 10,000 was drawn to Hackney Wick. The *Sporting Life* described the scene as follows:

> It is thought some 10,000 people attended the ground notwithstanding the cold cheerless weather. The fence around the ground had been thrown back some yards, and the entire course was railed-in. The railway embankment, which forms a portion of the grounds, had been turned to rare account, and formed an immense grand stand, which was so densely occupied that it could be likened unto nothing during the race but the Grand Stand at Epsom on the Derby Day. Although the main bulk of the visitors came by the totally inadequate, for such numbers, 'iron road,' the 'macadamised way' had also been enormously patronised and in front of the house was a great nest of vehicles of every description, but chiefly 'hansoms' and 'showfuls'. For hours the rush for admission was terrific, and it required a strong body of ticket takers and police to prevent the intrusion of the crowds en masse. Even after the men had been started thousands continued to arrive, and many hundreds of people returned to town rather than brave a battle with the roughs. Every nook and crevice from which a glimpse of the contest could be obtained was occupied, and no little merriment was caused by the

Samuel Barker, 'The Billingsgate Boy,' holder of the Ten Miles Champion Cup

repeated break downs of lottery platforms, which people had contrived to enable them to see over the heads of those in front of them. The double rows of trees around the course were soon stormed, and men and boys clung to the branches and boughs, which looked anything but calculated to bear the weight.

As to the race itself, the contestants paraded around the ground before the start, Barker attended by Richards, Deerfoot by Mower. Following the usual pattern of these races the Englishman led from the start and it was 16 laps (2½ miles) before Deerfoot came up to his man to increase the pace. The same happened on the 26th lap (four miles) after which the lead changed hands continuously until seven miles as each tried to assert himself. At this point Barker staggered from the exertions he had made and looked deathly pale, but battled on and was still in the lead at nine miles. Shortly after, however, he fell exhausted and was assisted off the ground by Richards and several friends. The mile times taken on the by now fashionable Benson's marking chronometer were: 4m.55s.; 10m.23s.; 15m.37s.; 20m.56s.; 26m.13s.; 31m.43s.; 37m.30s.; 42m.52s.; 48m.25s.; the time up to the fall of Barker was 50m.34s.

Deerfoot ran the remaining distance through a narrow path made by the crowd, and on finishing leapt in the air with a wild shriek of victory. He was surrounded by the mob; grasping him by the hand, and patting him on the back 'with all that generous enthusiasm which Englishmen bestow upon those who have distinguished themselves in our national sports'. Before the great body of spectators dispersed, there was a great roar for Deerfoot, who appeared at the window of the White Lion where the massive silver cup had stood for inspection throughout the afternoon, and the Indian grasped the prize then flourished it victoriously above his head with a shrill war whoop. There was a loud cheer for Barker whose great display of gameness had never been excelled. But the brave fellow was unable to leave the sofa; indeed it was some time before he recovered sufficiently to stand the fatigue of dressing.

SAMUEL BARKER (1833–?)

Samuel Barker of Billingsgate, born on 5 April 1833, was a small man standing only 5ft. 4in. and weighing just over 7 stone. He trained under the guidance of Bill Price at Hackney Wick where he ran most of his races, commencing with the win of a silver watch in a one-mile handicap on 25 January 1858. He began to have some success the following year, finishing second in the Ten Miles Championship and later taking the scalps of Toddy Ray and William Jackson. He ran a number of times for the Ten Miles Cup and after second places to Pudney and Deerfoot eventually held it briefly in 1862 when he beat W. Jones of Islington. Barker rarely ventured to race away from London, but at Worcester in June 1862 he won an eight miles handicap beating Mills, Richards and Stapleton. He ran occasionally in the 1870s and his last race was over two miles in Cambridge in 1875. He became proprietor of the Queen Catherine public house in Pollard's Row, Bethnal Green Road.

Mills, Brighton, Deerfoot, Lang and Barker at Cambridge in December 1861

Another highlight of these early months of Deerfoot's England visit came on 4 December, when, at the invitation of John MacDonald, a local solicitor and well known amateur runner on the professional circuit, he ran six miles on Fenner's cricket and recreation ground at Cambridge against Lang, Brighton and Barker. Edward Mills was also at the ground but unable to run because of a severe cold acquired during his exertions at Newcastle and Leeds the previous week. However, he was able to be part of a memorable photograph taken of the runners presented by George Martin to H.R.H. The Prince of Wales, who after the race gave to Deerfoot and to each of his rivals a purse containing monetary reward. The referee and timekeeper on this great occasion was Harry Reed who recorded a win for Deerfoot in 31m.54¾s. four yards ahead of Brighton, while Hackney Wick officials Bill Price, Dick Lewis and William Richards helped with the organisation and manned the entrance gates.

There was to be one last great race at Hackney Wick in 1861 – Mills against Deerfoot on 16 December. Their rivalry was enormous and in their two most important encounters Mills had been victorious at six miles and Deerfoot at ten miles. The meeting was destined to be gladiatorial. George Martin and William Price, the two promoters, agreed that a match at eight miles for £100 aside would bring out the best in both men as well as attracting a large betting crowd and drew up the following articles.

ARTICLES OF AGREEMENT entered into this 8th day of November, between Deerfoot (the Seneca Indian), and Edward Mills (*alias* Young England), they agreeing to run the distance of eight miles, for £100 a side, on Monday, the 16th of December, at the White Lion Race Grounds, Hackney Wick; to start at three o'clock precisely. The first deposit of £5 a side is now deposited in the hands of the Editor of the *Sporting Life*. The next deposit of £5 a side to be made good on Friday, the 15th of November, the next, of £15 a side, on Friday, the 22nd of November; the next of £25 a side, on Friday, the 29th November; the next of £25 a side, on Friday, the 6th of December; and the final deposit, of £25 a side, on Friday, the 13th of December. The Editor of the *Sporting Life* to be the final stakeholder, and to appoint a referee. Either party failing to comply with these articles to forfeit the money staked. The men to be on the mark at three o'clock precisely. All the deposits to be made good at the office of the *Sporting Life*.

GEORGE MARTIN (for Deerfoot)

WILLIAM PRICE (for Edward Mills).

Edward Mills 'Young England,'
Champion at six and ten miles

As was hoped the likely closeness of the outcome in a fair race led to more betting than usual and in the London clubs wagers as high as £4,000 were rumoured with race day drawing a vast throng estimated between 8,000 and 9,000.

For the contest over fifty-three laps and 200 yards, Mills just recovered from a severe cold and several visits to the Turkish baths, was attended by Barker and dressed in a white silk tunic with black short drawers over the top. Deerfoot attended by Lang wore the same English costume but with crimson drawers. Mills adopted different tactics for this race allowing Deerfoot to do most of the leading but making sure he put him under pressure the whole time. The contrast between the two runners, both in style and size, could not have been greater; Deerfoot lunging along with his rolling action, whilst his lesser opponent went over the ground as lightly as though running on air. The first time Deerfoot got away was around five miles when Mills' shoe burst open compelling him to run on his heel to prevent it slipping off. Eventually he discarded the shoe and continued the battle as if nothing had happened. Nothing separated the runners as they entered the final stages of the race and the crowd from all parts of the ground rushed to the finish and the course was so blocked up that it was almost impossible for the men to run. As they entered the straight run in, Mills was leading by about a yard, but when within forty yards of home, Deerfoot made a tremendous rush in an endeavour to pass Mills, but came in contact with one of the spectators causing him to cannon into Mills. Mills was the first to recover – but Deerfoot sprinted again as both passed the post together in 43 minutes with the six-mile mark passed in a time of 31m.38s. Much to Mills' dismay a dead heat was declared and Mills, who thought he had won, immediately challenged Deerfoot to race again on the same terms.

So who was the better runner, Mills or Deerfoot? Much has been written about the intense racing schedule undertaken by Deerfoot, whereas that of Mills is not generally recognised as being so arduous. In fact between their first meeting on 9 September and the end of November Deerfoot had eleven races and Mills ten. Unfortunately Mills was iil towards the end of November and had to take a break from racing while Deerfoot competed a further three times. During this period Mills and Deerfoot raced each other on seven occasions:

09.09.61	Mills beat Deerfoot over six miles in 32m.31½s. at Hackney Wick.
23.09.61	Deerfoot beat Mills over ten miles in 54m.20s. at Hackney Wick.
07.10.61	Deerfoot beat Mills and Levett over one hour. At ten miles Mills and Deerfoot were level in 54m.10s. at which point Mills retired. Deerfoot completed 11 miles 200 yards in the allotted time. In Dublin Deerfoot reached 12 miles in 65m.06s.
28.10.61	Deerfoot beat Mills in a four-mile handicap in Birmingham where ambitious handicapping gave Deerfoot 50 yards start.
04.11.61	In a one-mile handicap meeting in Sheffield, Mills ran close to 4m.30s. in his heat but did not qualify, while Deerfoot dropped out of his heat.

13.11.61	Deerfoot beat Mills over ten miles in 55m.15s. to 55m.16½s. at Portsmouth.
16.12.61	Mills and Deerfoot dead-heated over eight miles in 43m. at Hackney Wick.

Mills had, I believe, proved himself the better man at distances up to six miles and was Deerfoot's match at eight miles; at ten miles he had proved himself more capable than others to give Deerfoot a 'race'. For the final reckoning there was to be a year's wait.

4

1862, A Year to Remember

Amateurs at Hackney Wick

The top professionals continued to battle for dominance at Hackney Wick but there was also a move to accommodate the demands of amateurs. There had been a number of letters in the sporting press arguing that amateur races should be organised for those not involved with the universities and public schools; as yet there were no amateur athletic clubs, the first was to be formed in 1863.

William Price was the first to answer this need and he advertised Hackney's first amateur meeting in the *Sporting Life* on 9 July, offering:

> Four silver cups to be contended for by gentlemen amateurs only, at the following distances: – 100 yards, quarter of a mile, half a mile, and one mile to take place 26th July. Entrance 5s. and acceptance, 2s.6d. [expensive races to run in!] gentlemen to be fairly handicapped according to their previous performances. Entries to W. Price at the White Lion, who will forward a card of handicaps to any gentlemen sending his address, as the names of the gentlemen will not be published.

In professional circles it was viewed that gentlemen amateurs would not like to see their names associated with such an event, particularly as betting was in evidence.

The races took place on Saturday, 26 July with 19 entries, a reasonable turnout for such a daring venture. There were two heats and a final in the 100 yards won by Mr Green who had beaten Mr Martin in his heat. Mr Martin was in fact C.M. Callow of the Civil Service and later Ranelagh Harriers. Mr Spicer of the Honorable Artillery Company, off 20 yards won the half mile in 2m.09s. from Walter Chinnery, wearing a pair of running shoes lent to him by Teddy Mills; both running under their own names. In the 440 yards Mr Franks the long handicap man won easily. The final race over one mile was a very poor two-man affair.

Walter Chinnery, a founder member of Mincing Lane Athletic Club the following year, describes Hackney Wick in *The 'House' on Sport* published in 1898:

Walter Chinnery, amateur one mile record holder

> A small ground about 260 yards round, and the turns were awkward. The whole place had a decayed and melancholy appearance, and was practically like an untidy tea garden with a running path (as it were by chance) in the midst. In spite of the disadvantages of the ground and its turns some splendid performances were done upon it.

Chinnery ran at Hackney Wick again on 30 August, when a second meeting of amateur handicaps for silver cups was held. This time off 10 yards, Spicer again beat him off scratch by 15 yards in a three-quarter mile race. The meeting was a great success as far as the running was concerned but attracted little public interest. The followers of the pedestrians (four thousand turned out the following Monday to watch the race for the Ten Miles Champions Cup), found little interest in an amateur meeting.

WALTER CHINNERY (1843–1905)

Walter Chinnery was born at Norwood in Surrey on 19 August 1843. On leaving school he joined a City firm of stockbrokers. Chinnery is famed for being the first amateur to run a mile in four and a half minutes on 10 March 1868 at Corpus College, Cambridge. His running career started on Christmas Eve 1861 when he won the half-mile at Bolton's Cricket Club, Brompton in 2m.35s. on very heavy grass. In 1862 he ran in the first two amateur meetings promoted at Hackney Wick where on both occasions, in a half-mile handicap and then three-quarter mile handicap he lost to W.J. Spicer. In 1864 he was a founder member of the newly formed Mincing Lane Athletic Club which trained at the Prince of Wales Running Ground, Bow where the many professional runners using the ground advised members. In the Club's first meeting at Bow on 21 May, he easily won the mile in front of 500 spectators. Later in 1864 the club moved headquarters to the Old Brompton Ground and was renamed the London Athletic Club with Chinnery as the Honorary Secretary. In 1866 in the first Amateur Athletic Club Championship Chinnery finished third behind two university runners. His best season came in 1868 when he won the A.A.C. one mile and four miles championships. In the four miles he broke the British amateur record in a time of 21m.11s. His career ended in 1870 when pressure of work as a member of the Stock Exchange meant he had little time for athletics. Walter Moresby Chinnery died on 29 March 1905.

WALTER RYE (1843–1929)

Walter Rye was born in Chelsea on 31 August 1843 and qualified as a solicitor in his father's practice. His first public race was over 300 yards at Beaufort House in West London in 1861 and he took part in William Price's Amateur Handicaps at Hackney Wick the following year. He recorded times in amateur races at distances from 200 yards to two miles before turning to walking in 1865, and climaxed his career by winning the AAC Championship 7 miles walk in 1868. Rye was greatly involved in amateur athletics administration; he followed Chinnery as secretary of the LAC in 1869/1870 and became founder and secretary of Thames Hare and Hounds in 1868. While president of this famous club he takes credit for initiating the first cross country championship for athletic clubs in 1877. He was a founder member of the AAA although he resigned within in two years, in many respects due to his outspoken views on amateurs who he considered should be 'gentlemen by profession and education'. He was for many years athletic correspondent of the *Sporting Gazette* and wrote his autobiography in 1916. He was Mayor of Norwich in 1908 and died in Norfolk on 24 February, 1929.

In the 240 yards handicap Walter Rye was one of the competitors, listed as Mr 'R . . . e', 'as there was at the time a prevalent idea that an amateur athlete should conceal from the world his taste for athletics, and the report of this meeting is couched in these mysterious terms.' Walter Rye became an outspoken promoter of the 'gentleman amateur'.

Other events

Again there were a number of benefit meetings throughout the year. Local pedestrians Edward Mills and Sam Barker both profited from events arranged by James Baum and at Mills' benefit the heat winners received a copy of Newbold's print of Mills.

Many celebrity pugilists were also aided and one of the most memorable benefits was that for Jem Mace the Champion of England and Tom King his opponent in a recent 'slashing fight' for the Champions Belt. Jem Mace was not a bad pedestrian himself, reputedly covering as much as 40 miles on some days in training, and held the Champion Pugilist Racing Cup, won at Clay Hall, Bow in 1860. He was born in 1831 at Beeston, near Swaffham in Norfolk, but had settled locally and was host at the Old King John public house in Holywell Road, Shoreditch, until it was pulled down to accommodate the railway line. His trainers at one time included Bob Bunn, a well known Norwich pedestrian, and Alf Milner, a noted pedestrian trainer. The benefit meeting in March 1862 attracted 2,000 spectators to watch seven boxing bouts followed by Mace and King displaying their belts and partaking in a friendly three-round spar to tremendous cheering from the crowd. Benefits for the champion pugilists became an annual event at Hackney Wick and by the time the grounds closed at the end of the decade there were few who had not been recipients of the public's and Mr Baum's generosity.

As for the top pedestrian, Deerfoot returned to racing in February when he had an easy win at six miles over Job Smith at Wandsworth followed by a seven yard win at ten miles over John Brighton at Brompton in 53m.07s.

Deerfoot returned to Hackney Wick in early March to beat William Lang at six miles in 31m.16s. However, Deerfoot mania was definitely on the wane and none of these London outings attracted large crowds. George Martin took Deerfoot to the provinces in March and April where he won a number of unexciting races but realised that Deerfoot had to break records to attract big crowds and offered to back his man for any part of £1,000 to run 11¼ miles in the hour, a feat that would have to wait for another year.

In the meantime George Martin decided that to tour the smaller English towns where the population would in normal circumstances have no

Jem Mace and Tom King sparring at Hackney Wick in March 1862

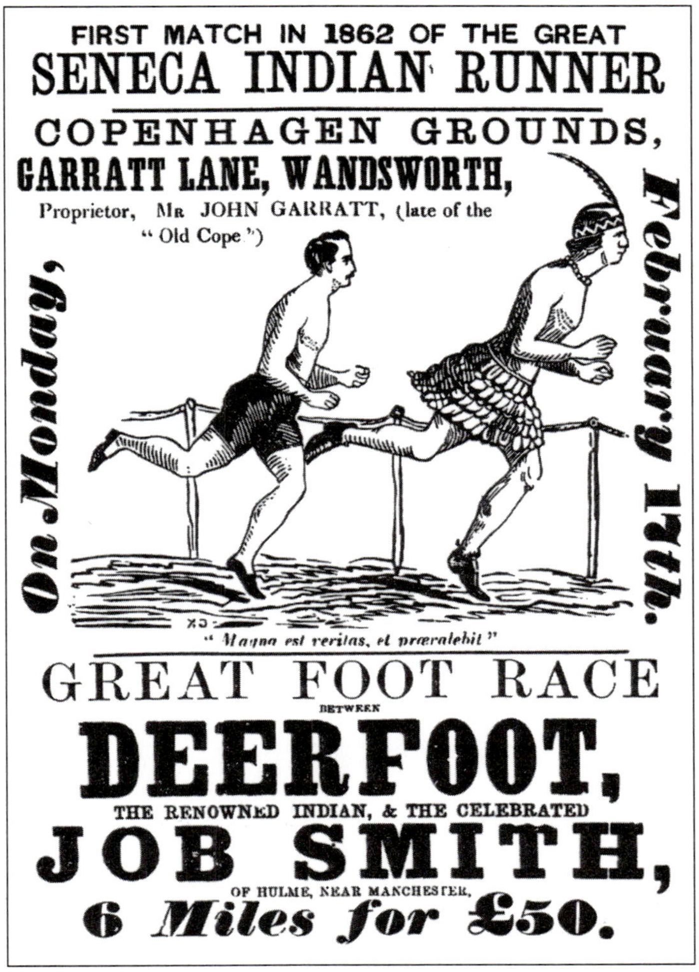

Poster featuring the race between Deerfoot and Job Smith at Wandsworth in February 1862

opportunity to see Deerfoot was a way to further their monetary interests and he placed the following advertisement in the *Sporting Life*:

> Deerfoot's Travelling Race Ground. – George Martin wishes to inform the public that, having received so many applications for Deerfoot to run at various parts of the country, and so few places being enclosed where a race can take place, Martin has, at enormous expense, built a portable race course, twelve feet high, and nearly a quarter of a mile in circumference, so that a race can take place in any town where an even piece of ground can be selected. Deerfoot, Brighton, Lang, Mower, Jackson and Andrews will contend in a four miles race every evening, and will run in the same costume as they appeared in before HRH the Prince of Wales. In addition to the above, prizes will be given for all kinds of English sports, such as

> sack racing, jumping, throwing the hammer, vaulting from a spring-board, &. &. Entries to be made at the ground, by two o'clock, to Geo.Martin. Route: – This day (Saturday), Aldershot; Monday May 12, Windsor; Tuesday 13 Harrow; Wednesday 14 St.Albans; Thursday 15 Hertford; Friday 16 Hitchin; Saturday 17 Bedford; Monday 19 Northampton. Agent in advance, Geo. Cassidy.

According to Harry Andrews, a member of the troupe, Deerfoot encountered some first class men in the north of England and elsewhere, who tried hard to win the first prize of £50 offered to any runner not in the troupe, but Deerfoot invariably proved himself too good for the outsiders. Throughout their journeyings the men had to put up with serious inconveniences. Nearly every day long distances had to be covered,

HARRY ANDREWS (1833–1885)
Harry Andrews was born on 28 May 1831 in Monmouth. At 5ft. 5½in. and only 7st. 9lb. he was typical of the pedestrians of his day. He ran his first race over one mile for £5 aside on Wanstead Flats, East London on 14 April 1854. His best performance was in beating Deerfoot and Jackson in a 12 miles handicap at Canterbury in September 1862. He briefly held the Four Miles Champion Cup presented by Charles Wilson at the Prince of Wales Grounds, Bow, and was a member of Martin's troupe that toured England, Scotland, Wales and Ireland with Deerfoot. When Bill Price bet him a 'dollar' that he could not run 11 miles in the hour and 15 miles in one hour and a half, he performed these feats at Hackney Wick showing his friends that he couldn't 'stand chaff'. According to the *Illustrated Sporting News* he travelled to France with the American Indian pedestrian Steeprock in 1865, but the speculation did not pay off and he returned to London as the assistant manager at the Brompton grounds. Although never a great runner he competed regularly to the end of the 1860s, and in his last race at the Lillie Bridge Grounds in 1871, finished second in a four miles handicap. In 1869 when living at 2 Little Cottage, Fulham, he began coaching at the nearby Star grounds and Beaufort House grounds and during the 1870s made a second career in athletics, training amateur athletes at the universities, Woolwich Military Academy and London Athletic Club. He also sold athletic equipment and managed the Lillie Bridge Grounds and later the Surbiton Recreation Grounds where he trained amateur and professional athletes. His book, *A Few Practical Hints to Amateurs on Training for Walking and Running, Rowing, Bicycling and other Athletic Sports*, was published in 1876 when he was living in Hammersmith. He died on 7 March 1885 leaving his widow and family totally unprovided for.

frequently on foot, from one town to the next. Once they walked through the night at least 37 miles from Macclesfield to Chesterfield, and ran again on the same day. On another occasion they actually ran twice on the same day in different towns. Deerfoot was successful in every match, but eventually an unpleasant feeling arose amongst the Englishmen, who did not like to see the Indian always winning and were determined to reverse the tables. This they accordingly did at Montrose in Scotland, when Deerfoot was run clean off his legs by three of the troupe. Afterwards at Glasgow, where upwards of 40,000 people had assembled to witness the racing, the Indian again had to lower his colours to two of the troupe. This latter race caused an immense amount of excitement at the time. Having suffered defeat on several other subsequent occasions, Deerfoot thought it time to return to his native shores but Mr Martin offered a valuable belt for a final race. In this last respect Andrews' memory had not got the facts quite right, as will be seen as events unfold in the following pages, and Deerfoot was to put up some wonderful performances before running his final race in England.

Edward Mills' 1862 season started at Newcastle towards the end of January. This was followed by three races on successive days in late February, a fast four miles at Hackney Wick on 24 February, when he beat William Cummings of Liverpool for £50 a side in 20m.18s., a win at six miles in 31m.20s. against good opposition at Wandsworth and an easy victory over four miles at Oxford. The result of this intense period of racing was a recurrence of injury and he pulled up lame in a two-mile match against W. Jones at Hackney Wick. Mills' big races would come later in the year.

Renewed battle for the Ten Miles Champion Cup

Deerfoot's Ten Miles Champion Cup had been returned to James Baum in December 1861, when it was realised that Deerfoot's stay in England would be too short for him to become the permanent holder. A new engagement for the title of Champion began with a race at Hackney Wick on 6 January 1862. Challenges for the Cup continued to draw large crowds and even on this inhospitable day 2,000 spectators assembled for a race which in the event proved a bitter disappointment. There were four entries, Edward Mills, Sam Barker and W. Jones all from London and John Brighton from Norwich. The path was now properly railed all round with only the starter and officials allowed in the centre of the ground. In the race Barker pulled up with an injured leg after one mile, while an 'out of training' Mills ran only five miles albeit fast enough to see off Jones. This left Brighton, after passing six miles in 31m.35s., to finish at his leisure. However, Brighton afterwards declined to defend the

JOHN BRIGHTON (1831–?)
John Brighton was born at New Leighton, Norwich, on 14 July 1831. Little Jack, as he was familiarly termed, lived for 14 years with Mr George Clark, an extensive dairy farmer at Tuxwood Farm, Leighton. The future pedestrian was noted when a child for running beside, not riding in, the milk-cart – hence his nickname 'Milkboy'. Brighton's first match over one mile was when he was backed for a small stake by his master against Brosh Sherman of Norwich in 1851, which he won on the Earlham Road in 5 minutes. From this he obtained a match with Bob Bunn of Norwich and was beaten by only 10 yards over a mile in 4m.31s. and proved to all he was a 'clipper'. Next, George Figg (the celebrated cricketer) then of the Boars Head in conjunction with Jem Mace, matched Brighton against Charley Mower for £50. With a following wind it was said that Brighton ran the mile in 4m.15s. Bunn doubted the fact, and measured the mile several times, and found the distance 12 yards over. From now on Bob Bunn became Brighton's manager and under his guidance he beat the likes of Mower, Lang, Sanderson and Rowan. Brighton had wins in the Ten Mile Cup and Six Mile Belt, and became outright holder of the Four Miles Champion Belt in 1862. On 27 October 1862 he also set a new British one hour record of 11 miles 370 yards finishing second to Deerfoot. When his good friend, Jem Mace, generally regarded as the father of the modern scientific school of boxing, took over the Strawberry Hill Grounds, Liverpool, Brighton became the manager. While in charge he ran a number of fast times over longer distances including 11 miles in eight seconds under the hour in the most appalling weather. As one of the most noted of the *Deerfoot troupe* he became well known all over England. In 1867 he took over management of the Middlesex County Cricket and Running Ground in Caledonian Road, Islington, where he trained many amateur athletes. Later he managed the nearby Tufnell Park Cricket and Athletics Ground, said to be the largest in the country. He continued running until he was in his fifties and in April 1875 beat Lang in a veterans' one mile in 5m.7¼s.

title, preferring to concentrate on his Four Miles Champion Belt at Brompton, which he retained by beating Barker in February and won outright against Jones in March.

In May there was another poor race for the Ten Miles Champion Cup between Barker and Jones (Jones pulling out after four miles,) and it was not until July that two 'heavyweights' met in a race worthy of a championship. The new challenger was William Lang 'The Crowcatcher' from Middlesbrough, who up till then had been considered a short distance runner whose best distances were one or two miles. Sam Barker, attended by Richards, was the favourite and with far more experience at

William Lang 'The Crowcatcher,' one mile record holder and
champion at one, five and ten miles

the distance made the running until eight miles when Lang began to test him. They were locked together for the next two miles until reaching the last lap when Lang made a rush and tried to take the lead. However, Sam would not allow this without a struggle, and for some yards they were shoulder to shoulder, going stride for stride rounding the Pagoda, then nature failed Barker. He reeled and but for his attendants would have fallen. Lang continued at the same pace to the finish – but as soon as he crossed the mark fell exhausted across the rails at the bottom of the course. Barker, after being led a short distance by his friends, became quite insensible, and remained so for some time. The time was a fast 52m.55¾s.

Mills immediately challenged Lang, who in turn challenged Mills for the Six Miles Belt which he had held unchallenged for nearly a year. September was the month agreed upon for these two matches with the ten miles scheduled to be run on Monday the first. Lang arrived in London with his backers on the Friday and took up quarters at Jesse Smith's Proud Peacock public house in Maiden Lane, Covent Garden. For the race a vast crowd of some 4,000 persons assembled in a scene reminiscent of Mills' great eight-mile race against Deerfoot, and at exactly six o'clock the contestants were 'off'. The initial pace was even faster than the Barker/Lang race with three miles reached in 15m.18s. But then Mills began to tire and at the six mile mark was compelled to cry 'enough', leaving Lang to finish at his leisure.

Six Miles Champion Belt decided

Lang remained in London, training at Brompton for the Six Miles Champion Belt race that followed two weeks later. Mills had only to defend the Belt for a further three months to become the outright holder and although he had been beaten by Lang over ten miles he was still confident of his ability over six miles. The ankle ligament injury incurred earlier in the year had been successfully treated by the eminent Mr Major of Park Lane and Mills' run-out two weeks earlier proved he was now fully recovered.

Six thousand spectators arrived at Hackney Wick, including Deerfoot who had just returned from a tour of Ireland and was keen to witness the fitness of England's two leading pedestrians. From the gun it was obvious this was to be a monumental contest, Lang led for the first mile in 4m.42s. but Mills immediately took over. Although the pace inevitably slowed, 15m.11s. at half distance, there was no let up in the nature of the race. From four miles Mills tried desperately to get away from his opponent, but coming into the last straight was still only a shoulder in front and for once the crowd was stunned into silence by the drama. At the line Mills flung himself at the tape and was home by a yard in a time of 31m.11s. Lang was by no means downhearted and during the evening's celebrations indicated he would challenge again for the Belt.

William Lang's backers soon indicated their willingness to sign articles for another contest and 27 October was set. Unfortunately for followers of the sport, the day clashed with the appearance of Deerfoot at Brompton where he was attempting to run 11¼ miles in the hour. Deerfoot's opponents were John White, John Brighton, Harry Andrews and Knowles from Canada. Deerfoot having suffered much criticism for his circus-style racing during the summer had something to prove to regain his self-respect. He did not let down his supporters running a new Allcomers Record of 11 miles 740 yards with John Brighton in second place setting a new British Record of 11 miles 370 yards beating that set by John Levett in 1854. Deerfoot who was presented with a silver cup was to be seen later that evening at the Alhambra Theatre with it secured round his broad shoulders by a leather strap.

Even though this great race attracted 4,000 spectators, a further 3,000 assembled at Hackney Wick to witness Mills and Lang. Never had two races of such calibre been contested on the same day and it was proof that the popularity of pedestrianism was still at its height in the metropolis.

Mills was attended by Richards, his training partner and adviser to Sam Barker who was also there giving advice and vocal support during the race. Lang was attended by his London mentor Jesse Smith. The pace although brisk was more even than in their last meeting with a first mile in 4m.51s. and the three miles in 15m.11s. But from this point there was no letting up until Mills came away by 12 yards on the last lap to win in a fast 30m.46s. Mills was brimming with confidence during the evening and hearing the result of Deerfoot's race at Brompton fearlessly expressed his willingness to meet the Indian once again in defence of his title.

Meanwhile Mills received a challenge from Jack White and it became obvious that to retain the Six Miles Belt through to the end of the year was going to be no easy task. In an already crowded race schedule he had only six weeks to prepare for the match against White. The race date of 15 December was anxiously anticipated, particularly as it was now known that Mills had also agreed to meet Deerfoot on Boxing Day. Although possibly past his peak, Jack White was still the quickest man in the country over two miles with a record of 9m.20s. and had recently been champion at four, six and ten miles.

'Young England' against the 'Gateshead Clipper' was truly a race of champions. The neighbourhood around Victoria Park was densely packed with pedestrians and vehicles of every description making their way towards Hackney Wick. There had been some concern over the possible recurrence of Mills' injury, but he had eased up on running during the

Mills and Deerfoot racing at Hackney Wick on Boxing Day 1862

preceding two weeks to concentrate on walking and seemed in perfect health. White, accompanied by George Martin and Deerfoot, had completed his training at Wandsworth and also looked in great shape. With the betting far greater than usual both stood bare-chested on the line and they were soon off. The pace was extraordinary: 4m.41½s. at the mile and 9m.44s. at two miles. Martin was now offering £20 to £10 on his man. Even though the path was cutting up badly and getting rather heavy, the three miles was reached by White in a new British Record of 14m.50s with Mills just a stride adrift. Soon after Mills badly cut his shoulder as he hit a tree and nearly fell, giving White a lead of some four or five yards, the biggest gap between the runners so far. Four miles came up in 20m.01s.with Mills twice spiked through running so close behind White. There was no let up in the pace. Five miles was passed in 25m.12s. and the two entered the last lap shoulder to shoulder; however, Mills was not to be denied and at the finish raced ahead by 10 yards to record a time of 30m.09s. – only five seconds short of William Jackson's British Record. The race had brought the best out of both men who unusually shook hands at the end.

There was just the Deerfoot race to come and Mills, although now outright holder of the Six Miles Belt, generously offered Deerfoot a match with his trophy as the ultimate prize. Boxing Day at Hackney Wick had always been an occasion when James Baum tried to produce something special for his patrons and 1862 was no exception. The draw of both Deerfoot and Mills and what was at stake brought another vast crowd of 5,000, paying the not inconsiderable sum of one shilling each.

Although the race was set for three o'clock, by midday vehicles of every description were already beginning to draw up, and soon the wide space in front of the White Lion (as well as all the stables in the neighbourhood) was crowded for upwards of half a mile. Inside the ground the reserved seats were crammed with notables of the turf, the cricket field and the ring as well as lovers of pedestrianism. The build-up for the race added to the excitement with Mills distributing handkerchiefs sporting his colours and Deerfoot appearing in all his regalia. Both pedestrians took a turn around the ground before stripping for the race. Deerfoot looked the fitter, Mills seeming to have partaken rather too freely of the Christmas festivities.

Unusually Deerfoot took the lead from the start, in previous contests a role normally undertaken by the Englishman. He set a cracking pace: 4m.41s. at the mile and 9m.48s. at two miles. Then Mills took the lead and raced through three miles in 14m.55s., close to the record, and putting Deerfoot under such pressure that he 'cracked' at 32 laps. Still Mills with a lead of 100 yards slowed only slightly before coming home to the delight of the crowd in 30m.46½s. thereby crowning a great year of pedestrianism at Hackney Wick.

This race, following so soon after the Mills and White contest for the six mile belt, was important for the reputation of the sport which had been demeaned by Deerfoot's 'exhibitions' throughout the summer and unusually warranted editorial comment in *Sporting Life* on 27 December for the second time in ten days.

> A tremendous congregation of spectators at Hackney Wick witnessed yesterday the defeat of the boasted savage, 'Deerfoot,' by Edward Mills. There was no deception, no approximation to a 'barney' in this contest, and the Indian's antagonist not being, as was the case with the un-English Jackson, hired to 'run behind,' did his best honestly, fairly, and left 'Deerfoot' hopelessly in the rear. The crowds who swarmed to Hackney yesterday went there from no admiration to the 'sensational' runner. They went there because they believed chiefly on our assurance and representations, that at last there was to be a genuine effort to beat 'Deerfoot.' Bells and feathers would not have gone down yesterday, and even the wily Martin saw this, and sent his 'noble savage' to the scratch in the ordinary running gear of an English pedestrian. It was plain that the spectators were not bent on witnessing one of 'Deerfoot's' meaningless 'exercises' with his stable companions. Mills seemed determined to uphold his character, and, after a magnificent display of finished pedestrianism, he beat the Indian, to borrow a Turf phrase, in a common canter. So much for the boastings of Mr. Martin, who pretended it was impossible for his American to be beaten! We do not, and never have denied the endurance and superior powers of 'Deerfoot,' but have always insisted that Mills could beat him whenever he wished, 'barring' accidents, and the result proves we were right. Some of the spectators yesterday were evidently under the impression that 'Deerfoot' on this occasion was not trying and that in fact he had got 'the strings on.' Let us say positively we do not believe for one moment anything else but that the race yesterday was thoroughly honest. For the sake of pedestrianism, we are glad to be able to make such an assertion, and we cannot help remarking that we feel something like national pride in the success of Young Mills. This little lad beat the be-praised and be-puffed 'Deerfoot' as he might have been beaten before, had our English pedestrians possessed proper courage, and manly pride. Now that 'Deerfoot' has been decisively beaten, we shall be relieved probably of the nonsense which has been talked and written about the superiority of 'savages' over the civilised 'palefaces'! Mills is entitled to the hearty support of the public for his conduct in this matter and if the professional followers of his occupation will make up their minds to go thoroughly on the 'square' they will never lack money – money honestly

obtained, we mean – or sincere and generous patrons, with the public and the Press.

While much attention was being paid to Deerfoot and the champion challenge trophies at Hackney Wick and Brompton, at one mile all eyes were on Manchester. In March 1861 Siah Albison had re-taken Thomas Hayes' Champion Belt at the Copenhagen Grounds from Mower, then defended it successfully against Lang and White to become the outright holder in October 1862.

Thus, of the four major championship trophies, three had been won outright in 1862; the six miles by Mills, four miles by Brighton and the one mile by Albison. Only the Ten Miles Cup held by Lang remained to be challenged.

Who would emerge as the new champion in 1863, a year in which some remarkable records were to be set?

5

1863, Champion of Champions

Hackney Wick continues to draw large crowds

The momentum that gathered in pedestrianism as a result of Deerfoot's performances continued into 1863 with James Baum and William Price ensuring that Hackney Wick remained at the forefront of distance running in England.

In addition to pedestrianism, James Baum expanded his area of activity with the purchase of the Crown and Anchor Booths, used for many years at race meetings and fairs by the late Sam Alger. The first part of this famous booth was a refreshment tent 120 feet long by 50 feet wide with 24 side and 4 end boards, three lamp baskets and crowns, one glory, front painting, seats, bar and other tables. The second part consisted of a tent 160 feet long by 50 feet wide containing dancing boards, illuminations, counters, flags, etc., and three other tents with seats and tables. In 1863 Baum took the booths to the fairs at Barnet and Croydon. At Barnet he advertised that the booth would be stocked with refreshment of the best quality at moderate prices with hot joints from 11 a.m. and at Croydon as providing hitherto unheard of amusements and accommodation. The splendid dancing-saloon would open until dusk, 'to allow the lovers of Terpsichore of all classes to enjoy the "merry and joyous dance" and "music's soft measure". Hackney Wick will be jubilant at Croydon, and

Hackney Wick meeting on Good Friday 1863

the noble White Lion will wag his tail in hearty welcome to all at the renowned Crown and Anchor.'

A report on the fair describes the booth where the Five Miles Champion Belt was exhibited:

> Alger's was this year in its old spot, and under the superintendance of Mr J.C. Baum, the enterprising proprietor of Hackney Wick pedestrian grounds, dancing on peculiar principles was carried forward with unflagging spirit, and light fantastic toe (by the way, we think the generality of the toes belonged to poor feet anything but 'light') swept in the mazy waltz. Alger's was, however, the promenade or lounge of the young Croydoners, or the Surrey men, who amused themselves with chaffing their companions, and 'guying' the alcoholic incapables.

James Baum used his love of pedestrianism to promote other causes and was keen that his running grounds should be used whenever possible for the benefit of those in need of help. Around this time he advertised Hackney Wick as being 'at the disposal Volunteer Corps, Members of City Firms, and all employed in the Great Establishments to get up any public, trade, or "shop" benefit for Lancashire, the London Poor, or other Charities', although it was James Baum himself who organised the largest benefit meeting for the distressed Lancashire weavers at the end of January 1863.

To attract all members of society, both as competitors and spectators, good prizes were put up for amateur and professional runners and walkers as well as for the military and Volunteers. The meeting was arranged for Saturday and Monday to allow those who normally did not work on a Saturday to take part. It was also understood that competitors would wear proper costumes so that ladies could attend and help in the 'Christian work'.

Many top pedestrians supported the event and the one-mile handicap, won by Edward Mills, included Lang, 'out for a breather', Andrews, Barker and others. The five mile handicap, on Monday, had even better support with Lang, running in flannels, Mills and Deerfoot all off scratch among the ten appearing at the start. Lang and Mills dead-heated in first place while Deerfoot stopped with a lap to go. All three demonstrated top form for the year ahead.

Although a considerable sum was raised, the support from the general public was not so generous as hoped and licensed victuallers in the locality who had derived so much benefit from the success of the grounds, were specifically condemned for giving nothing in support.

Fortunately larger crowds attended on other occasions especially at Easter when all the top London grounds put on first-class fixtures.

A CRY OF DISTRESS

FROM

Lancashire.

TWO DAYS' GRAND

Pedestrian Fete

For the Benefit of Our Suffering Brothers and Sisters in the North, at

HACKNEY WICK!!

Victoria Park Station, on

SATURDAY & MONDAY NEXT

January 24th & 26th, 1863.

THE APPEAL ON BEHALF OF LANCASHIRE.

"*Charity* is twice blessed—
It blesseth him that gives, and him that takes."

The cause for which the following programme is issued requires no comment—the object in view speaks louder than words—but it is a programme, in extent, never before equalled, the entries including the first of the athletic—Amateur and Professional. It is respectfully hoped, that the Public will render the work *truly blessed* by their good support

SATURDAY.—Gentlemen Amateurs' 440-*yds* RACE, for a Silver Cup; Entrance, 5s.

The Gentlemen Amateurs' Four Mile Walk-ING HANDICAP, for a Silver Cup; Entrance, 5s.

The Volunteer Handicap of 100 Yards, for a Gold Ring; for Volunteers only, to run in any Costume; Entrance, 2s. 6d.

The Volunteer Half Mile Handicap, for a Gold Ring, for Volunteers only; conditions as the preceding Race.

The Volunteer Walking Match of One Mile, for Volunteers in *full marching order*, for a Gold Ring; Entrance, 2s. 6d.

The Professional One Mile Handicap Race for a Silver Cup; Entrance, 5s.

For the Celebrated Professionals Engaged a reference to the Cards of the Day is requested.

The Great Military Quarter of a Mile Handi-CAP, for non-commissioned officers and privates of the Army, for a Silver Snuff Box; *Entrance Free.*

MONDAY.—200 Yards Handicap and a One MILE HANDICAP, for Men who never won £5, for Silver Watches. (For the large entry for both see Cards.)

The Great Champion Professional Running HANDICAP, of five miles. Amongst the Competitors of this Great Race, are Deerfoot, Mills, Lang, White, Barker, &c.

The Great Professional Walking Handicap, of Four Miles.—Miles, Hatley, Spooner, Thomas, &c., &c.

The Volunteer 100 Yards Race:

The Volunteer Half Mile Race:

The Volunteer 1 Mile Walking Handicap:

The above three Races are for Gold Breast Pins, and all include a large entry of the Brave Volunteers.

ADMISSION—Saturday, One Shilling; Monday, Sixpence.

All will run or walk in proper costumes, and Ladies are specially invited to witness the contests. Names of Competitors, Starts, &c., in Cards of the Day.

To Commence each Day at One o'Clock.

The Grounds are easy of access, as all Trains stop at Hackney Wick from Fenchurch Street up to Hampstead, Camden Town, and all intermediate stations.—Return Ticket, 6d.

NOTICE.—Volunteer Corps, Members of City Firms, and all employed in Great Establishments, are respectfully informed, that Mr. Baum will place at their disposal Hackney Wick Grounds (on any day not engaged for public running) to get up any public, trade, or "shop" benefit for Lancashire, the management to be left to themselves, subject only to the rules necessary to the proper carrying out the sports according to order and decorum. Mr. Price, the manager, will give his aid, and a letter addressed to him at Hackney Wick will be immediately responded to.

Luke and Pollard, Machine Printers, Hackney Wick.

Handbill for the Lancashire Pedestrian Fete at Hackney Wick

PRINCE OF WALES

"OLYMPIA" AND

Running Ground

White Swan, Devon's Lane,

BOW.

Proprietor — — Mr. CHARLES WILSON

GRAND OPENING DAY:

Tuesday, March 10th 1863

Bridal Day of the Prince of Wales

When the following Sports will come off:—

THE GREAT FOUR MILES'

CHAMPION CUP!

VALUE £50.

And £5 for the Winner; Second, £3; Third, £2; Fourth, £1.

The Winner to hold the Cup one Year against all Comers.

The following First-rate Men have entered, and will contend:

E. Mills, Young England
W. Lang, of Middlesboro' (Champion Runner)
Sam Barker, of Billinsgate
Marsh, of Brighton
Harry Andrews, of Holborn
C. Cook, of Marylebone
Toddy May, of Limehouse
J. Brown, of Oxford
And many other First-rates.

WALKING HANDICAP,

OF 4 MILES. First Prize, £5; Second, £3; Third, £2; Fourth, £1.

For this Race, 25 celebrated Men, including William Hatley, the Champion of Tall Walking.

600 Yds. Handicap

For this Race upwards of 40 Men have already entered

First Prize, £7; Second, £2; Third, £1.

TROTTING MATCH,

AGAINST TIME FOR £20;

MR. IZZARD'S PONY TO TROT TWO MILES IN EIGHT MINUTES.

All Men to run in Long Drawers and Guernseys. The First Heat of 600 Yards Handicap to take place at Half-past One precisely.

A First-rate BANDis engaged.

The Grounds are close to Bow Station of the North London Railway, and all Trains from Fenchurch Street and all intermediate Stations, stop at the Grounds.

For the Heats, Starts, Handicaps, Names of Competitors, &c., see Sporting Papers, and the Cards of the Day.

The whole under the Sole Management of the once-famed Champion,

James Pudney.

Admission 1s. Grand Stand Extra.

J. PHILLIPS, Printer, Russell Street, Mile End Gate, E.

Handbill for the grand opening of the Prince of Wales Ground, Bow

Brompton had always been an agreeable ground to visit on bank holidays. But this year there was also a rival ground at Bow. The aptly named Prince of Wales Olympian Running Ground, close to Bow railway station, was opened on 10 March, the Prince's wedding day, under the proprietorship of Charles Wilson of the adjoining White Swan Tavern in Devon Lane, Bromley-by-Bow, and managed by the former pedestrian champion James Pudney. The ground was huge, with a running path 543 yards in length, wide enough for 20 competitors abreast, and a straight level course of 160 yards for sprinting. The arena was surrounded by rising ground supposedly able to accommodate 50,000 spectators with at one end a covered grandstand capable of seating 1,000 spectators. The only drawbacks were the depressing surroundings, the dreadful smells from the nearby factories on one side and on the other the noise and smoke from the railway-yard.

The Easter meetings at the beginning of April showed that for the moment there was no diminution in the popularity of pedestrianism in London. It was said there were crowds of 7,000 at Hackney Wick, 5,000 at Bow and 5,000 at Brompton while a smaller number attended events at Wandsworth.

As well as the athletics at Hackney Wick, the 111th Annual Meeting of the Cornwall and Devon Wrestling Society was an added attraction. The most popular running event was the one-mile handicap for which there were 30 entries, while pole leaping provided a further diversion for the spectators. On this occasion Robert Musgrave from Keswick, the British

Grand Opening of the running grounds at Bow on 10 March 1863

ROBERT MUSGRAVE (1841–?)
Robert Musgrave was born at Cockermouth on 11 October 1841. He learned his pole vaulting skills competing in the various Cumberland and Westmorland Games where he also showed himself to be an excellent lightweight wrestler, hurdler and half-mile runner. In 1860 he met David Johnstone at Preston, for a £5 prize and although losing the match, vaulted 9ft. 4in. to Johnson's 9ft. 6in. The following year, however, he vaulted 9ft. 8in at Preston and then in the Flan Ring at Ulverstone cleared 9ft. 9in. In 1861 in Durham in front of the Durham collegians he cleared an unprecedented 10ft. 8in. to break the British record. Musgrave competed at the Hackney Wick Easter Sports in 1863 when he won with 9ft. 8in. the maximum height of the posts! He broke the British Record once again in 1866 when he reached 10ft. 10½in. Musgrave was several times credited with jumps indoors over 11 feet (11ft. 3in. on 26 March 1864, 11ft. on 19 April 1867 and 11ft. 6in. on 26 March 1869), all at the Agricultural Hall in Islington. He had a long career, winning at Grasmere as late as 1871, eleven years after his debut.

Robert Musgrave, pole vault record holder and champion

record holder at 10 feet 8 inches was competing and he easily cleared the maximum height of the posts (9ft. 8in.) to win the competition.

Benefits were held at Hackney Wick in 1863 for Bob Travers the lightweight boxing champion of England, heavyweights Jem Mace and Joe Goss, and the celebrated pedestrian sprinter George Seward. Seward was in London with his dog 'Venture', a renowned catcher of rats. They appeared at Mr Cheese's White Horse public house, Shepherds Bush on 12 October when the dog killed 100 rats in seven minutes. The occasion was also graced with the presence of William Lang who displayed his championship cup and belt. It was in the knowledge of his visit that James Baum took the opportunity of arranging Seward's benefit at Hackney Wick on 28 September, inviting Seward to run in a veterans' handicap against Westhall, Reed, Price, Jackson and Jemmy Patterson.

There was also some excellent walking at Hackney Wick during this period with James Miles, one of the best walkers the country would ever see, being the main attraction. He normally raced at his local track in Wandsworth where he had won a Ten Miles Champion Belt and had come within ten seconds of walking 21 miles in three hours, 'The Westhall Feat', on 29 September 1862.

Miles, soon to become the British record holder at seven miles, raced at Hackney Wick four times between September 1862 and December 1863 but had little success. His handicap over the shorter distances, much to the delight of Hackney Wick's regular punters, meant he was no match for William Hatley, a local walker of some note. His only win was against

GEORGE SEWARD (1817–1883)

George Seward was born in Newhaven, Connecticut, USA on 16 October 1817. He is supposed to have taken part in 100 yard sprints in America from 1838 until 1843 when he arrived in Liverpool, England, where he was soon beating all the noted sprinters in the north. He settled at Cockfield, a village mid-way between Barnard Castle and Bishops Auckland. His greatest claim to fame was his allegedly running 100 yards in 9¼ seconds in a match against William Robinson of Newton Moor on a measured course on the turnpike road near the Seven Stars public house, Hammersmith, London on 30 September 1844. The only full report of the race appeared in *Bell's Life* on 6 October 1844 and obviously casts doubt on the authenticity of the time; taken by William Jackson the American Deer. There was no doubt, however, that Seward was an excellent sprinter, far ahead of his time, and he later recorded other outstanding times – 19½s. for 200 yards on 22 March 1847 and 11½s. for 120 yards on 5 May 1847. He made his final track appearance at his own Staleybridge grounds on 24 February 1866 and died in Birkenhead on 10 April 1883.

William Hatley, two miles walk record holder

WILLIAM HATLEY (1840–?)
William Hatley, a walker from the City of London, known as 'the City Nonpareil' was born in March 1840. His first match of any note was with T. Underwood who he defeated in a two miles match for £5 a side. After further wins he was taken in hand by the famous trainer, John Smith, 'The Regent Street Pet', and matched with James Miles at Hackney Wick. With 100 yards handicap advantage he beat Miles over two miles in November 1862 and with 200 yards over four miles in January 1863. He was beaten by William Spooner at Hackney Wick in May 1863 but followed this with a win over Miles at five miles on level terms in December. During 1864 and 1865 he was not in good condition, suffering badly with rheumatism, and although he challenged Miles twice for the Seven Miles Challenge Cup, he was soundly beaten on both occasions. In 1866 he came under the training of Bob Rogers at Hackney Wick and backed by William Price won a two mile walk on 23 July, matched against the up and coming Joe Stockwell at Brompton in a record time of 14m.26s. accepted as 'quite fair' by *Bell's Life*. His comeback was short-lived, however, and little was heard of him after this.

W. Myers of Norwich. A thousand enthusiasts attended a benefit for Miles at Hackney Wick in November 1862.

Deerfoot's one hour records

12 January 1863 brought Mills and Deerfoot together once again, this time to do battle over one hour. The appearance the previous week of Deerfoot at Worship Street Magistrates Court for committing an assault in Hackney Wick at the end of December adding more than the usual excitement to such a contest. The rivalry between the Hackney Wick pedestrian troupe and those in the George Martin camp had never been greater and an encounter of classic proportions was expected. The match was scheduled for three o'clock and at ten past three the men appeared on the course, Deerfoot attended by his backer George Martin along with John White and the walker James Miles. Mills appeared waited on by his great friend Sam Barker. Deerfoot looked considerably fitter than his lithe little opponent, in fact Mills looked far from race fit; the locals being sure that he had been indulging too heavily in the 'victualling department' over the Christmas and New Year holidays. So strong was the apparent disparity of condition between the two competitors that the betting speedily rose to 2 to 1 on Deerfoot. The race, however, was to prove much closer, and in a hard-fought contest in which both men continually

tried to break the other, Mills was only 15 yards behind Deerfoot when the pistol fired to signal the end of the contest. Both athletes recorded new but short-lived records. Deerfoot improved on his one hour best by 50 yards to record 11 miles 790 yards while Mills set a new British Record of 11 miles 775 yards.

The editorial in *Sporting Life* was quite harsh in its comments on Mills' performance.

> Mills' defeat being ascribed by those most capable of forming an opinion to the fact that he had neglected the necessary training for such an encounter, living free, with flitting visits to the Haymarket, (at this time the Haymarket was the Victorian equivalent of London's latter day Soho) are apt to take something of the physical endurance out of a man, but we trust Mills, who is a most deserving young fellow, would not give way to either of these vulgar temptations. Still it was plain that Mills had what is coarsely, but correctly,

Deerfoot in a studio pose

known as 'a belly,' that is, he exhibited the signs of having paid no attention to his training duties. We do not know how his backers felt, but the result in favour of Deerfoot, when it might have been otherwise must have been most vexatious.

Deerfoot had not finished with his record breaking, however, and at Brompton on 23 February, when paced for alternate miles by White, Brighton, Richards and Jones, he ran 11 miles 880 yards in the allotted time. Then, at Easter, John Roberts, the proprietor of the Brompton ground, and George Martin successfully attracted many of the top distance pedestrians to meet Deerfoot in yet another attempt on the one hour record in a 12 miles handicap. The field of 11 and the smart handicapping looked to give Deerfoot an excellent chance to improve on his record. Deerfoot was on scratch, giving White 50 yards and Lang and Brighton both 100 yards start. The weather and conditions were excellent and the race was run at a remarkable pace; the first mile took 4m.41s. and three miles 14m.55s., only five seconds outside White's British record. At ten miles Deerfoot set a new Allcomers' Record of 51m.26s. and at 12 miles another record of 1h.2m.2½s. The winner of the handicap and silver cup, however, was Lang by half a yard to create a new British Record for one hour of 11 miles 871 yards to Deerfoot's new Allcomers' Record of 11 miles 970 yards in the same race. This was Deerfoot's third improvement in the one-hour record since the beginning of the year.

EARLY HISTORY OF RACES AT ONE HOUR

Prior to the performances of Deerfoot in 1862 and 1863 there had been comparatively few running matches over one hour in length. In 1845 Thomas Maxwell of Slough, the 'North Star', attempted to run 11 miles in one hour on the Bath Road, but failed, according to the referee by five seconds. Earlier the same year, however, William Howitt, better known as William Jackson, the 'American Deer' completed 11 miles 40 yards on the Hatfield Road, Barnet against William Shepherd. In 1852 at Copenhagen House, Islington, Jackson met John Levett for the first track race at such a distance. In the 20 mile race, Jackson reached the 11 mile mark in 59m.20s. although retiring lame after 15 miles, leaving Levett to finish at his leisure. In 1854 John Levett bettered Jackson's record at the Star Hotel grounds at Rock Ferry, Birkenhead with a distance of 11 miles 350 yards. In 1856 James Pudney ran 11 miles at Oxford in 57m.20s. and would obviously have set new one hour figures if he had continued. It was not until the arrival of Deerfoot that the distance was bettered with a run of 11 miles 740 yards on 27 October 1862, pulling John Brighton to a new British record of 11 miles 370 yards.

These British one hour records were not to be beaten until Walter George ran 11 miles 932 yards at Stamford Bridge in 1884, 21 years later.

John White's remarkable record

Deerfoot's last appearance in England was at Hackney Wick for a fifty guineas Ten Miles Champion Belt specially commissioned by Baum in a match against the English Champions on 11 May. The belt was given to decide the moot point as to whether or not Deerfoot, who had given up the Ten Miles Champion Cup in December 1861 because his stay in England was too short for a defence, was the best ten miles runner.

The area around the ground was buzzing from early in the day. With very heavy betting, spectators were anxious for a glimpse of the competitors before placing their wagers. The crowd eventually numbered 9,000 and Victoria Park and the ground outside the White Lion looked like 'Kennington Gate on Derby Day'. As the competitors lined up the odds were evens on Lang, 7 to 4 against White, 5 to 2 against Deerfoot, and 8 to 1 against Barker, Richards and Andrews. Mills, although entered and on the ground, did not feel sufficiently well to start. According to Chinnery's recollections of the race:

> All Martin's troupe, including Deerfoot, Jack White and Lang were entered. In the meantime White and Martin had quarreled, and the former determined to show up Deerfoot and beat him. Martin knew White could beat Deerfoot, but thought Lang, who was mile champion, might beat White. It got noised abroad that there had been a split in the camp, and that there would probably be a fast race run, and consequently a great crowd (and a very rough one) assembled.

As suspected the race was fast, 4m.40s. at one mile and 9m.37s. at two miles, then an unprecedented 14m.36s. at three miles as White broke his own British Record by 14 seconds. Deerfoot could not stand the pace and pulled out while White forged ahead, four miles in 19m.35s. five miles in 24m.40s., (all new best times on record) then at six miles a truly great time of 29m.50s., 14 seconds inside the British Record, and like the three mile time a record that would not be broken for many years. Lang, who had matched White stride for stride up to this point, was the next to go, staggering off the track exhausted just after six miles, and Andrews and Richards were lapped more than once. White's winning time, easing down in the last couple of miles, was 52m.14s., thereby proving himself that day to be *the greatest performer ever known*. There is little doubt that he could have run ten miles in 50 minutes if he had wished. The race was one of

DEERFOOT

The RENOWNED INDIAN RUNNER, and the

ENGLISH CHAMPIONS

FOR THE

10 MILES CHAMPION BELT,

Of 50 Guineas, Second, £5; Third, £3; Fourth, £2.

HACKNEY WICK,

VICTORIA PARK STATION.

MONDAY, MAY 11th, 1863.

The last RACE of the SENECA INDIAN before his departure for the

WESTERN PRARIES.

To fully test the powers of the Celebrated DEERFOOT, and before his departure from our shores, added to the fact that his stay could not be prolonged to enable him to "hold the Ten Miles Champion Cup," this beautiful belt will be given by Mr. BAUM, of the value of FIFTY GUINEAS, to set at rest the pretensions of the famed man of Seneca. To prove the genuineness of the transaction, the entries are thrown open free to the whole world; and whoever he may be, and whatever his colour or his country may be, who proves the winnner on MAY the 11th, will at once receive the beautiful trophy to become his own for ever. Other liberal prizes, are added up to the fourth in the race, and such liberality will produce a contest unprecedented before, as fully evidenced by the names of those given below who will strive for the mastery with the REDOUBTABLE INDIAN.

E. MILLS, (Young England), the 6 Miles Champion,
W. LANG, (Crow-catcher), the 10 Miles Champion,
J. WHITE, The Gateshead Clipper,
J. BRIGHTON, of Norwich, the Four Miles Champion.
PATRICK STAPLETON, the One Mile Champion,
SAMUEL BARKER, the Indomitable, H. ANDREWS, the Untiring,
W. RICHARDS, the Speedy Welshman, and others; "Good Men & True."

Whether the above Noble Prize is destined to adorn the wigwam of the Redskin, or whether it shall be won by a Pale-face, the 11th, of May will decide. It will be DEERFOOT'S

LAST APPEARANCE IN ENGLAND

And no doubt that many thousands will be there to cheer the Stranger on in his struggle for victory, or if defeated, in the spirit of Englishmen, still to award the full amount of praise to one who has dared, and successfully dared, to compete with Britons in one of the most popular and manly games of the country. The names and the pretensions of the English Champions need no mention, only to foreshadow the nature of the Contest to be expected.

TO START AT 6 o'Clock. ADMISSION One Shilling.

Trains every 15 Minutes by North London Railway from Fenchurch St., and Camden Town— Return Tickets only 6d.

W. A. LUKE, MACHINE PRINTER, HACKNEY WICK.

Poster featuring Deerfoot's last match against the English champions at Hackney Wick in May 1863

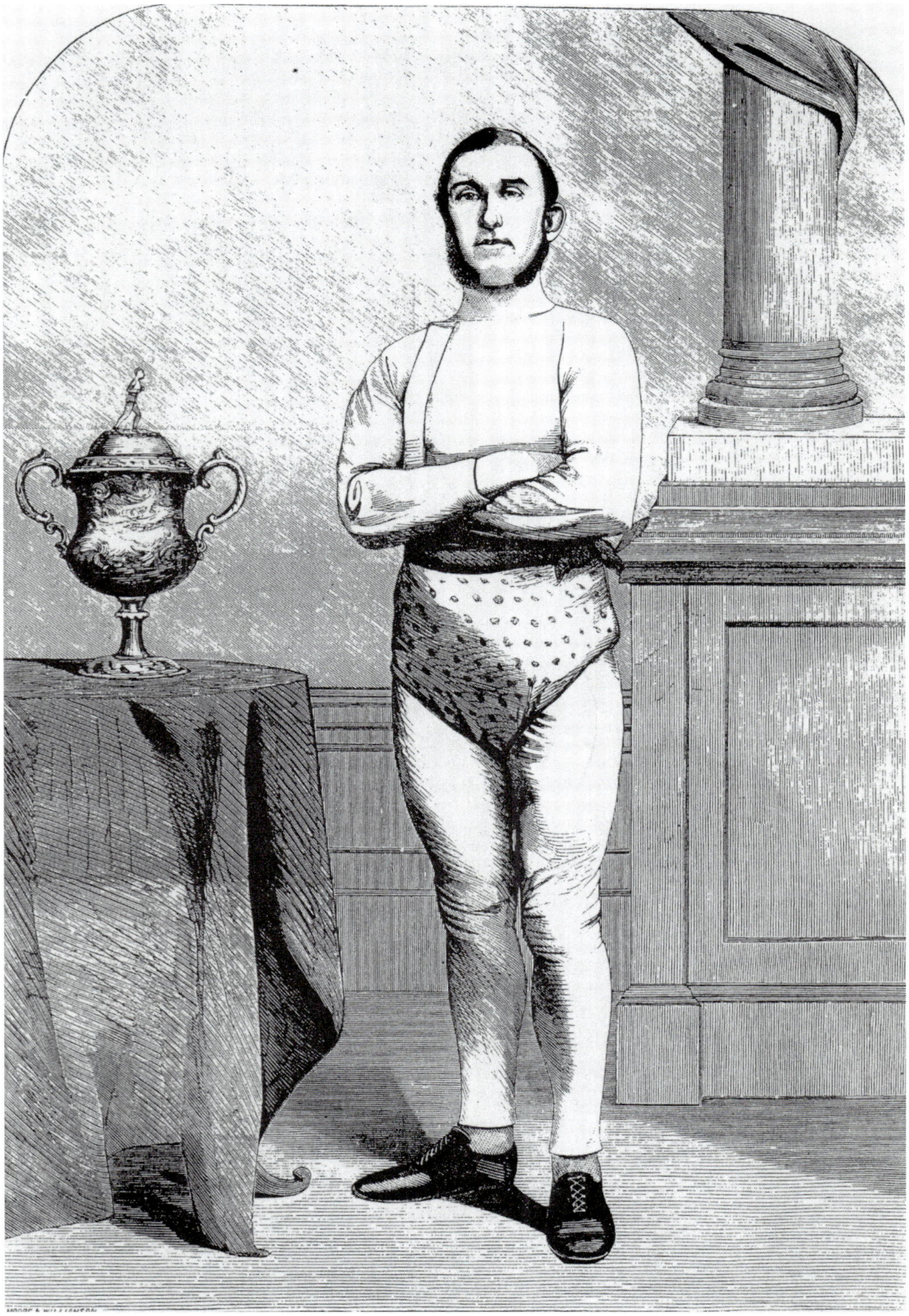

John White 'The Gateshead Clipper,' four, six and ten miles champion and three and six miles record holder the greatest ever; the three mile record lasted until 1880 and the six mile record until 1936!

Deerfoot left England for America aboard the Great Eastern on 13 May 1863.

Just two months before this race Hackney Wick had already seen some of the country's finest racing over ten miles involving Deerfoot. On 2 March, Deerfoot ran Lang to exhaustion, winning by a few yards in 52m.44s. The following week it was Mills' turn to challenge Deerfoot and he beat the Indian by seven yards in a time of 52m.24s.

Chequered history of the Ten Miles Cup continues

1863 had started with the Six, Four and One Mile Champion Belts having been won outright by Edward Mills, John Brighton and Siah Albison, leaving only the Ten Miles Champion Cup to be contested. This resulted in a proliferation of new challenge trophies at one, one and a quarter, one and a half, four, and five miles, and one runner in particular would make most headlines to become the champion amongst champions.

First though, there was the future of the Ten Miles Cup to be decided. The next challenge took place in the most appalling conditions at Hackney Wick on 2 February. In torrential rain 1,000 ardent spectators sheltered under every piece of cover they could find. Lang, the holder since July 1862, was attended as usual during his visits to London by Jesse Smith of the Proud Peacock in Maiden Lane, and Mills by Sam Barker who, like so many pedestrians, had recently become a publican with the purchase of the Queen Catherine in Bethnal Green Road. The race was scheduled for half past four and with both runners keen to get started they were soon away. As lap followed lap they became blacker and blacker, being completely covered back and front with the black ashes which formed the track. The going was becoming heavier and heavier. Even so they maintained a miling pace of 5m.05s. for the first seven miles and although slowing in the last three miles, with Mills feeling the effects of his record-breaking one hour race against Deerfoot only three weeks earlier, a winning time of 52m.36s. brought Lang home just ten yards to the good.

Lang's defence of the Cup was scheduled for 30 March, when he met John Brighton making his first individual challenge. Brighton had trained hard for the match and through the opening miles constantly tried to break away from Lang until, just after five, his efforts caused him to pull a calf muscle and he withdrew at six miles.

The form of Jack White in his record breaking victory for the Ten Miles Belt in May made him the next obvious contender. But it appears that Martin, his backer, was dilatory, so more than once White had to forfeit

GREAT RACE

FOR THE

CHAMPIONSHIP of ENGLAND

HACKNEY WICK ! !

Victoria Park Station,

MONDAY, FEB. 2nd, 1863

The Important Contest between

E. Mills

Young England, "Challenger," and

W. LANG

Of Middlesboro', Crowcatcher, "Defender," for the

TEN MILES

Champion Cup

Of England,

AND £50 !

THE CHAMPION CUP.—The "Ten Miles Champion" is ever considered the *Champion Runner of England*, and whenever two pedestrians, by their speed and endurance, and by their superiority above all others, single themselves out, as both likely to maintain their proud position, the contest is *the* one to which the greatest interest is attached by the public. Therefore this great national prize is the height of the ambition of all our long distance runners, and well worthy is this splendid trophy of the struggles of the trained man, and proud ought that man to be who can maintain the "pride of place," on the day of the great trial for the mastery. The Cup is nearly 24 inches high, and contains 83 ounces of silver beautifully chased, with emblematical figures, and a plain shield, on which can be engraven the name of him who shall obtain the proud distinction, and hold it against all comers the stipulated time. The sum of £50 is also awarded to the winner, as a still further incentive for their perseverance to the end.

Noble as the prize is, and high the honour to be attained, the two men who will meet on Monday next are well worthy of the occasion, the great doings in the pedestrian arena for which they are so celebrated requiring no recapitulation. EDWARD MILLS has run the quickest Six Miles on record, and has become possessed of the splendid Belt at that distance as his own for ever; but his last great race with the Indian, when *eleven miles and 790 yards* was covered in one hour, gives a foreshadowing of his capabilities as a "long distance runner" and no other remark is needed of what may be anticipated from him on the day in question. He is therefore the "Bold Challenger" for the Ten Miles Cup. WILLIAM LANG, the "Speedy Man of Middlesborough" is renowned as having run one mile in the shortest time—4 min. 22½ sec.; he is the present "Holder of the Cup," and his capability to maintain his own, when he surprised the pedestrian world by defeating the Indomitable Sam Barker, for the same trophy (which he has held ever since) in a contest which is supposed to exceed the celebrated one between the American Deer and John Levett.

Both are in the pride of youth and strength, perfect models of the *athlete*, although Lang has the advantage in weight and height, standing 5ft., 9 in., and is 23 years old; Mills 21 years of age, and stands 5 ft. 5 in. Each enjoys the confidence of their friends, and are as fine as stars, so that the important nature of the race may be easily imagined by all classes of the community, sporting or otherwise—and more especially by those who do not usually patronise such sports, except on occasions like the race in question.

Pluck, stamina, the pride of winning, the endurance under difficulties, honest endeavours, and the Briton's resolve to "do, or die" must decide the question on Monday next, 2nd of Feb., 1863.

The start will take place at

HALF-PAST 3 O'CLOCK.

And the men will bound from the mark by report of pistol, to enable all who choose to "time the race" in all parts of the grounds.

The Grounds are rendered still further easy of access, as all trains stop both ways at Hackney Wick from Fenchurch street, and all intermediate stations up to Camden Town, Hampstead, &c.—Return Tickets, 6d.

Notwithstanding the importance of the Race, the Admission will be

SIXPENCE.

NOTICE.—Volunteer Corps, Members of City Firms, and all employed in Great Establishments, are respectfully informed, that Mr. Baum will place at their disposal Hackney Wick Grounds (on any day not engaged for public running) to get up any public, trade, or "shop" benefit for Lancashire, the London Poor, or other Charities, the management to be left to themselves, subject only to the rules necessary to the proper carrying out the sports according to order and decorum. Mr. Price, the manager, will give his aid, and a letter addressed to him at Hackney Wick will be immediately responded to.

Luke and Pollard, Machine Printers, Hackney Wick.

Handbill for the Ten Miles Champion Cup race in February 1863

THE GREAT

CHAMPION

RACE

OF 1863.

FIVE MILES

CHAMPION

Belt OF England!

HACKNEY WICK,

Victoria Park Station,

Monday, August 17th.

IT has ever been the mission—the aim and the end—since the establishment of the famed grounds of Hackney Wick, to bring out the

Decided Champions of England among the "Fleet of Foot,"

and although the public generally, and the lovers of pedestrianism especially, will not be surprised, all classes of the community will be pleased to learn, that another of those GRAND PRIZES will be given for competition on Monday next August 17th, which will not only outvie all other trophies of a similar description, but will also excel any previously given; more especially when the object in view to be obtained is considered as the first among pedestrians at One Mile is considered the "Short Distance Champion Runner," so is the one at 10 Miles as mostly considered the "Long Distance Champion Runner," at which distances both have their unmistakeable and "Deoided Defenders." It is thought, and rightly too, that between the *unit* and the *decimal* the exact half should be attempted, and the question of the

FIVE MILES CHAMPION!

satisfactorily set at rest, for which purpose the Great Race announced for the above day will take place. The often-expressed wishes of the Public will be responded to by Mr. Baum in conjunction with his manager Mr. William Price, and the Head Quarters in the "*World for Pedestrianism*"—Hackney Wick—will decide the question. Mr. Baum has had Manufactured a BELT specially for this purpose, which in itself is worthy even to contend for, and the very height of the ambition of the Swiftest Runner to obtain—to "have and to hold," and eventually be his "own for ever." A worthy and priceless heirloom to his children, his children's children, and his descendents in future ages. To still further bring out a genuine race the liberal plea usual with Hackney Wick will on this occasion be adopted, and therefore

FOUR MONEY PRIZES

Will be given, an incentive for all to persevere, namely:—

£6 for the WINNER of the CUP, Second Man £4; Third £2; Fourth £1.

The public will not be surprised at the following entry, which will embrace a field of runners, before which all previous ones pale—their names alone are their warranty—their deeds speak for themselves:—

WILLIAM LANG,
The "Middlesboro' Wonder" and 10 Miles Champion.

JAMES SANDERSON,
One Mile and a Half Champion.

SAMUEL BARKER,
The Renowned "Indomitable,"

BEN BRUNELL,
The Bounding Antelope.

JOSEPH SPENCER,
Yorkshire's Hero.

EDWARD MILLS,
"Young England the Bold" and Six Miles Champion.

PAT STAPLETON,
One Mile Champion.

ROBERT MARSH,
Brighton's Pride.

WILLIAM RICHARDS,
The Speedy Taffy.

HARRY ANDREWS,
The Lasting Man of Holborn.

Verily the above need no comment; to see them alone will be worthy a journey, and as they bound along the "Curriculum," the very pride of the *athlete*, each and EVERY MAN IN DISTINCTIVE COLORS, properly inserted in the Cards of the Day, it will be a sight in which even Hackney Wick—famed as it is for such displays—has rarely if ever witnessed before.

CONDITIONS OF THE BELT.—To hold it for 12 months against all comers, to run in six weeks any one who may challenge for it, for a stake as low as £10 a side, if any one can win it three times consecutively, then it shall be his own for ever. Any third or fourth man can enter at the same time that any challenge is accepted by staking £10, the winner to take the whole of the stakes and the Belt.

Notwithstanding the importance of the above race, the celebrity of the men engaged, and its being the

First Race for the Five Miles

CHAMPION BELT OF ENGLAND !

And to enable all classes of the community to witness this

GREAT NATIONAL CONTEST!

The Admission will be 6d., Reserved places extra.

Trains extra & Special on August 17th, will run to the Victoria Park station, adjoining the Grounds, every 10 minutes, from all Stations on the North London Railway—there and back 6d.

At Five o'clock, the deciding HEAT for the HALF MILE RACE, first Prize £3; second £1 5s; third 10s; fourth 5s. S. Sutton, 60 yards start; Lake, 90; G. Parker, 90; Wilkinson, 80; Riley, 60; and J. Coe, 90, will run off, being winners in the previous trials on Monday, August 10th.

*** The Grand Five Miles Champion Belt of England can be seen until 12 o'Clock on the morning of the Race, at Mr. Wilson's, the "Spotted Dog," 298, Strand, opposite "Bell's Life."

Great Champion Race at half-past SIX.

W. A. LUKE, Machine Printer, Hackney Wick.

Handbill for the Five Miles Champion Belt race in August 1863

the opportunity to race, at a time when he was undoubtedly at his best. As a result William Price backed Mills, who had never been beaten by White, for another match against Lang at the beginning of August. Again, however, there was a forfeit, this time because of the death of Mills' father, and the match had to be rearranged for October, when an unfit Mills again forfeited. Another challenge came from White towards the end of the year, but by this time Lang's exertions had taken their toll; he had 'broken down' and was forced to forfeit the Cup with only a month remaining to win the trophy outright.

A Five Miles Champion Belt at Hackney Wick

With the Six Miles Belt having been won outright in December 1862, few challengers for the Ten Miles Cup and a general dearth in top class pedestrian matches around the metropolis with the departure of Deerfoot, James Baum decided to offer another challenge belt for competition at Hackney Wick. The distance decided upon was five miles, mid-way between the championships at one and ten miles and likely to attract more interest. Less severe conditions were set. To be won outright the belt 'had to be held for 12 months against all comers, the holder to run in six weeks any one who may challenge for it'. Anyone winning three consecutive races would retain the belt as his own property 'for ever'. Furthermore a third or fourth man might enter when any challenge was accepted by staking £10, the winner to take the whole of the stakes and the Belt.

The entry for the belt was advertised in flamboyant terms:

William Lang, 'The Middlesboro' Wonder and 10 Miles Champion'
Edward Mills, 'Young England the Bold' and Six Miles Champion
James Sanderson, 'One Mile and a Half Champion'
Pat Stapleton, 'One Mile Champion'
Samuel Barker, 'The Renowned Indomitable'
Robert Marsh, 'Pride of Brighton'
Ben Brunell, 'The Bounding Antelope'
William Richards, 'The Speedy Taffy'
Joseph Spencer, 'Yorkshire's Hero'
Harry Andrews, 'The Lasting Man of Holborn'

Sanderson, Barker and Spencer were non-starters but Toddy Ray was added to the field and eight runners lined up on 17 August. Richards was in the field to make the pace for his stable companion Mills and set off in the lead, but with two miles run in 9m.56s. the race soon became a match between the two great rivals Lang and Mills, and once again Lang outsprinted his opponent in the last 50 yards to win in a time of 25m.15s.

However, Mills, although defeated by Lang on so many occasions, challenged again, but did himself no favours in the subsequent race held on 5 October, as following report from *Sporting Life* relates:

> Lang took up his quarters at Wandsworth, and being in fine form had comparatively little to do; while Mills, not having run for sometime, had lost all form, and thus had a much more arduous time before him – he as usual took his breathings at Hackney Wick. The race seemed to excite but little interest among the regular followers of pedestrianism, for they could not forget the brilliant performance achieved by Lang, when he last met White, of Gateshead, on these grounds, in the race for the ten miles belt, and the unprecedented time made by them on that occasion. Teddy's immediate backers, however, fancied he had a chance, he having defeated White at six miles, and as the belt has only to be won three times in succession to become the property of the holder, at once matched him for it, and he left no stone unturned to render himself fit for the great task before him. ... A few minutes after five o'clock, Mills came on the course in his flannels, attended by W. Richards (the Welshman). Lang, accompanied by Alf Crudgington and his backer, G. Martin, followed him in about five minutes. The betting was at a complete standstill, the only wager coming to our knowledge being a solitary halfcrown. ... The men then went to the mark, and doffed their flannels. Lang (although a few pounds bigger than we have seen him) was in the best condition, his muscles standing out like bosses of bronze at each motion; while Mills looked comparatively soft, although thin. They started with the aid of a pistol at exactly twenty minutes past five o'clock. Mills made the running at a fair pace, Lang following about a yard in the rear. As they bounded up the hill, they were greeted by loud cheers from those assembled, who were hoping to see a good race, but to an experienced eye it looked all over, for in Teddy's style of going there was wanting that elasticity and light springing step for which he has been so celebrated. He was evidently doing his utmost to keep the pace something near the mark, while Lang was running with the greatest ease, and each time he passed his backer gave him a confident smile and nod. Thus they paced over the first mile in 4 min. 47 sec., and Mills looked to be going more freely. Still the pace did not alter, neither did their relative positions, Lang seeming quite content to bide his time until he got the 'office' from his mentor to increase the rate of going. The second mile (thirteen laps and 200 yards) was got over in 9 min. 56 sec., and as they swept past the referee for the fourteenth time, Martin told his man to 'go,' and go he did, and at such a pace as soon to leave Mills some distance in the rear; he kept increasing his advantage at each succeeding lap, until coming down the straight

to finish the nineteenth lap, Mills, to the surprise of all present, pulled up, being some fifty yards in the rear. Mills seems bent on destroying his popularity by his neglect, and he could not be surprised at the outburst of uproarious indignation which broke forth from the spectators on Monday.

The following week Bill Price let it be known that there was just one more opportunity to relieve Lang of his belt and invited both White and Sanderson to challenge, with the result that a match was made for 30 November, to include Mills, White, Sanderson and Brighton.

Lang who had recently become landlord of the Navigation Inn, Ancoats Lane, Manchester, broke down while training for the race and George Martin, who had himself bought a public house in Manchester, the Royal Oak Hotel at Newton Heath, at one time feared that his man would have to forfeit. However, by regular massage and visits to the Turkish bath Lang appeared on the line looking in splendid condition. James Sanderson, 'The Whitworth Flyer', making his debut at a London ground, was predominantly a miler, while Brighton now one of the older pedestrians on the path, was hardly in the running. It was considered that White was the only opponent Lang should fear; Mills it should be said, although on the ground, did not run and gave no reason for his withdrawal.

GREAT RACE
OF THE
CHAMPIONS
OF 1863 !

Hackney Wick

"White Lion" Tavern, Victoria Park Station,

MONDAY, NOV. 30, 1863.

FIVE MILES
CHAMPION BELT OF ENGLAND
☞ AND £50 !

On the 17th of last August this Great National Trophy was given for competition, and was on that occasion won by Lang; again, the second time did the Crowcatcher keep the "pride of place;" and should it prove that the Speedy man of Middlesborough can "hold his own" on Monday, November 30th, the finest Belt ever put forth will become his own for ever. The "Third time of asking" is a critical period—so the following men will contend with

William Lang The Noted Champion, viz:
Edward Mills, Famed Young England,
John White, The Gateshead Clipper,
John Brighton The Norfolk Phenomanon
AND
Sanderson, The Whitworth Flyer.

Antecedents of the Champions, and Anticipations of November 30th.

THE LAST TRIAL FOR THE FIVE MILES CHAMPION BELT OF ENGLAND !

When the Belt was first won on the 17th of last August, the victor was informed, that if he could win it three times in succession it would become his own for ever. Twice has he been successful, but the conditions also stipulated that, on the third time as many as choose could enter, and the then "holder" must contend against all comers. Hence the entry of the four celebrated men who will strive to the uttermost to make William Lang cry "Hold! enough," on Monday next, November 30th.

It is scarcely necessary to speak of the performances of *William Lang*; a mile in 4 min. 2 sec., and 2 miles in 9 min. 11 sec., need no comment, and he has been either the "holder" or "defender" of more trophies than any other pedestrian for years. It will be a treat to see the celebrated man; he will try all he can to win the third time, to make it his own; and it will require the great powers of the game and gallant men opposed to him, to wrest from him the much-coveted prize. But who are those who come forth to dispute the Crowcatcher's title? Four of the most renowned of the fleet-footed of this or any time! *Edward Mills*, as the Six Miles Champion has conquered all at that distance, even Lang *twice* among the number! Many a time and oft, have the victories of Mills been recorded at Hackney Wick, and, again in fine fettle, his friends will once more cheer him on in his trial for another victory. Tarry not by the way my bold Middlesborough hero, nor must you let Little Teddy be far in the van, if you wish to be girt again, like a noble Knight, with the Belt of Honor. Of *John White's* powers no one is a better judge than Lang himself, for his wonderful speed is world-famed. It may be remembered that in May last, on the occasion of the great race for the Ten Miles Belt, contended for by the noted "Indian and the English Champions," he made Deerfoot give in at three miles, accomplished six miles *under thirty minutes*, and ran even William Lang to a stand-still at seven miles, the time not only never equalled, but never approached. Speedy indeed must the Speedy Man of Middlesborough be, beyond compare, if he shakes off John White. Next comes *John Brighton*; although his friends may wish him a "few days younger," still the famed Four Miles Champion will give a taste of speed, pluck, and endurance never surpassed, as he dashes up the back stretch of the famed Curriculum. Pull-foot you must Billy Lang, whether you be in the front or in the rear of the Norfolk Phenomanon. *James Sanderson* will make his first appearance in a London Ground, and has been preparing for the coming fray, determined to make Lang put forth all his powers. His first race in London will be another great feature of the contest, but it may be as well to state that in Lang's quickest race on record at two miles, he was only beaten by the latter by three yards, and since then has beaten the celebrated Siah Albison in one mile. Although Sanderson may be a "dark'un" to London visitors, it would not be the first time that a "Black Knight" has borne off the honors of the Tournament, and it may again be proved so on Monday, November 30th, 1863.

It can truly be said, that at no previous period have five such celebrities of the "fleet of foot" met to strive for the mastery; the prize in view is worthy of Champions to contend for, and honorable for a Champion of Champions to wear. Special arrangements will be made; all the vast resources of the establishment will be brought to bear; and as the Hackney Wick Curriculum is noted for bringing out the very *elite* of our Athletæ, so is it equally famed as the best *locale* to witness such displays, where all can have a view of the competitors during the whole journey, the running course being surrounded by a vast ampitheatre capable of accommodating 20,000 spectators.

To Start at 3 o'Clock. Admission 1s., Reserved Places extra.

NOTICE.—Mr. WILLIAM PRICE, the Manager, wishes respectfully to ask for an early attendance to see the most renowned champions of any day, and trusts to the kind aid of all true sportsmen to bring this great national contest to a satisfactory issue.

W. A. LUKE, Machine Printer, Hackney Wick.

Handbill for the Five Miles Champion Belt race in November 1863

James Sanderson 'Treacle,' one mile and a half champion

There was a good crowd of 3,000 to witness the race. White took an initial lead but Sanderson led through the early laps before all three kept changing the lead as each tried to stamp their authority on the other. As the contest progressed it became anyone's race with the result in doubt up to the finishing straight when a much-distressed Lang pulled away to win by 12 yards from Sanderson with White third. The time was a fast 25m.05s. with Lang the outright holder of yet another title – but now suffering from the effects of the effort needed to defend all his trophies, including the one and four mile cups.

Charles Wilson had introduced the new Four Mile Cup at Bow at Easter and Mills became the first winner. Unfortunately, through the death of his father he was unable to defend the cup, which was again open to allcomers on 3 August. This time Andrews beat a poor field in the slow time of 20m.50s. and Lang saw the opportunity for an easy win. He challenged Andrews and three weeks later won an undemanding race in 20m.13s. in front of a crowd of only 200.

Lang had to defend the cup just one week after his exhausting five mile race at Hackney Wick. His challenger was Sanderson who had run him so close a week earlier. However, on this occasion the injury to Lang's foot proved too much of a handicap and in obvious difficulty he resigned after three miles, well down on Sanderson who had set a cracking pace from the start.

Lang cleans up and sets new records at one and two miles

In the north of England the search for a new one mile champion after Albison's outright win of the cup at the Copenhagen Grounds, Manchester in October 1862 becomes rather confused. Thomas Warren, whose Snipe Inn Grounds, Audenshaw, near Manchester, boasted a track 540 yards round with a 140 yard finishing-straight on a dry turf surface, offered a silver cup valued at £50 which was first competed for on 6 December 1862. The terms of the cup were the normally accepted ones that it was to be held for 18 months against all challenges. But in this case for the first 12 months Albison was to be handicapped 20 yards; hardly making it a true champion's cup. In the first race the entries were Alfred Day of Brighouse, Patrick Stapleton of Mossley, Charles Mower of Dereham and James Sanderson, better known as Treacle, of Whitworth. Siah Albison, although on the ground, was matched to run, in his mind, a more important race for £50 a side at the City Ground, Manchester on 3 January 1863 against Sanderson and decided not to compete. Stapleton won the Audenshaw race in a time of 4m.30½s.

The City Ground, managed by Mr Holden of the White Lion public house, Long Millgate, Manchester, was a vast circular course, 807 yards

PATRICK STAPLETON (1831–?)
Patrick Stapleton, born in Tipperary, Ireland, reportedly did not know his date of birth, though he is believed to have been 34 in August 1865. Trained by Joe of Nancy's at Mossley, he was 5ft. 5in. tall and weighed 7st. 7lb. In 1863 Stapleton was holder of the One Mile Champion Cup presented by Thomas Warren of the Snipe Inn Grounds, Audenshaw. He pushed Edward Mills to a new British one mile record in 1864 and beat him in a re-match the following month. He was always there or thereabout in major races but although running under 4m.30s. on a number of occasions never quite pulled off a major win.

round, with a stand opposite the starting post leaving the finish of the mile some 146 yards away. Albison must have regretted not competing in the earlier competition, because he had now been ill for some days and, far from fit, dropped out after three quarters of a mile leaving Sanderson to finish at his leisure.

Back at Audenshaw on 24 January, Alfred Day was challenged and beaten by Stapleton in a respectable 4m.30¼s. Although Stapleton was now the holder of the Cup, Lang soon afterwards beat him soundly in a non-title race on the City Ground. William Lang then went on to challenge Sanderson, the other main contender for champion at one mile, to run one mile and two miles, for £25 each match at the much improved City Ground. The first match, over one mile on 11 July, attracted 1,500 paying sixpence each – a great compliment to the two pedestrians considering the depressed state of the cotton industry. The crowd's admission fee was handsomely rewarded, however, as those present watched one of the great races in English miling with Lang winning by between eight and ten yards in a new British Record of 4m.21¾s. This left him with just the Snipe Inn One Mile Champions Cup to win to be acknowledged as the true champion. This match took place on 30 August and Stapleton, overawed by Lang's recent form, resigned after two of the three laps leaving Lang to win at his ease. Lang faced no challenge for this cup during the following 18 months.

William Lang, holder of probably more pedestrian titles than any previous professional, claimed two more that summer. On 18 July, at the City Ground, he won a mile and a quarter sweepstake beating Stapleton, White and Albison in 5m.35½s. for 'One Hundred Golden Portraits of Her Majesty' (£100), before a crowd of 3,500 including 'the great M.C., Bill Price of Hackney Wick notoriety, and Jesse Smith, of the London Proud Peacock', who had 'just dropped down to take stock, so that the "Land of Cockayne" might not be behind the provinces.'

The date fixed for Lang and Sanderson's two miles confrontation was

3 August at the City Ground. An immense crowd gathered to witness the race in the full knowledge that both men were at the height of their careers. Sanderson took up the running from the start and set a tremendous pace, passing the mile mark in 4m.28½s., but Lang who had dropped back some six yards gradually clawed back Sanderson's lead and with 450 yards to go had drawn level. The two raced head to head entering the straight run home, but the superior stride of Lang gave him the advantage and he came home a gallant winner by six yards in a new British Record of 9m.11½s. fully nine seconds inside Jack White's record. The new record was truly a remarkable one and would remain unbeaten by either an amateur or professional for nearly 40 years.

William Lang, backed and trained by George Martin, could now claim to be the champion at one, two, five, ten and twelve miles, and was probably the holder of more pedestrian titles than any professional runner before him; a true Champion of Champions. Jesse Smith, proprietor of the Proud Peacock public house in Covent Garden, was delighted with his association with Lang and announced:

> Verily Juno's favourite has cause to be proud, for another grand trophy has 'landed', on Monday last, for this 'house of call' for Champions, by the speedy Lang, who is now stopping under the shadowy wing of the 'Argus-eyed one', the latter now more jubilant than ever. The Great Ten Miles Champion Cup, the Five Miles Belt, and the Twelve Miles Cup, of which the Middlesbrough Wonder is still the 'proud defender', are now on view, and are trophies worthy of a visit alone to see. Jesse Smith has a secret of supplying 'the speedy beverage' which brings out the speed; of providing beds for his 'ped' patrons, made from the 'down of the done' and as quiet as the lovely dell, to ensure balmy and refreshing sleep, with wines worthy of the presiding goddess of this, one of the first sporting houses in London. Lang will be glad of a call.

His main rival throughout the year had been Sanderson who, although beating Lang for the four miles belt, had to give best to Lang in his record-breaking races at one, two and five miles. Sanderson finished his year as outright holder of the 1¼ mile and 1½ mile cups, won at the expense of Edward Mills at Sheffield in February 1863.

William Lang was also famous in 1863 for his celebrated 'down-hill' mile. He had agreed, for a bet of £50 to £25, to run a mile in 4m.15s. at Newmarket on 30 October. Lang appeared on the 'down-hill' course at 9.30 a.m. and commencing at the starting post on the Cambridge turnpike road, finished his mile opposite the betting-rooms in 4m.02s., the fastest ever run. The first quarter took 55s. and the second 59s. thus also making it the fastest ever half-mile. An account of the race in *Bell's Life* states

William Lang, with Jesse Smith, proprietor of the Proud Peacock, Covent Garden

that 'the down-hill business was only in the latter half of the journey,' which makes the performance even more outstanding.

Lang's exertions throughout the year left him injured by December and he would be an infrequent competitor in 1864 as Teddy Mills returned to his best form.

6

1864, A Year for Miling

Meagre times at Hackney Wick

Hackney Wick was not able to maintain its momentum through 1864. In the early part of the year James Baum was pre-occupied with having his victualler's licence reinstated and it was not until the end of March that the objections of local residents were overturned. As a result only three poorly attended matches of any note were held at the Hackney Wick Grounds in the first few months. The most important was on 8 February, when the Ten Miles Champion Cup match, originally intended to take place on Boxing Day, was eventually run off.

Handbill for the Ten Miles Champion Cup race in February 1864

Jack White, now backed and trained by Bob Bunn of Norwich, defended against the challenge of Edward Mills in a disappointing race attended by 1,000 spectators. Mills was quite obviously ill-prepared and to the disgust of his supporters completed less than three miles before retiring. During the evening, however, Mills challenged White to a match at Hackney Wick over one mile to take place on 21 March; a distance over which Mills quite fancied he could overcome the dominance of the pedestrians from the north of England.

When the day arrived, word had got round that 'Teddy' Mills, under the guidance of his training companion William Richards, was now in good shape and his many supporters turned out prepared to take a pecuniary interest in the result. This time they were not quite so disillusioned. With Charlie Westhall as referee the pair were soon away. A fast half a mile in 2m.5s. caused the pace to drop somewhat as both men prepared themselves for a tight finish. It was a desperate battle at the end with White throwing himself at the tape to win by 18 inches in 4m.31s. For Mills, though, it was a triumph and he now felt confident to travel north to meet the best at one mile.

The Royal Oak, Manchester becomes the main venue for middle distance running

As mentioned in the previous chapter, George Martin, considering the metropolis well supplied with running grounds, had purchased the Royal Oak, Newton Heath, Manchester situated on the Manchester to Oldham turnpike road, in December 1863. Two thousand pounds was spent on preparing its 17 acres of ground, where 2,500 loads of cinders were delivered to prepare a sprint ground over a quarter of a mile in length and a round course of 660 yards; both nine yards wide. The whole course was railed on the outside, with a footpath, so that '20,000 can see with comfort. A shower-bath on a new principle has been erected, enabling pedestrians to have a cold shower-bath, soap, and towel, all complete for a penny.' At the starting post there was a portable dressing room for the competitors – a four-wheeled wagon, covered in, divided into two compartments each carpeted and fitted with every convenience. The ground soon became one of the most popular for middle distance running in the north of England and, under the management of George Martin, attracted the top pedestrians on a regular basis to the detriment of Hackney Wick.

Some four years later in February 1868 a columnist for the magazine *Freelance* gives a vivid description of his visit to the Royal Oak:

> At the top of a queer collection of advertisements that add a doubtful interest to the sporting columns of the Manchester dailies, frequent announcements of pedestrian contests arranged to take place at the Royal Oak or Copenhagen can hardly escape notice. These establishments, we will be bound to say, not one in a hundred of our readers has visited. Perhaps one in fifty has even the faintest notion of their whereabouts. And yet – strange as it may seem, – they furnish the chief and almost only amusement of a very large section of the Lancashire population, and are, on this account well worthy of a few moments' attention. Two of these places are situate on the Oldham Road, perhaps half-an-hour's walk from the Infirmary ...
>
> Just at this point where Oldham Road begins to be bearable, to shake off its connection with the city, and to indulge in an occasional

George Martin, promoter of pedestrianism and proprietor of Royal Oak grounds, Manchester

> stunted tree or scrap of hawthorn hedge, which has survived the poisonous fumes of neighbouring chimneys, we came upon the first of these places, the Royal Oak – a busy looking public house, energetically engaged in swallowing up and vomiting forth a talkative and excited crowd. Passing through the bar to the back of the house, we found a gate at the end of a cindered path, admission through which to the grounds beyond was allowed on the payment of a shilling. The place is of no small size, as may be inferred from the fact that, on recent occasions, some sixty thousand persons managed to pack themselves within the enclosure, two-thirds of whom had paid at the door, the remaining twenty thousand finding their way over the wall without troubling the gate-keeper.
>
> In the arrangement of the ground there is no pretence at ornament. A grand stand of the simplest and barest construction, with rooms for dressing and so on, is provided for the accommodation of the runners and the general public. In one room we noticed a shower bath for the use of competitors whose nerves require bracing at the critical moment. The course is of considerable extent, perhaps a quarter of a mile or more in circumference. For pedestrian purposes, no doubt it is everything that can be desired, there being no irregularity in the shape of the ground, and no very sharp turns at the corners. The interior of the ring is an unbroken area of unwholesome-looking swampy grass, which gives, when necessary, scope for the display of canine talent. A fence surrounds the course on every side, high enough, on ordinary occasions, to preclude the possibility of a surreptitious enjoyment of the Olympic sports by needy outsiders, but not lofty enough to shut out the mills and factories which are the prominent accessories of the scenery of Newton Heath. As these hem in the ground on all sides, and as the wooden fence is painted a cheerful black, modified in places by the effects of the wind and weather to an almost equally cheerful slate colour, the view is somewhat depressing. But the patrons of the Royal Oak do not go there to enjoy the view.

The opening meetings on 16 April and 23 April 1864 both gave prominence to one mile matches. The first featured Sanderson and Albison, and although both runners had a fine record over the mile Sanderson ran in an easy winner in 4m.34s.

The second match on 23 April was between Patrick Stapleton and Edward Mills who, accompanied by Bill Price, had arrived in Manchester the previous week for the opening of the Royal Oak Grounds. Patrick Stapleton was attended by John Woolley, his principal backer, and his trainer Joe of Nancy's from Mossley. Mills drew the inside for the start and led off to pass the quarter-mile post in an unbelievable one minute; at

EDWARD MILLS (1841–1894)
Edward 'Teddy' Mills, known as 'Young England' was born at Pearson Street, Kingsland, Bethnal Green on 25 August 1841. One of five brothers, all runners, he became a dyer's assistant and, at one time, a cat's-meat man. He was small in stature, only 5ft. 4½in. and just 9 stone. Of his brothers, William or 'Billy', became a pedestrian of some note with many wins and good times to his name. Edward made his first public appearance at Hackney Wick in a half-mile handicap in January 1860, after which William Price, with whom he took up residence, immediately took him in hand. During the next three years at distances from 440 yards to ten miles he was virtually unbeaten against all the well-known pedestrians of the day, and in a series of matches against Deerfoot at the end of 1861 frequently proved himself the better man. He briefly held the 10 Miles Champion Cup in 1865 and won the 6 Miles Champion Belt outright in 1862. On 12 January 1863 he broke the British One Hour Record with a distance of 11 miles 775 yards just 15 yards behind Deerfoot. The following year he broke the British One Mile Record on 23 April 1864 when he beat Patrick Stapleton at the Royal Oak Grounds, Manchester in a time of 4m.20½s. Although his best races were now behind him he continued to race through the whole decade. His last recorded match was at Bow on 26 December 1871 when George Hazael beat him over one and a half miles. Outside of pedestrianism he took a keen interest in pugilism and in 1863 helped train Tom King for his fight with John Heenan. He became the proprietor of the Northampton Arms public house in Cambridge Heath Road, Bethnal Green in 1865 but lost everything in a house fire in August 1868, a few months before his wife died. A benefit was held at the Brittania Theatre, Hoxton. He recovered from these misfortunes and throughout the early 1870s owned a number of public houses including the Hand in Hand public house in Islington and the Crown and Anchor in Mile End. From 1875 to 1890 he was proprietor of the Cock Inn, off Jermyn Street, St. James', London. In 1872, as manager, he was instrumental in putting on some of the best meetings at the famous Agricultural Hall in Islington. Although Mills could neither read nor write, by the time of his death he owned more than one prosperous licensed house and was worth £55,000 – the equivalent of more than a million pounds today. He died on 16 July 1894 at the affluent address of 41 Gloucester Road, Regents Park, London.

the half-mile post, passed in 2m.8s., he led Stapleton by 2½ yards and continued to press on, still leading by 2 yards at three quarters of a mile in 3m.16s. With the possibility of a new mile record, the excitement among the one thousand crowd was intense and Stapleton, cheered on by his supporters, passed Mills to take the lead by three yards as the two men entered the home straight. Mills though, with a 'do or die' effort was again in front with 25 yards to go and broke his man, finishing comfortably in 4m.20½s., to set a new British Mile Record by 1¼ seconds.

The miling stakes were raised again before the end of the week, when first Mills accepted a return match on 28 May against Stapleton, who felt that if he had delayed his final effort a little longer he would have won their previous encounter. Then George Martin offered a new 76 ounce silver cup and £25 to be contested for in a sweepstake of £20 each in June.

The pattern of Mills and Stapleton's next race at the Royal Oak grounds was much the same as before with Mills leading through the first three-quarters in 62s.; 2m.10s. and 3m.20s. but this time Stapleton, leaving his challenge to the final bend, left Mills with no response and came home the winner in 4m.27s. The pedestrian pundits, however, were going to have to wait a little longer to be certain who could claim to be the best miler of the era.

Miling returned to Hackney Wick the following week when Mills'

Patrick Stapleton, a champion at one mile

opponent was Siah Albison making a very rare appearance in London. His performance unfortunately did nothing for his reputation with the crowd of 1,000 who had gathered hoping that they might once again see some racing of note in the East End of London. Mills trailed Albison for two laps, then ran away as he pleased to win in the moderate time of 4m.34¼s. and £50 richer.

Meanwhile the entrants for the One Mile Sweepstakes at the Royal Oak had all made good their money and George Martin erected a new grand-stand to hold 2,000 persons with special trains laid on from Leeds, Manchester and other nearby towns. The betting was Lang 5 to 2; Nuttall, Stapleton and Sanderson 3 to 1; Mills 4 to 1 and Albison 6 to 1 with active books being run by George Martin and Bill Price at the Royal Oak and George Hardy at the Rising Swan public house in Manchester. The prize money was to be split £110 for the winner, £25 for second and £10 for third, providing the competitors with a tremendous incentive to be at their peak. William Lang was favourite based on his virtual invincibility the previous year and he invited his friends from London to stay at his public house, the Navigation Inn, during the preceding weekend and accompany him to the big race.

On the Saturday before the race the pedestrian's colours and details were announced:

> Siah Albison of Bow Lee, near Middleton (black and green) age 24; weight 10st. 9lb.; height 5ft. 11in.; trained by Rocker of Failsworth.
> Patrick Stapleton of Mossley (orange) age 30; weight 7st. 6lb; height 5ft. 5in.; trained by Joe of Nancy's at Mossley.
> Edward Mills of London (white and blue spots) age 23; weight 8st. 4lb; height 5ft. 5in.; brought to the post by Bill Price.
> William Lang formerly of Middlesbrough (black) age 26; weight 9st. 9lb; height 5ft. 8½in; prepared by Billy Fish of Royton.
> James Nuttall of Manchester (magenta) age 22; weight 10st.; height 5ft. 8in.; trained by Billy Beswick at the City Ground, Manchester.
> James Sanderson of Whitworth (blue) age 27; weight 8st. 4lb; height 5ft. 7in.; trained by himself.

George Martin acted as starter and referee, whilst Mr Barber of Sheffield officiated as timekeeper. With the track measuring 660 yards there were different coloured flags marking the quarter-mile points; a union jack at the start, red at the quarter, white at the half, blue at three quarters and the Royal Standard on the winning post. The rules were strict; runners were allowed two attendants in the enclosure but they were not allowed to wait on their man over the last 200 yards of the race.

When 25 June arrived the scene at the ground about one hour before the start was almost indescribable, with the officials at the gates unable to

Edward Mills 'Young England,' one mile record holder

take the sixpences fast enough from the thousands who wanted to gain admission. At one point the barriers at the great gate gave way and hundreds surged in for nothing. Eventually, with order restored it was estimated from the takings in excess of £500 that some 25,000 people were present; the largest crowd to attend a pedestrian meeting since the early appearances in England of Deerfoot. Betting at the ground was immense with the odds swinging away from Lang in favour of Mills.

Once the preliminaries were over the runners were soon away with the lead frequently changing hands. By the half mile Sanderson led, with Lang and Mills in close attendance, an order maintained until the three quarter mile mark when Lang and Mills surged past Sanderson and ran shoulder to shoulder until five yards from the tape when Mills surged ahead to win by 12 inches. Sanderson finished third with the others tailed off.

The official times were quarter mile 1m.1½s.; half mile 2m.8s.; three-quarter mile 3m.17s.; one mile 4m.21s. – only half a second outside the record. In what was the equivalent to today's 'Golden Mile' the crowd were delighted.

William Lang was now considering retirement but was keen to have one more match with Mills, offering several challenges throughout October and November. Mills was not keen to venture north for another showdown, however, and it was only after a large amount of paper warfare that he eventually signed articles to meet Lang at the Royal Oak grounds on 14 January 1865 for £50 a side.

Seven Miles Walk Champion Belt

Before returning to the affairs at Hackney Wick mention should be made of the champion belt contested in Liverpool by the London walker James Miles.

In August 1863 the proprietor of the Strawberry Hotel Running Grounds, West Derby Road, Liverpool, announced he would be giving a champion belt for a Seven Miles Walking Handicap. The belt was displayed at Thomas Wilson's Spotted Dog in the Strand, London, during September and the response from the country's walkers was overwhelming. Twenty-six entered, as a result of which two heats had to be contested on Saturday 3 October with Charles Westhall acting as referee to ensure that the walking was 'fair'. James Miles of Brixton, (scratch) won both his heat and the final to become the first holder of the belt. William Spooner was an early challenger but no match resulted and it was not until 18 January 1864 that the next walk took place, between Miles and John Allen of Wednesbury, who was given half a minute start. Miles walked brilliantly and won in a new British Record

James Miles, seven miles walk champion and record holder

of 55 minutes. Two months later, a very unfit William Hatley from London was soundly beaten by Miles, retiring after being lapped. In July Allen was in the frame once more, this time allowed three minutes start. However, he was no match for the ever-improving Miles, who set another British Record of 54m.30s. In February 1865 Miles again easily beat Hatley. On 3 April 1865 Miles, now living in Liverpool, had a disagreeable match against Henry Smalley of Birmingham. Smalley was given 4 minutes 30 seconds start but before the race commenced there was a long dispute over who should be referee. Then, once started, Smalley walked with a far from fair style and in order to overtake his opponent Miles was himself warned for lifting and eventually reeled off and fell from exhaustion. Smalley finished in 60m.10s. but the referee refused to give a decision because neither man had walked fair heel and toe. Following court action, and in order to avoid useless expense the two men agreed to race again on 15 May, when Miles won by a quarter of a mile. The final race for the belt was on 23 December 1865 when Miles at last met William Spooner, the other great walker of the time. Unfortunately, Miles had been troubled by his legs in recent training and walking with his legs bandaged, was no match for Spooner who performed well within himself to win. When the match was concluded and everything settled Spooner sold the belt to the proprietor for £14

JAMES MILES (1840–?)

James Miles, born at East Grinstead on 24 July 1840, was living in Brixton when he started his pedestrian career. He was 5ft. 8½in. and 10st. 6lb. and his first recorded race was a ten mile win at Garratt Lane, Wandsworth in 1859. Most of his early walking was at Wandsworth where he won a ten mile champion belt in 1862 and had a most famous win there against J. Oliver when he walked eight miles in 1h.8m.37s. for £200. Throughout his career Miles was noted for the high stakes for which he was prepared to walk. He won the Seven Miles Champion Belt at Strawberry Grounds, Liverpool, on 5 October 1863 and held it against six challengers until beaten by Spooner in December 1865. In his races for the belt he broke the British record for seven miles in 1863 in 55m.00s. and again in 1864 in 54m.30s. both at Liverpool where he had moved to further his walking career. Miles made three attempts to walk 21 miles in three hours and failed every time; once by just a few seconds. He maintained his position as the leading walker in England until the arrival of George Topley and George Davison in 1867 when they too battled for very high stakes. He turned to longer distance walking in 1876 and although beaten in a 24 hour race at the Agricultural Hall, Islington, on 8 and 9 May, he walked 50 miles in the then unprecedented time of 8h.48m.28s. and was still walking strongly at Lillie Bridge the following year.

and it was suggested he might offer it for a ten miles sweepstake Championship of the World. Spooner, who only once walked at Hackney Wick – on 18 May 1863 when he beat William Hartley over four miles – was nearing the end of a magnificent career that started in 1849.

Steeprock provides new interest at Hackney Wick

During this time pedestrianism in London continued to struggle, with matches at the established grounds attracting crowds of no more than 300–400. One exception was Jack White's defence of his Ten Miles Cup against the challenge of James Sanderson at Hackney Wick on 25 April when the crowd numbered nearly 1,000. It was not only in London that it was difficult to put on popular meetings. In Manchester, George Martin offered a handsome Six Miles Cup and 100 guineas to be run for at the Royal Oak Ground which had to be cancelled due to a lack of interest from the top pedestrians. At Audenshaw a match for the One Mile Cup could not be arranged. Even for the Four Miles Champion Cup held at the Prince of Wales Ground in Bow; James Sanderson had to plead for a challenger before the time limit was up and receiving no response became outright holder.

James Baum continued to give considerable time to publicising the Crown and Anchor Booths taking them to the Peterborough, Barnet and Croydon Fairs where in the 200ft. long dancing saloon customers were entertained by Bradsill's Original Quadrille Band illuminated by thousands of lamps.

James Baum and Bill Price were, however, still keen to revive the status of Hackney Wick as the centre for distance running in the metropolis and in October announced two new events, a 'Great Twenty Miles Handicap' with a £20 first prize and a 'Great Five Miles Handicap' with a £50 first prize.

A successful 20-mile race had been held at Hackney Wick earlier in the year on 13 June when Steeprock an American Indian and his squaw, who had been staying with George Martin in Manchester, arrived in London. Steeprock was a friend of Deerfoot and in later years they became noted for their races against horses in North American cities such as Boston and Cleveland. In London Steeprock and his squaw took up residence with Jesse Smith at the Proud Peacock where they attracted attention by displaying beadwork, moccasins and dresses made by the squaw.

Steeprock, now 39 years of age, made it known that he would accept a challenge from any man to run at Hackney Wick providing he could name the distance. When asked the distance, to everyone's surprise he

Steeprock and his squaw

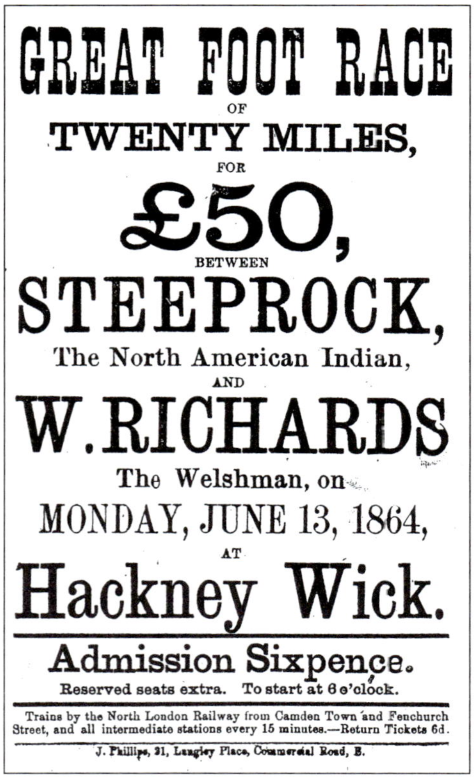
GREAT FOOT RACE
OF
TWENTY MILES,
FOR
£50,
BETWEEN
STEEPROCK,
The North American Indian,
AND
W. RICHARDS
The Welshman, on
MONDAY, JUNE 13, 1864,
AT
Hackney Wick.
Admission Sixpence.
Reserved seats extra. To start at 6 o'clock.
Trains by the North London Railway from Camden Town and Fenchurch Street, and all intermediate stations every 15 minutes.—Return Tickets 6d.
J. Phillips, 31, Langley Place, Commercial Road, E.

Handbill for the twenty miles race between Steeprock and Richards in June 1864

answered 'twenty miles,' and it was one of Bill Price's troupe, William Richards the Welshman from Millwall, who took up the challenge and went into three weeks' hard training. There had been some doubt before the race as to whether this was the same Steeprock who in 1844 at the Beacon Course at Hoboken, New Jersey, USA had run so well against the visiting Englishmen, John Barlow, John Greenhalgh and Ambrose Jackson (not to be confused with William Jackson). However, once the race was underway there was no doubt amongst the 2,000 spectators, Hackney Wick's largest crowd of the year, that this was the same man. At ten miles the Indian was ahead by some 80 yards in 57m.10s., but running with a now badly injured foot. Although calling to Jesse Smith, his backer, that he wished to stop in order to cut off his shoe, Jesse would have none of it and forced his man to carry on. At 15 miles he was still ahead in a time of 1hr.26m.40s. but was forced to pull up: 'The right foot presented a painful sight; his shoe had worked round in turning the corners; and the "pad parted on the waste" had to be dragged out of the raw and bleeding flesh and Bill Richards was declared the winner.'

With the intention of bringing out a champion at this distance the race on 10 October was advertised as the 'All England Handicap of 20 Miles'. The entry was good with ten runners, with Edward Mills off scratch, Richards with 2½ minutes start and Steeprock with five minutes.

A good crowd attended on race day but were disappointed to find that Mills had met with an accident the previous weekend and had withdrawn, as had Brighton and Shaw; leaving Richards the favourite. At four o'clock the runners streamed away at the start of their 136 laps! At ten miles J. Brown, 'the Fulham Street Pet' (later and better known as Henry 'Blower' Brown), led in 57m.10s. off a five minutes handicap from Ray, Steeprock and Andrews; Richards having retired at 6 miles. At 15 miles reached in 1hr.28m. Brown was still leading from Ray with Steeprock tailed off and running with the hope that the others would retire. At 128

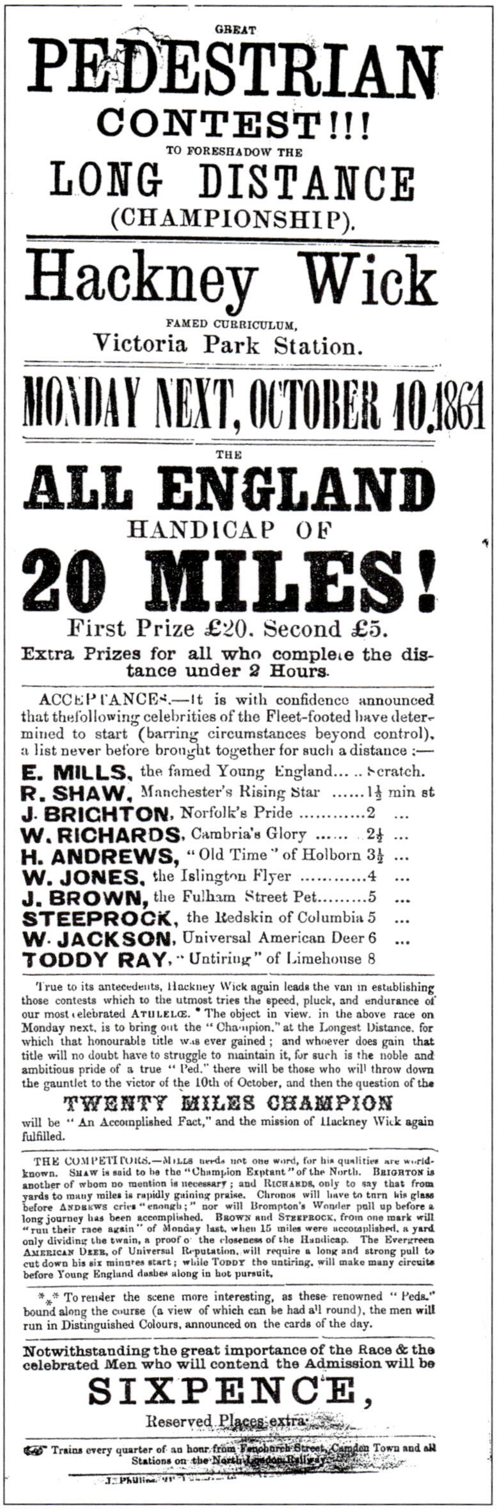
GREAT
PEDESTRIAN
CONTEST!!!
TO FORESHADOW THE
LONG DISTANCE
(CHAMPIONSHIP).

Hackney Wick
FAMED CURRICULUM,
Victoria Park Station.

MONDAY NEXT, OCTOBER 10.1864
THE
ALL ENGLAND
HANDICAP OF
20 MILES!
First Prize £20. Second £5.

Extra Prizes for all who complete the distance under 2 Hours.

ACCEPTANCES.—It is with confidence announced that the following celebrities of the Fleet-footed have determined to start (barring circumstances beyond control), a list never before brought together for such a distance :—

E. MILLS, the famed Young England... .. Scratch.
R. SHAW, Manchester's Rising Star ......1½ min st
J. BRIGHTON, Norfolk's Pride ....2 ...
W. RICHARDS, Cambria's Glory ...... 2½ ...
H. ANDREWS, "Old Time" of Holborn 3½ ...
W. JONES, the Islington Flyer ....4 ...
J. BROWN, the Fulham Street Pet.........5 ...
STEEPROCK, the Redskin of Columbia 5 ...
W. JACKSON, Universal American Deer 6 ...
TODDY RAY, "Untiring" of Limehouse 8

True to its antecedents, Hackney Wick again leads the van in establishing those contests which to the utmost tries the speed, pluck, and endurance of our most celebrated ATHLETÆ. The object in view, in the above race on Monday next, is to bring out the "Champion," at the Longest Distance, for which that honourable title was ever gained; and whoever does gain that title will no doubt have to struggle to maintain it, for such is the noble and ambitious pride of a true "Ped." there will be those who will throw down the gauntlet to the victor of the 10th of October, and then the question of the

TWENTY MILES CHAMPION

will be "An Accomplished Fact," and the mission of Hackney Wick again fulfilled.

THE COMPETITORS.—MILLS needs not one word, for his qualities are world-known. SHAW is said to be the "Champion Exptant" of the North. BRIGHTON is another of whom no mention is necessary; and RICHARDS, only to say that from yards to many miles is rapidly gaining praise. Chronos will have to turn his glass before ANDREWS cries "enough;" nor will Brompton's Wonder pull up before a long journey has been accomplished. BROWN and STEEPROCK, from one mark will "run their race again" of Monday last, when 15 miles were accomplished, a yard only dividing the twain, a proof of the closeness of the Handicap. The Evergreen AMERICAN DEER, of Universal Reputation, will require a long and strong pull to cut down his six minutes start; while TODDY the untiring, will make many circuits before Young England dashes along in hot pursuit.

*** To render the scene more interesting, as these renowned "Peds." bound along the course (a view of which can be had all round), the men will run in Distinguished Colours, announced on the cards of the day.

Notwithstanding the great importance of the Race & the celebrated Men who will contend the Admission will be

SIXPENCE,
Reserved Places extra.

Trains every quarter of an hour from Fenchurch Street, Camden Town and all Stations on the North London Railway.

J. Phillips

Handbill for the All England Twenty Miles Handicap in October 1864

laps, however, it was obvious this would not be the case and he too retired, leaving Brown to come in the winner two laps in front of Ray in a time of 2hr.4m.5s.

Steeprock ran at Hackney Wick again a fortnight later, when he easily beat Ray in a race over 15 miles that attracted little attention. The widely advertised five miles handicap at the beginning of November similarly received little support and a better crowd was attracted to a benefit for the widow and family of the late station master of Hackney Wick railway station when, with the gardens illuminated, there was a giant bonfire with fireworks, dancing and a successful balloon ascent forming the major attractions.

Hackney's final meeting of the year, on Boxing Day, had been intended to feature a challenge for the Ten Miles Champion Cup, but it had to be postponed because most of the top pedestrians were already engaged in matches at shorter distances. Even so, this last meeting of a disappointing year at the running ground proved a resounding success for James Baum and Bill Price. There were 66 entries in the heats for the one-mile handicap, and consequently plenty of betting opportunities. In the big race of the day Mills met Brighton over two miles, giving the recent winner of a three-lap race at the Royal Oak in Manchester a start of 60 yards. The starting marks were at the top of the course, the men having the pagoda between them, Brighton

HENRY 'BLOWER' BROWN (1843–1884)
Henry Brown was born in Fulham on 16 January 1843 and became a famous 'wobbler' (a 'go-as-you-please' long distance pedestrian) in the 1870s. He was a brickmaker by trade and wonderfully fond of beer, indeed his trainer, John Smith, the Regent Street Pet, could always get that extra spurt from his man with a shout promising a barrel of beer if he won! Henry's first running prize was a timepiece for a one mile handicap, at Garratt Lane, Wandsworth in December 1862. He ran at Hackney Wick three times in 1864 recording wins over William Richards and Albert Smith, better known as the North American Indian 'Steeprock'. His first attempt at a six day competition came in March 1878 at the Agricultural Hall, Islington where he won third prize behind the American, Daniel O'Leary, covering a distance of 477 miles in the first race for the Astley Belt. Then in the November he was second to William Gentleman, better known as 'Corkey', in another race for the Belt, this time covering 505 miles. In April 1879 he beat George Hazael, 'Corkey', and the American, Edward Weston to win the John Astley Belt and £400, covering a distance of 542 miles 440 yards and successfully defended the Belt in February 1880, this time reaching 553 miles 165 yards. He visited the United States in the 1880s but had little success. Henry Brown died on 9 March 1884.

being at the entrance of the straight run in, and Mills at the top of the back stretch. Mr. H. A. Reed was both referee and starter, and when he had taken his post the competitors doffed their flannels, and two finer specimens of condition could not be seen. On getting the signal they dashed away at a tremendous pace, Brighton electrifying the spectators by the style of his going and the great form displayed by him. He went over the ground at a long low stride, while in his rear came Teddy, bounding along with his high and light action, seemingly scarcely to put his toes on the ground. It could easily be seen that a fine and exciting race would ensue, and the loud cheers of approbation from the assembled thousands were almost deafening. Mills from the commencement of the struggle began gradually but surely to gain on his opponent, and when two laps had been run, had reduced the gap by about ten yards; at five laps he was within thirty yards of his man, and at the end of the first mile (4m.40s); not more than twenty five yards separated them. As the competitors went along the back stretch in the fourteenth and last lap they were all but level, and after a fine spurt on the part of both to the goal, Mills, who succeeded in coming to the front as they came down the straight run to the finish, went in a winner by a yard and a half; the two miles being run in an excellent 9m.37s.

7

1865, Manchester Makes the News

Hackney Wick in decline

Hackney Wick was definitely in the doldrums at the start of 1865. Edward Mills, the ground's favourite pedestrian, had his mind on other things, not least his Manchester re-match with Lang over one mile in January. Without top pedestrians, the few meetings that were promoted failed to attract large crowds although there were good entries from the local runners.

The first meeting to draw a crowd of any size (and that was a small one) was a benefit for Jackson, who had recently injured his hand. The meeting received good support from his colleagues and the events included a veterans' 80 yards between John Smith the Regent Street Pet, and Jemmy Patterson, the Flying Taylor; a four miles between 'Corkey' whose real name was William Gentleman, Sam Barker and James Pudney; a two

WILLIAM GENTLEMAN better known as 'CORKEY' (1839–?)
'Corkey' as he was known was born at Virginia Row, Bethnal Green in 1839. His first races were at Hackney Wick in 1862. He raced at the Agricultural Hall in 1865 with limited success then with 560 yards start won the Five Miles Handicap at Hackney Wick for the Copenhagen Belt on 25 September 1865. He appeared only occasionally until 1871 and then only at Hackney Wick and Bow. He turned to ultra-distance races in the mid 1870s and completed 405 miles and 4 laps in 139 hours, receiving a prize of £45, in the original six-days' competition instituted by Sir J.D. Astley, at the Agricultural Hall, Islington, on 18–23 March 1878. He won the Long Distance Champion Belt and £500 at the six-days' competition from 28 October to 2 November 1878, completing 520 miles 503 yards in the allowed time to create a new record. Most unusually for an ultra-distance pedestrian, 'Corkey' was looked after by his wife throughout the race, and they did the last few laps together, arm in arm. According to John Astley, Mrs 'Corkey' was a real treasure, she never left him day or night, and was always ready to hand her 'Corkey' a basin of the delicious and greasy eel broth, which he loved so well, and which evidently agreed so famously with him.

William Gentleman 'Corkey' (middle), Henry 'Blower' Brown (on his left) and Daniel O'Leary (on his right) at the end of the six day race at the Agricultural Hall, Islington in 1878

miles walk between an out of condition and 'fat as a pig' Topley, and Gilder and a one mile handicap with 59 entries and 30 starters.

There were no meetings of note until Easter, when there was a new race for the Ten Miles Champion Cup which John White had announced he would not defend. A reasonably good field – John Brighton, Edward Mills, Sam Barker, B. Brunel, William Richards, Markham, B. Brown, Joe Rowe and Toddy Ray – assembled and despite the awful weather several thousand turned up to watch an entertaining programme of events. In the big race Mills beat Brighton with ease in 54m.53s. to hold the Cup for the first time.

The year ticked away for James Baum and Bill Price struggling to keep Hackney going. In September they made another big effort to revive the ground's fortunes with a two day Pedestrian Fete, at which Corkey won a 5 miles handicap for the 'Old Cope Belt' they had redeemed from their 'uncles' where it had been lying for some time. Other events included nine heats, semi-finals and final of a 250-yard handicap, a three miles walk with 14 entries and a one mile handicap of 38 entries in four heats.

In September Edward Mills would announce his retirement to concentrate on business, in particular his public house, the Northampton Arms in Cambridge Heath Road, Bethnal Green, and at the same time

JAMES SANDERSON (1837–1905)
James Sanderson, known as 'Treacle', was born at Cowclough, Whitworth, near Rochdale on 29 December 1837. His nickname of 'Treacle' seems to have come from his fondness for molasses. Although a blacksmith by trade he had a pedestrian's slight build being 5ft. 7in. tall and weighing 8st. 10lb. He first entered the running scene in 1856 under the patronage of George Parkinson of the Three Crowns, Rochdale and ran one mile in under five minutes, for £1 on the Whitworth Road in May, 1856. His first race of note was when he beat Job Smith over two miles. Training under the guidance of Billy Fish of Royton he then beat most of the best pedestrians in his time, including Albison, White, and Mills, mainly in the provinces. He won both the Mile and a Half Champion Cup at Ash Inn Grounds, Stockport and the Mile and a Quarter Champion Cup outright at Hyde Park, Sheffield in February, 1863 and then the Four Miles Champion Cup at Bow in December the same year. His greatest race was probably when he finished six yards behind Lang in his two miles British Record breaking race with a time estimated at 9m.12s. He held the Ten Miles Cup in 1865/1866. Sanderson was still running well into the mid-1870s; in 1875 he had a six miles win over Brighton in 30m.55½s. and in 1876 had two wins over George Hazael.

return the Ten Miles Cup to James Baum to be competed for once again.

Baum and Price decided that they would use their traditionally well supported Boxing Day meeting to promote a race for the Cup, giving them time to put together a good field for what was still regarded as one of the most desirable prizes amongst middle and long distance pedestrians. They did not fail the large crowd of 4,000. James Sanderson, John Brighton, William Lang, Robert McKinstray and William Richards, all champions and record holders at their specialised distances, toed the line. As word had it among the betting men that Richards, Lang and McKinstray were not in condition and Brighton had recently sprained his ankle, Sanderson, attended by his backer George Parkinson of the Three Crowns public house in Rochdale, was favourite. The pundits were not wrong. Although there was a competitive race to nearly half distance it was only Sanderson, followed by a very distant Brighton, who finished the race with Sanderson taking home the Cup and a first prize of sixty 'sovs'.

New records at Manchester

Before Mills' much publicised one mile against Lang he was matched over two miles against Sanderson at the Royal Oak Grounds on New Year's

Eve. Bill Price accompanied him, and although the pair had high hopes it was the favourite Sanderson who won the day with Mills retiring at 1½ miles.

The 'Great One Mile Race' for £50 aside was held at the Royal Oak on 14 January and a crowd of 4,000 braved the heavy rain, sleet and wind to witness Lang's attempt to beat the champion miler. William Lang was the favourite as it was well known he had trained unstintingly for many months under the guidance of William Fish, of the Hare and Hounds Inn at Royton, and had pulled his weight down from 11st. 9lb. to a mere 9st. 10lb. Considering the weather conditions and the heavy state of the ground, the performances of the two athletes were extraordinary. Mills led from the start, passing 440 yards in 63 seconds and the half-mile in 2m.9s. At ¾ mile Mills still made the pace with 3m.20s. but now Lang, who had been at his heels the whole time, began to pressure Mills around the final turn of the 651 yard track as they raced shoulder to shoulder into the straight. Then 60 yards from the tape, a gap opened and Mills,

Robert McKinstray, half-mile record holder and Scottish champion

ROBERT McKINSTRAY (1835–1881)
Robert McKinstray was born at Maybole, Ayrshire in August 1835 and started his running career at the age of 18. He was trained first by Bill Thomas and Hugh Dunachie in Glasgow and then by William Straker of Newcastle. Competing at the various Highland Games he was soon carrying off all the pedestrian honours of note, becoming the One, Two, Three and Five Miles Champion of Scotland. By the mid 1860s he was making a name for himself in northern England and in 1865 was only five yards down on Lang and Richards in their record-breaking 4m.17¼s. mile. In 1865 at the Royal Oak Grounds, Manchester he beat Heywood and Richards in a half-mile sweepstake to break the British record with a time of 1m.56½s. and briefly held the One Mile and One Mile and a Half Champion Cups before losing to the up and coming John Fleet. He became proprietor of Bank Tavern at 33 Trongate, Glasgow, before retiring in December 1869. He died in his home town of Maybole on 27 September 1881.

suddenly eight yards down, found he had nothing left and came to a halt leaving Lang to finish at his leisure in 4m.35¾s.

The next great middle distance race at the Royal Oak came in May when George Martin brought together Robert McKinstray of Glasgow, commonly called the Scottish Champion, John Heywood of Rochdale and William Richards the Welshman, born in Glamorgan but now from London, for a half mile sweepstake of £25 each. The three men, all at the height of their fame and expecting a fast race, arrived in Manchester the week before the match to finalise their training. McKinstray worked under J. Booth of the Kings Arms public house in Newton Heath, Heywood, with Lang's adviser Billy Fish of Royton, while the self-trained Richards stayed at the Royal Oak.

The race was held on Saturday 20 May, at five o'clock – not a popular time for pedestrian followers – and only 2,000 spectators attended to watch the fastest ever half-mile. The runners started on the slightly uphill 400 yards straight before turning on to the circular track and kept the same order – McKinstray, Heywood, Richards – for 550 yards. Then Richards challenged Heywood but could make no impression on McKinstray, leading by six yards. McKinstray was in total control and looking over his shoulder twice in the final yards, came home the winner five yards ahead of Richards who in turn was two yards ahead of Heywood, the favourite. The time was a magnificent new British Record of 1m.56½s. beating the previous record set by Harry Reed in 1854 by 1½ seconds.

The Golden Mile

George Martin announced on 17 June what he hoped would be the greatest mile race ever run. In order to attract the best field 'in the world' he offered a gold champion cup (a massive two handled silver tankard, partly gilt, ornamented with oak leaves, and surmounted by acorns, symbolic of the Royal Oak) to be run for on Saturday 19 August, with one-half of the gate money to be divided between the first four competitors. The cup was to be held against all-comers for a period of 12 months, with the winner holding himself in readiness to run at six weeks' notice for not less than £25 aside.

Within weeks a field containing the current stars of the pedestrian world had been formed: Siah Albison, running into form with a recent win at Leeds, when as back marker off 45 yards in a 1050-yard handicap he won in a fast time against 42 other runners. Robert McKinstray, the half-mile record holder and Scottish champion; William Richards, who ran second to McKinstray in the half-mile record race then went on to beat him in Glasgow in early August over one mile in 4m.24s.; William Lang, who had been out-sprinted by Mills in the Great One Mile Sweepstake at the Royal Oak the previous July, but won a return match earlier in 1865; James Sanderson, holder of the Ten Miles Champion Cup who had beaten Lang over one mile in June in 4m.27¼s. and Patrick Stapleton, who finished second to Mills in his record breaking mile. Charles Mower, John Neary and James Nuttall made up the excellent entry. The only star not putting in an appearance was Edward Mills, holder of the mile record set the previous April, who did not feel at his best.

The race created immense interest in the pedestrian world and 13,000 spectators made their way to the Royal Oak grounds. The betting made Lang favourite at 7 to 4, with Albison 5 to 2, Richards 7 to 2, Mckinstray 5 to 1, Sanderson 6 to 1, and almost any odds available on the others. The race was described in *Sporting Life*:

> Mr. George Martin filled the triple duties of starter, referee, and timekeeper, and securing a favourable opportunity, fired the pistol. As the race commenced a hoarse roar arose from the assembled thousands, and on the men settling down into their places the first to show in front was Nuttall, behind whom, in Indian file, came Neary, Sanderson, McKinstray, Richards, Lang, Stapleton, Albison, and Mower in the order named. In this way Nuttall led the way at a rare pace past the stand for the first time, when the running was taken up by the Champion of the land of Burns, the Welshman being second, Lang, who had by this time got through his men, going on third, and Sanderson fourth, the lot sticking close together. About fifty yards behind 'Treacle' came Stapleton (fifth), who was a similar distance in

front of Albison immediately behind whom struggled on hopelessly in the rear Neary, Nuttall, and Mower. The terrific pace soon told its tale, for on entering the straight for the second time, Neary, Nuttall, and Mower seeing their hopes of victory already extinguished pulled up and resigned the contest. On passing the stand, the men were vociferously cheered to renewed exertions, and it soon became evident that the contest was virtually confined to McKinstray, Richards, Lang, and Sanderson. So close were the first four that a sheet would have covered all of them, each trying his utmost to gain pride of place. At the factory chimney the Scotsman began to fall slightly back, on which Richards and Lang showed prominently in front and on entering the straight run home were abreast. Simultaneously the pair put forward their final efforts, and, locked together, dashed down the straight at a terrific rate. The excitement now became tremendous, the immense concourse of spectators moving to and fro like surging billows. Each made almost superhuman efforts to cut down his opponent, the pace being more like sprinting than at the conclusion of a mile race. It is almost impossible to describe the scene as the two approached the tape, when the referee, being unable to separate them, declared a dead-heat for first place between Lang and Richards; McKinstray was third, five yards behind the dead-heaters, twenty yards behind whom came Sanderson, fourth; Stapleton was fifth, and Albison sixth. The first quarter was completed in 1 min., half a mile in 2 min.5½ sec., three quarters in 3 min.14 sec., and the one mile in a British Record of 4 min.17¼ sec., the shortest time on record, and 3¼ sec., less than Teddy Mills unparalleled time above referred to. It was subsequently agreed to run off the dead-heat between Lang and Richards next Saturday afternoon, at five o'clock, when a brilliant struggle is sure to result.

A crowd of 5,000 attended the deciding race for the Gold Champion Cup the following Saturday, with Lang once again the favourite. Keeping in close attendance Lang allowed Richards to take the lead through the quarter mile in 58s., half in 2m.05s. and three-quarters in 3m.15s. They were still locked together with 120 yards to go when Lang put in his noted sprint to leave a tired Richards 30 yards behind. The final time was 4m.22s. George Martin presented William Lang with the Cup for all to see at the window of the Royal Oak and the health of the two runners was drunk from the trophy filled with champagne.

Lang continued his celebrations in London the following Wednesday when he was entertained at Edward Mills' Northampton Arms, and a host of celebrities led by Bill Price witnessed Lang claiming his forfeit of wine from Teddy for beating his mile record. Finally Lang entertained his friends from the north at his own establishment, the Navigation Inn, the

WILLIAM LANG (1839–1905)
William Lang, known as the 'Crowcatcher', was born in Stockton-on-Tees on 22 December 1839 and later moved to Middlesbrough. At 5ft. 9½in. he was one of the tallest pedestrians of his day and also stood out because of his beard. His first recorded race over 100 yards for £3 was at the age of 16. He was soon spotted by George Martin who backed him in matches at Sheffield and Manchester where he beat the likes of Sanderson over two miles in 1859 in a time of 9m.49½s., Brighton, Barker and Job Smith. Then in 1862 he won the Ten Miles Champion Cup and held it for 12 months. He was trained by Mr W. Fish of Royton and when in London was normally backed from Jesse Smith's Proud Peacock in Maiden Lane, Covent Garden. His best year was undoubtedly 1863 when he created new British records at one mile 4m.21¾s. and at two miles 9m.11½s., in addition to a new British One Hour record of 11 miles 871 yards and winning the Champion Cups at one, four and five miles. The same year on 30 October, it is claimed he ran one mile downhill on the Cambridge Road at Newmarket in 4m.2s. At the end of the year he took up residence in Manchester as proprietor of the Navigation Inn, Anscotts Road at around the same time his mentor George Martin bought the Royal Oak. The Navigation Inn became a famous sporting house in Manchester where Lang exhibited his trophies and was frequently 'at home' for visiting pedestrians with matches in Manchester. Lang's greatest race came at the Royal Oak, Manchester on 19 August 1865 when in a dead heat with Richards he reduced the one mile record to 4m.17¼s. In a run off the following week he won the One Mile Gold Cup. In 1868 he announced that he was to leave the English pedestrian scene and disposed of the Navigation Inn to John Fleet before leaving for the USA to challenge the American Champion William Harding. Unfortunately no match was made and a disappointed Lang returned to England the following year. He was sued for divorce in 1869 and raced rarely after this, retiring in 1871. He remained involved with the sport and is known to have trained the A.A.C. Four Miles Champion, James Edgar in 1872. He was proprietor of the Robert Burns Inn on the Oldham Road, Manchester in 1874 but died penniless in his home town of Stockton-on-Tees on 29 July 1905.

following Saturday before going into training for a valuable two mile sweepstake being arranged by George Martin to take place in October.

That race never came about, however, possibly due to George Martin's ill health. The *Sporting Life* of the 18 October reported that George, who had recently been staying at a private asylum in Buxton, had escaped and made his way to London where he stayed with friends for some days in a very disturbed state. Finally his mental state was so bad he had to be

GEORGE MARTIN (1827–1865)
George Martin was born at Blackwater, near Sandhurst in Berkshire on 28 August 1827. His father was a shoemaker, and George, at an early age, adopted the same trade, and showed such aptitude for the business that at the age of 17 he was sent to London. In consequence of this visit to London, Martin became acquainted with John Smith (the Regent Street Pet), and showing a great liking for pedestrian sports, was put through the 'mill' by Smith, who found him good enough to be backed for a winning 'tenner' against Berry, of Lambeth. From this period he gradually advanced until he became known as one of the fleetest runners in the metropolis, competing regularly until 1858, winning several races for his backers. In his last race at Hyde Park, Sheffield he won £20 in a 300 yard handicap. Later Martin moved to Manchester, where his great talent for putting the fleet of foot together, and obtaining many victories for his 'stable', brought him into greater notoriety than ever. He was located near to, and was in great measure the promoter of, the noted Salford Borough Gardens, in which grounds he gave the first silver cup to be run for in a 200 yards handicap. After this he gave his whole attention to finding out good novices, travelling hundreds of miles in the process. His first 'novice' was Ralph Wheatley, the Oyster Lad, of Leeds; he then found and brought out such men as John Nevin, John White, William Lang, Charles Mower, and Davenport, and for some time the celebrated Harry Reed was located with him. Martin being of an enterprising disposition then formed a troupe for America, taking with him White, Mower and Nevin. The group met with huge success and their offers of matches brought forth, amongst others, Deerfoot. Martin, with his great acumen at once saw that there was the making of a great runner in the American Indian. He spared neither expense nor trouble to engage him for a trip to England, with great success. One of his most extraordinary exploits while managing Deerfoot, was the building of a travelling race course (12 feet high and a quarter of a mile in circumference) with which he toured England, Scotland and Ireland with Deerfoot and a small group of runners for a period of four months with races virtually every day. Martin was one of the greatest promoters of pedestrianism, and many men owe the position they held to him. In 1863, he again took up quarters at his favourite town, Manchester, and at great expense made the ground attached to the Royal Oak public house into one of the most complete pedestrian arenas ever known. Success attended his efforts until he showed unmistakeable signs of derangement, which terminated in his decease in Hanwell Asylum on 20 October 1865 at the young age of 39. He was buried after a private family ceremony (with the exception of the attendance of Bill Price), at Finchley Cemetery in London. He left a wife and six children totally unprovided for and it was left to his friends to raise a subscription on their behalf.

severely restrained and the physicians had him taken to Hanwell Lunatic Asylum where he died after a few days.

The year finished quietly with James Holden managing the Royal Oak, William Lang becoming more involved with managing pedestrian matches and Edward Mills retiring to manage his public house.

THE BEST PERFORMANCES OF LANG, WHITE AND MILLS COMPARED

	Edward Mills		John White		William Lang	
	Ranking	Time	Ranking	Time	Ranking	Time
1 mile	3rd	4:20.5	11th	4:26.0	1st	4:17.5
2 miles	4th	9:37.0	3rd	9:20.0	1st	9:11.5
3 miles	3rd	14:52.0	1st	14:36.0	1st	14:36.0
4 miles	3rd	20:01.0	1st	19:35.0	1st	19:35.0
6 miles	3rd	30:09.0	1st	29:50.0	2nd	29:51.0
10 miles	2nd	52:36.0	1st	52:14.0	3rd	52:36.0

8

1866, Walking at Hackney Wick

A small revival at the 'Wick'

By the beginning of 1866 the running grounds at Hackney Wick were at a very low ebb and the description given in *Sporting Life* on 17 January that year summarises the situation quite clearly:

> Hackney Wick – alas! what a falling off! Time was when the announcement of a race between two good men would draw thousands of spectators and speculators to the above rendezvous; but now how changed! W. Richards (the Welshman) and W. Lang, who some short time back ran a mile (a dead-heat) at Manchester in the shortest time on record (4min. 17¼sec.), had on Monday last to contend for, it was said, £25 a side, in a race, distance one mile; but the names of even these clippers failed to draw more than a thousand visitors to the place, although, from the fact of the battle between Rooks and Ryall being so near, an unusual number of countrymen were present, and the members of the Ring mustered in force, prominent among them were Jem Mace, Joe Goss, Rooke, Bob Travers, Gannon and several other notables in the PR. The pedestrian circle was also pretty well represented, several ex-champions, including Pudney, Teddy Mills, Sam Barker, old Jack Smith, etc., being there. The energetic M.C., W. Price, had done all that lay in his power to make such arrangements that would give satisfaction to all who attended to witness the contest, but from the supineness of the proprietor the place has been allowed to fall into such a state of decay that it is enough to give one the horrors to look at it. The once vaunted monster dancing platform is a mere mass of rotten wood; the pagoda, whose turn has oft been mentioned as having been a 'turning point' in many a spin, seems now to be only waiting some friendly blast to lay it low; the very rails even, that separate the so-called reserved seats from the running track, are humbly bowing their heads at such an acute angle that the slightest pressure must inevitably bring them down; so that, altogether, the whole wears such a woebegone aspect as to plainly betoken that the once famed Hackney Wick must soon be numbered among the things that have been. And now for the race – Lang led but made no effort at a

reasonable pace and after 5 laps Richards took the lead and won by 60 yards in the slow time of 4m.53s.

Between January and Easter there were few matches of any note, although a race between Edward Mills' brother William and Edward Golder from Canterbury attracted reasonable numbers, when Golder won over four miles in a mediocre time of 21m.15s.

By Easter, however, James Baum had regained his enthusiasm for pedestrianism. He had set to work in earnest over the preceding month sparing no expense or trouble in renovating the ground, and it looked as bright as it did in its palmiest days. The reserved seats had been completely renewed and the fencing made so good that the spectators were able to comfortably watch the proceedings. Considering the other major attractions available in the metropolis that Easter there were reasonably good crowds at Hackney Wick each day for a programme that included boxing and wrestling to supplement the pedestrianism.

One should be under no illusion, however, as to the type of place that Hackney Wick could be; as demonstrated on August Bank Holiday Monday at the second Hackney Wick Grand Annual, 'Ye Roasting of ye Bullocke'. There was a programme of pedestrianism, ball gathering, jingling matches, old English sports, dancing on the monster platform and fireworks as a finale. A whole bullock was roasted as the main attraction of the proceedings which were open all day and drew together *the very scum of the East End*, some thousands of whom assembled during the day for a cheap dinner. As for the pedestrian events, there was a walking match between two aspirants whose names were never discovered and a mile handicap that for no apparent reason did not take place.

Walking at Hackney Wick

For some time the metropolis had sported some fine walkers, although few had been attracted to race at Hackney even though Bill Price had introduced a Four Miles Walking Handicap Challenge Cup in 1865 that boasted entries from William Hatley and William Spooner. The most important pedestrians walking in 1866 were Spooner, now a veteran of 40 from Turnham Green; James Miles aged 26 from Brixton, the British Record holder at seven miles and holder of the Seven Miles Champion Belt for many years; William Hatley, also 26, from the City of London; and then the younger men, George Davison aged 22 from Hoxton, Joe Stockwell aged 22 from Surrey and finally George Topley aged 21 from Fulham who was considered the champion walker having beaten Miles the previous year and also broken Westhall's long-standing record of 21 miles in three hours with a time of 2h.58m.24s. on Boxing Day 1865.

George Topley, reported to have walked 21 miles in three hours

George Davison's first appearance at Hackney was on 6 August 1866 when he beat William Howes of Haggerston by 50 yards in a seven-mile race. The event proved a success and William Price immediately offered prizes of £50 for first place and £10 for second in a seven-mile handicap walk to take place on 3 September.

Entries came from Topley (scratch) who had walked a disputed 50m.52s. for the seven miles distance at Brompton on 12 March, when he beat Miles in completing 13½ miles in another attempt on his own 21 miles record; Stockwell (½ min.), Miles (1 min.) and Davison (3½ min.). Topley again proved that he was the best walker at that time, having an easy win in 55m.30s. while Davison showed good style and form for the future.

Walking at Brompton

At this stage the subject of walking cannot be left without mention of some of the matches held at Brompton between 1864 and 1866. George Topley, born in 1845, a real find at such a young age, was a fast walker with a good style trained initially by Jem Howes at Hackney Wick. He was unfortunate to fall ill in 1864 after making his mark in a two miles walk at Brompton earlier in the year. However, by May 1865 he was at his best again. Although disqualified for lifting when storming away from Stockwell in a four mile match he went on to beat Miles in June. Next, on Boxing Day 1865 he walked his doubtful 21 mile record. This race, with Charles Westhall acting as referee, was meticulously recorded in *Sporting Life* with times for each quarter of a mile, finishing with a new Record of 2h.58m.24s. which seems to warrant its acceptance as the record even though the last laps were walked in darkness. On 12 March 1866 the two leading walkers at 21 miles, Topley (now trained by John Smith, the 'Regent Street Pet') and Miles, met in a match over the distance for £50. Topley again confirmed his superiority when he lapped Miles for a second time at the 13½ mile mark, at which point Miles retired, exhausted.

William Spooner and John Smith, the ten mile walking champion and his trainer

On 3 June Topley met Spooner over the same distance, with the ground a quagmire, and surprisingly lost to the much older walker, who was now nearly 40 years old. Topley was obviously not well but was soon back

GEORGE TOPLEY (1845–1877)

George Topley was born on 29 October 1845. His walking career started in 1862 when his employer, a well known East-end publican, fancying the 'boy' possessed a turn of speed at walking, took him to some rural sports at Canterbury, and was both surprised and pleased at Topley's prowess. Having discovered that he was worth backing, Topley was matched against George Wild and then Charley Dixon at Bow, winning both matches. With his rapid rise his backers had no option but to match him with Jack Underwood, at that time looked upon as a most promising performer. The match, which was for £25 a side, distance two miles, took place at West London Grounds, Brompton, early in 1864 and after one of the fastest (15m.10s.) and best races on record Topley, trained by Jem Howes at Hackney Wick, was again declared the winner. Shortly after this Topley was taken seriously ill and it was feared his pedestrian days were over. For the remainder of that year he was compelled to be idle, but phoenix-like, trained by John Smith, the Regent Street Pet, of the Norman Arms, Fulham, he rose again and in a match against time for £100 in January, 1865, walked seven and a half miles in the hour: 'Completing the distance in so fair a manner that not a murmur was heard even from those backing the scythe-bearer – a most remarkable thing in these days of "mixing" and disqualifications.' After that he accomplished the great Westhall feat of walking 21 miles in three hours (2h.58m.24s. on 16 December 1865 at Brompton), the last named great pedestrian being referee. Then in 1866 he walked eight miles in one hour and supposedly two miles in 14 minutes. Soon after this he married and entered business at the Hole in the Wall public house, Leader Street, Chelsea. In February 1868 he visited the USA and in his first race for $250 a side easily walked 7½ miles in the hour against time, but in May failed to walk 50 miles in ten hours on the Fashion Race Course, Long Island. While in America Topley made repeated attempts to compete against the great American long distance walker, Edward Payson Weston and eventually a match was made for a race over 100 miles on 19 June 1868 at the Mystic Park racecourse near Boston. At 75 miles Weston was two miles ahead of Topley, at which point Weston stated he could not go on. Topley continued to 74 miles, when he stopped to rest. While the spectators waited for him to return to the track it was announced he had withdrawn and Weston was declared the winner to an astonished and highly suspicious crowd. In 1869 he visited Australia with Frank Hewitt and Alf Bird at the invitation of a Melbourne promoter and won a series of races in Melbourne and Sydney before returning to England in September 1870. He died of heart disease at his home in Chiswick in August 1877.

WILLIAM SPOONER (1832–?)
William Spooner was born in Hadleigh, Suffolk on 24 July 1832 and married the daughter of John Smith, the Regent Street Pet. In his first race, a six miles walk at Turnham Green on 28 May 1849 he won a silver watch. By the following year he had improved dramatically and on 11 September beat G. Bradshaw over seven miles in 57m.29s. at Wexham, Bucks and raced regularly at the Flora Gardens Battersea. On 8 December 1851 he won the Ten Miles Champion Belt for walking at Copenhagen Grounds, Islington, in a time of 1h.22m.5s. Spooner won a Champion Belt seven miles walking handicap in 57m.04s. at the Royal Oak Grounds, Barking on 16 May 1853 and defended the belt in a time of 57.20s. on 11 July 1853. Neither of these marks appear as records although he was off scratch in both races and *Bell's Life* who sometimes criticised his style made no comment on his not walking fair. In 1858 he beat Westhall over 20 miles and walked the same distance on the Newmarket Road in 2h.57m.03s. However, at Manchester he failed in his attempt to walk 21 miles in three hours. In October the same year he walked 50 miles in 8h.27m. at Garratt Lane, Wandsworth. In his last race, 21 miles for £100 at Brompton, on 1 July 1867, he was beaten by Topley, having vanquished him the previous year also at 21 miles for £50. Spooner was a prolific walker and during the years 1849–1866 was virtually unbeaten except by time. In one of his more extraordinary feats at Newcastle on 17 September 1855 he beat James Rowan who had to run ten and a half miles while Spooner walked seven and a half miles. He won in a time of 57 minutes. When unable to find walking opponents Spooner took up prize-fighting, but retired from the ring after a particularly gruelling fight.

to his old form and on 30 July won an eight mile walk against time in 59m.39s.

On 10 December Topley again met Miles, given one minute start, this time over seven miles with another £50 at stake. Although Topley had closed the gap to 80 yards by the fifth mile it took too much out of him and he gradually faded before retiring at six miles. The overweight Topley no longer appeared the great walker he was and no doubt his recent acquisition of the Hole-in-the-Wall public house in Chelsea had something to do with this. Even so, he would be prepared to stake up to £100 to race Miles again.

Another walking record was set at Brompton on 23 July 1866 when William Hatley met Joe Stockwell. Stockwell's debut race had been at Hackney Wick in September, 1862 when he won the Great Exhibition Four Miles Walking Handicap in such convincing style he found some trouble in meeting with further matches. On this occasion Stockwell gave

Hatley 30 seconds start over two miles and in a race where both competitors were complimented for their fast and fair walking it was Hatley who retained the lead finishing in a new record time of 14m.26s. (*Bell's Life* 14m.25s.) Although the fastest time on record it seems not to have found its way into the record books.

Events in Manchester

After the death of George Martin there was little top-class middle distance pedestrianism at the Royal Oak, Manchester, until George Hardy promoted a three-quarters of a mile sweepstake with £85 for the winner, on 30 June 1866. His invitation was answered by five of the country's speediest pedestrians – William Richards, William Lang, Siah Albison, James Nuttall and Robert McKinstray. The race attracted 3,000 who despite steady rain were entertained by a close race won by Richards,

WILLIAM RICHARDS (1839–?)
William Richards, known in pedestrian circles as 'The Welshman', was born in Glamorgan on 11 October 1839. He moved to Millwall in London as a young man and began a running career in 1858 when he forfeited £1 to Bill Price at Hackney Wick in a match to run 880 yards. Many of his early races were at Hackney Wick, mainly over 880 yards against the likes of Sam Barker and Toddy Ray before moving up distance to beat Harry Andrews and William Jackson, then, in his first outstanding win, he beat James Rowan over three miles (with 100 yards start). On 13 June 1864 he defeated Steeprock over 20 miles, reaching 15 miles in 1h.26m.40s. He was one of Bill Price's school and many pedestrians were helped in training by Richards in the time he spent there. He moved to Manchester when his running career took off in the mid-1860s and became proprietor of the Black Horse public house in Oldham Road, close to the famous Manchester running grounds. His most successful racing came in 1865 over one mile. First he beat McKinstray at the Stonefield Grounds on 29 July in 4m.24s; then on 19 August he dead-heated with Lang to jointly hold the British one mile record at 4m.17¾s. He finished second to Lang a week later in the race to decide the Cup. On 30 June 1866 at the Royal Oak, Manchester, he beat Albison, McKinstray and Nuttall over three quarters of a mile in a British record time of 3m.07s., winning £85 in the sweepstake. He was consistent over all distances; as well as his mile time he ran 880 yards in 2m.00¼s, three miles in 15m.26s. and ten miles in 55m.40s. He visited America in 1869 and on 29 June was beaten by Deerfoot over five miles for $2,000 at the Fair Grounds Cleveland, Ohio.

three yards ahead of Nuttall, in a new British Record of 3m.07s. Having moved to Manchester early in the year Richards was trained by Ike Hughes, and acquired the Black Horse public house on the Oldham Road, close to the Royal Oak and Copenhagen grounds.

James Holden Junior, George Martin's brother-in-law (son of the 'pedestrians banker' of Manchester and district), managed the Royal Oak Grounds during the first part of the year. A lack of resources, however, led to a gradual decline until it was eventually bought at auction by John Taylor, a brewer from Ardwick, in September 1866 and soon afterwards sold to John Cooper. By this time the place had become a complete wilderness. But under Cooper's management the 'Oak' soon regained its old appearance and prime position as a middle distance pedestrian venue. By November Cooper was encouraging pedestrians to inspect the newly renovated path as well as facilities for trotting, pigeon shooting and rabbit coursing – and looking forward to 1867.

9

1867, A Revival in Middle Distance Pedestrianism

Top pedestrians continue to appear at Hackney Wick

1867 was an 'up and down' year at Hackney Wick. There were further challenges for the Ten Miles Champion Cup after no competition the previous year and the further promotion of walking matches. A two miles championship sweepstake was introduced in March and there were a number of races for a two miles handicap cup that had been introduced by Bill Price the previous year. In addition regular handicap meetings took place most Mondays.

Bank holiday meetings retained their popularity and the ground was again completely renovated for Easter, attracting a crowd said to number 8,000 on Good Friday. There were 122 competitors for a programme which included wrestling and pedestrianism with a two mile walking handicap in which Davison and Topley competed. The programme continued on Saturday and Monday when further large crowds were additionally entertained to a number of boxing bouts. At Whitsun the Crown and Anchor Booth was erected in the grounds and many people again flocked to Hackney Wick.

James Sanderson, the holder of the Ten Miles Champion Cup, forfeited to John Fleet in December 1866 shortly before he could have become the outright holder. The first challenge to Fleet took place on 6 May 1867 when Lang, who had retired the previous year to spend more time on business, showed his determination to test the young champion's abilities. Teddy Mills with whom he had occasionally trained attended the unassuming Fleet, making only his second appearance at Hackney. Lang came to the line in determined mood taking Fleet through three miles in 15 minutes and there was a fine race up to six miles when Lang was forced to withdraw. The uneven surface of the path had caused the leather in his shoes to give way and the spikes to enter his foot. In view of this unfortunate end to the race, Lang challenged Fleet shortly after his defeat but Fleet was not prepared to meet him. So once again Lang became the holder of the cup.

Lang accepted the challenge of John Brighton on 27 October and although the challenger had been racing regularly he was even older than Lang and moving towards veteran status. The race was not fast and Lang won by 20 yards in a time of 56m.40s. Brighton expressed dissatisfaction at the result and Lang offered him a return but it came to nothing. The next race for the cup would be the following February.

John Fleet's earlier outing at Hackney had been in March when Bill Price attracted the top men to run in his Two Miles Champions Sweepstake, advertised as having as competitors the champions of England, John Fleet; Wales, William Richards; and Scotland, Robert McKinstray. James Sanderson joined this trio bringing the prize money to £50. Unfortunately prior to the race Sanderson withdrew. Then, the day before, McKinstray, who like Richards had been staying with Jem Pudney, slipped off a kerbstone and sprained his ankle. So it was left to just Richards and Fleet, who had arrived from Manchester the previous

John Fleet, champion at one mile

Thursday to race for the £50. Fleet stayed with Teddy Mills who introduced him to the different running grounds in the metropolis and on Saturday took him for a spin at Brompton. It was Fleet, recent winner of the one and a half mile cup in Manchester, who showed he was undoubtedly the man of the moment beating Richards easily in 9m.53s.

The terms of the Two Miles Handicap Cup bearing the name of Bill Price were that, if held for six months against challenges at six weeks notice from any of the original entry, according to their original starts, for not less than £10 aside, it would become the holder's outright. First held on Saturday 29 September 1866, the event proved extremely popular with metropolitan pedestrians who were all content with Bill Price's handicapping skills. There were 38 entries for the first race won after three heats by William Mills, brother of Teddy, with a start of 170 yards. Bob Rogers from Chelsea off 130 yards, was the first challenger in November 1866, but Mills was able to hold his own. Next Curley (Goulding's Lad) off 300 yards, ran Mills in December 1866, winning after Mills fell. Then on 28 January 1867 Curley beat Alec Austin, who received a 200 yard handicap, by 20 yards. At the end of May Curley forfeited the cup to Mills who was challenged in July by Thomas Cox of Canterbury off 250 yards. Mills, trained by Springhall, won a fast race to retain the Cup and although he subsequently advertised for a challenger, by the end of the year none was forthcoming so he became the outright holder.

Fine walking at Hackney Wick

George Davison, the local Hackney walker, improved again in 1867. He started the year in January giving Howes an increased handicap of two minutes over seven miles and won convincingly.

In February it was the turn of George Topley and James Miles, with a win apiece, to make a match at Hackney Wick to decide for the last time who was the better man. The stakes had been upped yet again and their match over seven miles on 4 February was for £150! The race was walked at a furious pace with two miles passed in 14 minutes (*Bell's Life* commented: we leave it to our readers to imagine what it is which these men call walking) and it was soon obvious that this could not continue. Indeed at 2½ miles, Miles was seized with cramp and had to retire leaving Topley to walk just two more laps before the referee, Harry Reed, called a halt.

Davison was at Hackney again in July, this time beating Kempster easily over seven miles. A few months earlier he had two great walks at Brompton, first he set the walking world talking by walking 7¼ miles against time in 59m.29s., then, two days later he was given a one-minute

WILLIAM HOWES (1839–?)
William Howes was born in Felthorpe about seven miles from Norwich on 25 March 1839. He later moved to Haggerston and made his first appearance as a walker at Hackney Wick on 4 August 1866, when George Davison, also making his debut there, beat him over seven miles. He became a familiar figure at the 'Wick' winning races from 1867 through to 1872. His best performance at Hackney was probably his race against time in May 1870 when he walked ten miles in 1h.16m.45s. With the opening in Islington of the Agricultural Hall (affectionately known as the 'Aggie'), he became involved in long distance walking. He made further attempts at the Westhall Feat with varying degrees of success and on 31 March 1877 walked 21 miles in 2h.57m.57⅘s. In a famous race against Perkins at Lillie Bridge in 1877 he walked 22 miles 20 yards in three hours, his opponent 22 miles 218 yards. At the Agricultural Hall in 1878 he won the Champion Belt presented by Dick Lewis for the 26 hours walk and a 50 miles competition in 7h.57m.44s. in which all the miles from 26 were new records. He failed to get a place in the 'Astley' tournament (won by Corkey), at the Hall in October 1878, but walked 370 miles and 4 laps during the week. Billy Howes was an early centurion in 24-hour races in 1878 and 1880 when he completed the distance in 18h.8m.50s. However, as a professional, he was never given recognition by that esteemed organisation, the 'Centurions'.

start over seven miles by Miles who could not hold him without 'lifting' and was disqualified. Davison finished his year in October with wins over Joseph Stockwell at ten miles in 1h.21m.23s. (56m.10s. at seven miles) and against George Topley over 14 miles with Topley resigning at nine miles. There was no doubt that Davison was the coming man.

More records in Manchester

John Cooper, the new proprietor of the Royal Oak Grounds in Manchester, honoured his commitment to be a worthy successor to George Martin by attracting the very best of middle distance pedestrians through the introduction of two new challenge cups in 1867. The first was a One-Mile and a Half Champion Cup worth 80 guineas to be held for 12 months on the usual conditions.

The field for the first race on 23 February comprised six pedestrian stars; John Fleet, John Neary of Hulme, Robert McKinstray, Ike Hughes of Manchester, William Richards and James Sanderson. A huge crowd of 10,000 attended from all over the country to see Fleet win in a new British Record of 6m.50s. Neary was second, 12 yards behind, followed by Richards a further 30 yards back. McKinstray became the next holder of the cup when he beat Fleet and Sanderson on 3 August. For Fleet it was his first defeat on level terms and to some extent was put down to him suffering a recent assault while out running on Sale Moor. Even so McKinstray successfully defended the Cup against Fleet in November. Challenges continued on a regular basis in 1868 but McKinstray defended it only one more time, on 7 March, when he beat Sanderson. On 23 May he was beaten by Fleet who then defended the cup successfully against Lang in July. In December he beat a challenge from Albert Bird of Sheffield, a good half miler and miler not a well-known name outside of his native city but with Lang and Richards in America, Ike Hughes in retirement and Neary and McKinstray out of condition, challengers were limited. Finally Fleet won against John Neary on 26 June 1869 to become the outright holder.

Albert Bird was one of three pedestrians who took up an invitation in September 1869 to compete in Australia. George Coppin a well-known Australian theatrical manager was taking a company of English players to Australia and keen to cash in on the remarkable running boom and huge wagering in professional running in that country decided to include a team of athletes in his venture. He selected Frank Scurry Hewitt, George Topley and Albert Bird. Of the three only Hewitt made a true success of his visit. Hewitt was born in Limerick of English parents in 1845 and later lived in Millwall. He won a Sheffield Handicap at the famous Queens Hotel Grounds in 1865 and was frequently scratch man over distances from 130 yards and 220 yards thereafter. In Australia, where he finally settled, he became virtually unbeatable and was credited with a time of 1m.53½s. for 880 yards on the road in Lyttleton, New Zealand in 1871. George Topley no longer at his best had only partial success and returned to England the following year. Albert Bird made a reasonable living for a while but in the early 1890s, according to J. Bull in his book *The Spiked Shoe*, he was picked up in the streets of Port Melbourne in a starving and dying condition. Friends rallied to his support, but he did not live long.

Back in England, John Cooper donated his second cup in June 1867 for a race at one mile that had only to be won twice in succession before becoming the property of the holder. The first race was held on 1 June, before a crowd of 3,000. Unfortunately the entry was poor, most pedestrians it seems preferred money prizes to plate and afterwards very few new challenge cups were offered. Nevertheless, five entered; Robert McKinstray, John Neary, John Nuttall, Teddy Mills and Ike Hughes with McKinstray the outstanding favourite. Neary provided McKinstray with his only real challenge but was still 20 yards adrift of the Scotsman at the line. In July Fleet beat McKinstray and defended the cup against Lang and Neary in September to become the holder of yet another trophy.

JOHN FLEET (1845–1884)
John Fleet, known as 'Young Fleet', was born in Manchester on 6 April 1845. He made his first appearance at Manchester's Royal Oak Grounds in 1865, winning a mile handicap. He was spotted by William Lang and put into the hands of the Manchester trainer G. Hardy. The race which brought him to the attention of the whole pedestrian world was the one in which he won the One Mile and a Half Champion Cup against a top class field at the Royal Oak Grounds, on 23 February 1867 in a British record of 6m.50s. He won the cup outright in 1869. In 1867 he ran at Hackney Wick, winning a Two Miles Cup in 9m.53s and the Ten Miles Champion Cup from Lang, but he was not a great traveller and declined to defend it, preferring to concentrate on the shorter distances in Manchester. He was only two yards down on James Nuttall when he broke the British half-mile record in a time of 1m.55¾s. at the Copenhagen Grounds, Manchester, in August 1867. At one mile he won the Champion Gold Cup outright at the Royal Oak in September 1867 in a time of 4m.28¾s. and recorded a personal best of 4m.23½s. in 1868 in winning a Champion Cup at the City Grounds, Manchester. He married in 1869 and little more was heard of him. In 1870 he claimed to have retired but ran two four-mile races against Hazael in 1871 beating him at both Hackney Wick and the Royal Oak. Fleet became proprietor of the Tatton Arms public house in Derby Street, Regent Road, Salford where he died at the age of 39 on 10 January 1884.

John Fleet was to win one further One Mile Champion Cup the following year. Peter Waddacor the proprietor of the City Grounds, Manchester, with two other well-known supporters of pedestrianism, donated a massive solid silver, two handled cup, capable of holding one gallon and a half, richly and elegantly chased, and engraved: – 'City Grounds, Manchester, One Mile Champions Cup, given by Messrs. Peter Waddacor and Co., on April 10, 1868'. Fleet, McKinstray, Nuttall and Rogers took up the challenge on the 800 yards City Grounds course with four very tight turns but Fleet proved once again he was now the best miler in the land winning in a time of 4m.23½s.

Saturday, 31 August saw a long-pending match between James Nuttall and John Fleet (ten yards start) to race half a mile for £25 aside at the nearby Copenhagen Grounds. A level bet of £50 was made between the men when the match was ratified, thus making the total amount to be contested £150. Each runner had a host of friends and such was the confidence of all in their man that other bets of amounts up to £100 were also placed. There was no doubt both had prepared well for the match and were in excellent condition. Nuttall was prepared at George Beddow's, Manor Arms Hotel, Golborne, near Newton in the company of William

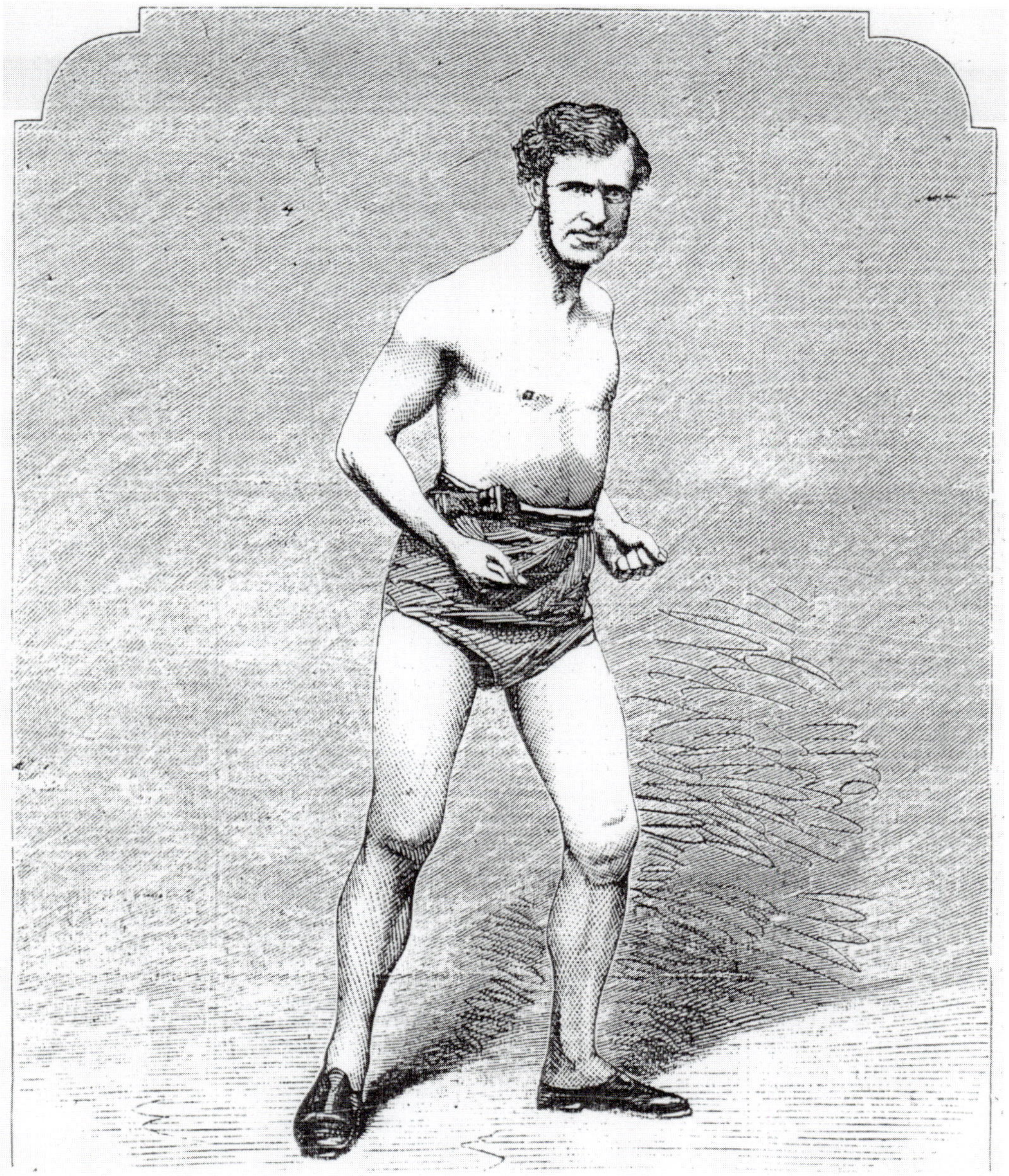

James Nuttall, record holder at the half mile

Lang. Fleet, as usual, trained at the Quarry Bank Inn, Timperly, Cheshire under Charley Cooper of Leeds.

> Mr. T. Hayes (the starter and referee) despatched the pair to a moderately even start, Nuttall, if anything obtaining a slight advantage. The pair bounded along amidst great excitement, Nuttall gradually reducing the gap between himself and his young formidable opponent. On arriving at the garden turn leading into the straight for

JAMES NUTTALL (1840–1907)
James Nuttall was born in Stockport on 29 December 1840 and started his long running career in 1859. He was self-trained and ran all distances up to a mile, winning against such runners as Albison, Fleet and Stephen Ridley of Gateshead whom he beat over 1,000 yards in January, 1872 in a time of 2m.19¾s. His most important success was at the Copenhagen Grounds, Manchester on 31 August 1867 when conceding ten yards start in half a mile he defeated John Fleet, and broke the British record with a time of 1m.55¾s. He recorded 51½s. for 440 yards in 1869.

> home, Nuttall collared his man, and after a brief struggle went to the front. Both now sprinted to the tape at a tremendous pace, but notwithstanding Fleet's game and strenuous efforts, he was not fleet enough, and Nuttall won a severe race by two yards. The record time occupied by the winner was 1min. 55¾ sec.

James Nuttall was the last professional to hold the half mile British Record.

Christmas at Hackney Wick

As usual the year ended with the Christmas meetings when the promoters of pedestrianism catered liberally for their patrons. Handicaps (more particularly in the north) had become immensely popular and large sums were given as prizes; but this year the money advertised was without precedent. Manchester – some years before – was the first to inaugurate the system of handicapping. Then £10 was considered a handsome prize. But now in one week alone at Sheffield there was one prize of £120, another of £200. The betting on these races was immense. Large 'books' were opened, and not infrequently men were kept for a year or two before sent for a stake, and when sent, were heavily backed. The proprietors of the metropolitan grounds provided some sport for their supporters, although the prizes sunk into insignificance in the face of those in the north. At the 'Wick', James Baum gave £5 for a 440 yards handicap with a silver watch and money prizes for a mile race. Unfortunately London was blanketed with fog and the Boxing Day meetings had to be postponed until the following Saturday, when a very small gathering watched a dreadfully poor turnout, only four coming to their marks in the mile and only 15 in the 440 yards. It was as if Messrs Baum and Price had lost all enthusiasm for the type of promotion they had offered only a few years before.

10

1868, Changes at Hackney Wick

Upheaval

The omens of Boxing Day 1867 at Hackney Wick were borne out during 1868 when the manager, Bill Price, gave up the post he had held for ten years to spend more time on his bookmaking business, particularly making books for matches in the north.

With the departure of Bill Price, the management of the ground was taken over by John Cole, who spent much time at the 'Wick'. The first major event he presented was a very successful Easter meeting:

> The meet at the old grounds yesterday, Good Friday, was as usual at holiday times, a large one, some 2,000 people being present. Mr. Baum catered for the public with his well-known liberality, not only inside but also outside the ground. On the green in front of the house was quite a fair, the chief features of which were Professor Hewlitt's Exhibition of Waxworks and a steam roundabout, thus giving all an opportunity of enjoying themselves. The course under the superintendance of young Cole, was in splendid order, and soon after 2 o'clock sport commenced.

The entries were first class, 40 for the 300 yards handicap and 39 for the one-mile handicap with a full programme of Cornish and Devon wrestling. Dick Lewis, who was once a pedestrian in Bill Price's stable and trainer to Deerfoot, took over from Cole as manager before Whitsun and set about constructing a 130 yard sprint track and continuing the successful Saturday handicaps that had been introduced by Cole.

Walking at Hackney Wick

On 11 February, the week previous to the race for the Ten Miles Champion Cup there was another large gathering at Hackney to witness George Davison walk 12 miles against James Miles for £25 aside. *Sporting Life* wrote:

> Seldom lately has the 'Wick', or any of the metropolitan running grounds, been so largely attended as it was on Monday, and we

> should say that over 1,000 persons were present, giving the place a resemblance of old times, which must have been highly encouraging to the management.

The crowd was entertained by a great race with the two walkers never more than a few yards apart, Davison winning by just one yard in 1h.41m.32s. (57m.56s. at seven miles).

In the following months Davison met Miles twice more at Hackney Wick, both times over eight miles. At Easter, when a crowd of 1,000 was privileged to witness one of the closest walking races ever seen, a magnificent tussle between the two men ended in a dead-heat. Next time they met at the end of June for much increased stakes of £100 a side (£200). Miles, at one time considered the best walker in Britain, was now finding the much younger Davison gradually becoming his superior and in this race he retired exhausted after just three miles.

Davison, now reckoned one of the best and fairest walkers ever seen, lacking only the advantage of a trifle more speed, set his sights on what was considered the greatest proof of a fine walker in those days: the 'Westhall Feat', or walking 21 miles in three hours. The attempt was made at Brompton on 20 July. Davison's backer against Time, with £100, was his good friend Bill Price. On an extremely hot evening Davison walked well; the first seven miles were completed in 56m.24s; at half distance the time was 1h.25m.16s; at 14 miles 1h.56m.15s. At close to 16 miles, however, the heat got the better of Davison and he had to stop. The general feeling of those who watched was that with more favourable weather he should certainly accomplish the feat. But that attempt would have to wait a while.

Final race for the Ten Miles Champion Cup

On 19 February the *Sporting Life* wrote:

> Pedestrianism in the metropolis has for some time been at a low ebb, but the last two Mondays at the 'old Wick,' prove that when genuine matches are to be decided between two good men, the love of the sport is still as strong as ever. Monday last was quite a field day, and the appearance of the old ground was as animating as in its most palmy days, reminding one forcibly of the time of Deerfoot, Teddy Mills, Pudney, etc., for the railings were completely surrounded by spectators three or four deep, while the reserved seats and the embankment were covered with eager faces, and there must have been at least 4,000 congregated.

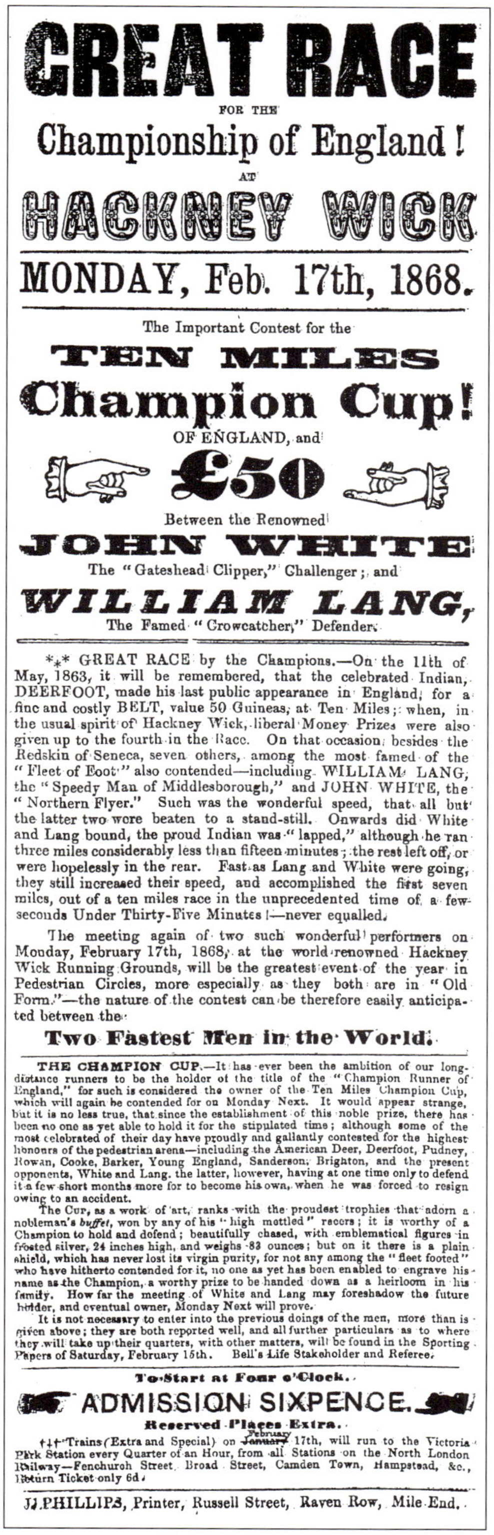
GREAT RACE

FOR THE

Championship of England!

AT

HACKNEY WICK

MONDAY, Feb. 17th, 1868.

The Important Contest for the

TEN MILES

Champion Cup!

OF ENGLAND, and

£50

Between the Renowned

JOHN WHITE

The "Gateshead Clipper," Challenger; and

WILLIAM LANG,

The Famed "Crowcatcher," Defender.

*** GREAT RACE by the Champions.—On the 11th of May, 1863, it will be remembered, that the celebrated Indian, DEERFOOT, made his last public appearance in England, for a fine and costly BELT, value 50 Guineas, at Ten Miles; when, in the usual spirit of Hackney Wick, liberal Money Prizes were also given up to the fourth in the Race. On that occasion, besides the Redskin of Seneca, seven others, among the most famed of the "Fleet of Foot" also contended—including WILLIAM LANG, the "Speedy Man of Middlesborough," and JOHN WHITE, the "Northern Flyer." Such was the wonderful speed, that all but the latter two were beaten to a stand-still. Onwards did White and Lang bound, the proud Indian was "lapped," although he ran three miles considerably less than fifteen minutes; the rest left off, or were hopelessly in the rear. Fast as Lang and White were going, they still increased their speed, and accomplished the first seven miles, out of a ten miles race in the unprecedented time of a few seconds Under Thirty-Five Minutes!—never equalled.

The meeting again of two such wonderful performers on Monday, February 17th, 1868, at the world renowned Hackney Wick Running Grounds, will be the greatest event of the year in Pedestrian Circles, more especially as they both are in "Old Form."—the nature of the contest can be therefore easily anticipated between the

Two Fastest Men in the World.

THE CHAMPION CUP.—It has ever been the ambition of our long-distance runners to be the holder of the title of the "Champion Runner of England," for such is considered the owner of the Ten Miles Champion Cup, which will again be contended for on Monday Next. It would appear strange, but it is no less true, that since the establishment of this noble prize, there has been no one as yet able to hold it for the stipulated time; although some of the most celebrated of their day have proudly and gallantly contested for the highest honours of the pedestrian arena—including the American Deer, Deerfoot, Pudney, Rowan, Cooke, Barker, Young England, Sanderson, Brighton, and the present opponents, White and Lang. the latter, however, having at one time only to defend it a few short months more for to become his own, when he was forced to resign owing to an accident.

The Cup, as a work of art, ranks with the proudest trophies that adorn a nobleman's *buffet*, won by any of his "high mettled" racers; it is worthy of a Champion to hold and defend; beautifully chased, with emblematical figures in frosted silver, 24 inches high, and weighs 83 ounces; but on it there is a plain shield, which has never lost its virgin purity, for not any among the "fleet footed" who have hitherto contended for it, no one as yet has been enabled to engrave his name as the Champion, a worthy prize to be handed down as a heirloom in his family. How far the meeting of White and Lang may foreshadow the future holder, and eventual owner, Monday Next will prove.

It is not necessary to enter into the previous doings of the men, more than is given above; they are both reported well, and all further particulars as to where they will take up their quarters, with other matters, will be found in the Sporting Papers of Saturday, February 15th. Bell's Life Stakeholder and Referee.

To Start at Four o'Clock.

ADMISSION SIXPENCE.

Reserved Places Extra.

††† Trains (Extra and Special) on ~~January~~ February 17th, will run to the Victoria Park Station every Quarter of an Hour, from all Stations on the North London Railway—Fenchurch Street, Broad Street, Camden Town, Hampstead, &c., Return Ticket only 6d.

J. PHILLIPS, Printer, Russell Street, Raven Row, Mile End.

Handbill for the Ten Miles Champion Cup race in February 1868

The crowd gathered on 17 February 1868 to see a race for the Ten Mile Championship Cup. Lang had come into possession of the Cup in May 1867, when Fleet declined to defend and in October that year defended it against the 36-year-old John Brighton. The pedestrian world was then taken by surprise in November 1867, when a challenge for the Cup appeared from the 'Gateshead Clipper', John White, as it was generally supposed that he had retired altogether. Richards also wished to enter, but this was objected to by White, and he was justified in doing so as the conditions upon which the cup was held stated that only in the last race could other competitors insist upon contesting. Lang who still had three more months before a final challenge had to be met arrived in London on the Friday and stayed at the Fox and Hounds in Tottenham Court Road while White on the Sunday stayed with a friend in Oxford Street. During the race White ran in a very determined style, continually holding off the challenge of Lang. As they entered the last mile Lang's running became more aggressive and the two runners ran head to head until the last 100 yards when Lang eventually took the lead and White, unable to live with the pace, fell just 40 yards from home. It was a great race in a time of 53m.50s.

The following month Lang, announcing his retirement from the English pedestrian arena, resigned the Cup. However, since no challenger came forward in the months that followed he became the first athlete in the ten years history of the Cup to hold it outright. The reason for Lang's decision had been his resolve to travel to America to challenge William Harding. Harding, a Canadian by birth, was a New York City newspaper reporter, who having defeated the leading runners of the United States in the years immediately following the Civil War, claimed the title of 'Champion of America'.

An international match?

In August 1867 Harding had offered to run Teddy Mills in America over three miles for \$5,000 a side. The physical condition of Mills at this time made the challenge impossible to accept but through Bill Price he offered to meet Harding in England for £500 plus £100 expenses. In December 1867 Harding stated he was involved in negotiations for a \$10,000 race from Portland to St. Louis but would meet Mills '*home and away*' in August and October 1868. The conditions to be: (1) the distance to be three miles for the Championship of the World; (2) the gate money to be equally divided between the contestants; (3) the first race to take place at Hackney Wick or Brompton; (4) the second race to take place at the Union Course, Long Island, NY; (5) the match to be for £500 a side, or increased to \$1,000 at the option of Mills. Price, however, would only accept the terms he had offered previously.

It was therefore Lang who took up the challenge and, accompanied by William Richards, sailed for America in September 1868, arriving in Philadelphia a few weeks later in search of a match with Harding. Efforts to bring the two parties together were in vain. Harding stated that he had not raced in nearly a year and had actually retired from running to concentrate on his newspaper career. However, to accommodate Lang, he stated that he would race him in the spring. Lang stayed on into the New Year only to find that when the time came for the principals to meet to sign the articles of agreement and put up the money, Harding failed to appear. A disappointed Lang returned to England in February 1869.

Sad end to 1868 at Hackney Wick

James Baum, who had not been too well, died quite suddenly on 30 December 1868, aged 45. Some four to five hundred local people attended his funeral at Bow cemetery. The *Illustrated Sporting News* for 9 January 1869 reported:

> Baum's funeral was attended by 400/500 spectators consisting of friends and neighbours, and those who had benefited by his bounty. The presence of the upper classes was conspicuous by their absence, but working men and women who were benefited and poor neighbours who he had served, and made the 'tablesmoke' often, came to pay respects in his memory. James Collins Baum supported the various charities with no niggard hand in his own parish and those adjoining; the rector of Hackney and vicar of Homerton will testify; while his support for the Licensed Victuallers Schools, the Asylum, and other charities are well known. These things should be remembered but are not; the good deeds will be forgotten, his faults will only be remembered, except by those who knew him as a kind friend and good neighbour. Mr. Baum was interred in the family vault where lay his father, mother and others. He was borne to his grave from the little church by eight men, the massive coffin being of immense size, for he was a man large in stature. There were two mourning coaches containing his surviving brother, Mr. Joseph Baum and Mr. Bernard his brother-in-law. Mr. W. Price, with whom Mr. Baum was associated with many years, was on the ground, having come especially from Manchester; but as no time or place of sepulchre had been mentioned many were absent who would otherwise have been present, including sportsmen of every degree. There were those there who knew his worth.

Even before the death of James Baum, Dick Lewis, the manager at Hackney was finding it increasingly difficult to generate crowd pleasing matches and the *Illustrated Sporting News* wrote:

> The once famous Hackney Wick is seldom heard of. Brompton grounds are let for building purposes and the fine grounds at Islington are not to be used any more for athletic purposes. Bow grounds apparently are the only resort for pedestrians next year.

The *Sporting Life* wrote:

> Boxing Day sports in London are not what they were – the glories of Hackney Wick have departed; Bow is in the sere and yellow leaf; and Brompton's race is finally run, the latter place having, after a gallant struggle and a plucky spurt at the finish, yielded to bricks and mortar. Not withstanding this, we are not called upon to deplore the extinction of Pedestrianism. The only thing worth notice in the metropolis is the race between Teddy Mills and George Hazael, who run for the Four Miles Champion Belt and £100 at the Prince of Wales Ground, Bow.

A race won easily by Hazael, with Mills retiring before three miles.

11

1869, Hackney Wick Under New Ownership

New proprietor and manager at Hackney Wick

With the death of James Baum, from a diseased liver and congestion of the brain, there was no activity at Hackney Wick in the early months of 1869. The closure of Hackney Wick meant that the ground at Bow owned by Mr Russell and managed by W. Wearden was virtually the only metropolitan running ground holding regular meetings for pedestrians until the end of March when John Smith (the Regent Street Pet) opened the Star Grounds at North End, Fulham.

James Baum's various property assets were put up for auction on 14 April and included as well as the White Lion public house, stables and running ground, the two Alger booths and a wealth of other property and land that he held for rental, development and investment. There were nine houses in Park Street; eleven cottages in Wick Lane, six known as Baum's Cottages and five as Deerfoot Cottages; thirteen houses in Cowdry Street of which seven were still being built; building land in Park Street, Cowdry

JOHN SMITH 'THE REGENT STREET PET' (1819–?)
John Smith was born on 2 March 1819 and his first recorded race was a win against Charley Jenkinson (the London Stag) over 120 yards at Turnham Green in 1841. He raced regularly throughout the 1840s both on the flat and over hurdles at distances up to 880 yards including matches against George Seward, William Jackson, Harry Reed, Jesse Smith and George Martin among many others. He raced rarely in the 1850s but when Hackney Wick opened he ran there in 1858 and won a veteran's 80 yards race at the venue in 1865. In addition to a successful career as a pedestrian, John Smith was an extremely successful and kind trainer of athletes in many sports, (he was also a good cricketer) developing several champions. Among his protégés were George Martin, George Topley and Henry 'Blower' Brown the famed ultra-distance star and winner of a number of Lord Astley trophies. His daughter married William Spooner. He was landlord of the Norman Arms in Fulham and later the Prince of Wales Tavern in Turnham Green. He was the first manager of the new Star Grounds at North End, Fulham in 1869.

VICTORIA PARK, HACKNEY.

ELIGIBLE LEASEHOLD PROPERTIES.

Particulars and Conditions of Sale

OF SEVERAL VALUABLE

LEASEHOLD ESTATES,

COMPRISING THE OLD-ESTABLISHED

WINE AND SPIRIT VAULTS,

WITH POSSESSION, KNOWN AS THE

"WHITE LION,"

With the Celebrated Running Ground & Extensive Stabling,

FOUR MESSUAGES,

Nos. 1 to 4, PARK STREET, VICTORIA PARK,

With Spacious Yard in the Rear, occupying a large Area, and available for

BUILDING PURPOSES;

FIVE SIMILAR HOUSES, Nos. 1 to 5, Park Street;

The Dwelling Houses and Business Premises,

Nos. 6 to 11, BAUM'S COTTAGES, WICK LANE, HACKNEY WICK,

AND

Nos. 1 to 5, DEERFOOT COTTAGES;

AN IMPROVED RENT OF £20 per ANNUM,

Arising from the houses erected and to be erected in

COWDRY STREET, PARK STREET;

The whole estimated, when complete, to produce a Rental of about

£455. PER ANNUM.

ALSO A VALUABLE

CORNER PLOT OF BUILDING LAND;

AND THE WELL-KNOWN

ALGER BOOTHS and Appurtenances,

Which will be Sold by Auction by Messrs.

WINSTANLEY & HORWOOD,

At THE MART, Tokenhouse Yard, Lothbury, E.C.,

IN THE C ROOM, ON THE GROUND FLOOR,

On WEDNESDAY, the 14th of APRIL, 1869,

AT ONE FOR TWO O'CLOCK, IN 16 LOTS.

By Direction of the Administrators of the late Mr. J. C. BAUM.

The Houses may be viewed by permission of the respective Tenants, and printed Particulars obtained of Messrs. MORRIS, STONE, TOWNSON, & MORRIS, Solicitors, 5, Finsbury Circus, E.C.; at the Mart; the "White Lion," Hackney Wick; and of Messrs. WINSTANLEY & HORWOOD, Auctioneers and Valuers, 10, Paternoster Row, St. Paul's, E.C.

Auction of the White Lion and running grounds in 1869

Particulars.

LOT 1. No Bid Withdrawn

The "White Lion," Hackney Wick.

A Valuable Leasehold Property,

CONSISTING OF THE OLD-ESTABLISHED

WINE AND SPIRIT VAULTS,

KNOWN AS THE

"WHITE LION," HACKNEY WICK.

Occupying an important position on the main road near the Victoria Park Railway Station, and possessing every requisite for carrying on an extensive trade.

THE HOUSE CONTAINS:—

ON THE SECOND FLOOR.

Five Bedchambers, four with Fireplaces.

ON THE FIRST FLOOR.

Club Room, with two Fireplaces, Sitting Room, and Bedchamber.

ON THE GROUND FLOOR.

Bar, Public Parlour, Tap Room, Large Assembly Room, with two Fireplaces, Kitchen, Scullery, and Water Closet.

AMPLE CELLARAGE for Beer, Wines, and Spirits.

On the South Side of the House is a Yard, with open Skittle Ground, Kitchen, Coal Store, Pot-washing Place, Water Closet, &c.

ON THE NORTH SIDE IS THE

about 1 acre

CELEBRATED RUNNING GROUND;

About 1 acre

A Large Stable Yard in Wick Lane, with Four-stall Stable, Loose Box, and Coach House.

Held by Lease for a term of 21 *years from Michaelmas,* 1850, *at the nominal Rent of* £100 *per annum.*

Possession may be had on completion of the Purchase.

The Purchaser is to take at a Valuation, to be made in the usual way, all the Furniture, Fixtures, Stock-in-Trade and Effects, upon the Premises, belonging to the Vendors.

It is believed that the Purchaser may have the option of buying the Freehold of this Lot at a moderate price.

(8)

LOT 14. £215 Sold

A Similar Leasehold Estate,

CONSISTING OF

TWO DWELLING HOUSES,

Nos. 1 and 2, DEERFOOT COTTAGES,

Each containing similar accommodation to Lot 13,
With the SHED adjoining.

No. 1, Let to Mr. Kelly, at 7s. 6d. per week, amounting to per annum	£19. 10. 0
No. 2, Let to Mr. Wilson, at 7s. 6d. per week, amounting to per annum	19. 10. 0
	£39. 0. 0
An Underlease of this Lot will be granted for the same term as Lot 6, at a rent of per annum	6. 0. 0
	£33. 0. 0

180
5
90
15
200
5
10

Cost 240 or 80

Lot 14 £215 Sold

THE ALGER BOOTHS.

The following LOTS are sold subject to the undermentioned SPECIAL CONDITIONS.

I. No person to advance less than One Pound at each bidding, and no bidding shall be retracted.

II. The highest bidder shall be the purchaser; and if any dispute arise between two or more bidders, the auctioneers shall be at liberty either to decide upon such difference or to put the lot up again at the last undisputed bidding.

III. The lots are sold with all defects and errors of description, and each purchaser will be required to pay the whole amount of the purchase-money on the fall of the hammer. After which time the lot to be entirely at the risk of the purchaser, and must be cleared from the respective premises where they now are, on or before Saturday the 17th inst., at 12 o'clock.

LOT 15. No offer

AN EXCELLENT REFRESHMENT TENT,

Consisting of a portion of the well-known

"Alger Crown & Anchor Booths,"

BEING 120 FEET LONG BY 50 FEET WIDE,

And having 24 Side and 4 End Boards, 3 Lamp Baskets and Crowns, 1 Glory, Front Painting, Seats, Bar and other Tables,

And used for many years at all the Principal

RACE MEETINGS, PLEASURE & OTHER FAIRS,

AT

PETERBOROUGH, NORTHAMPTONSHIRE.

This Lot is now in the care of Mr. Jackson, "Painters' Arms," Peterboro', where it may be viewed on application, and whence it will be delivered to the Purchaser.

LOT 16. No offer

A Similar Refreshment Tent,

Comprising another Portion of the

"CROWN AND ANCHOR BOOTHS,"

BEING 160 FEET LONG AND 50 FEET WIDE,

With nearly new Canvas Covering, and having Dancing Boards, numerous Illuminations and Lamps, Service Utensils in Boxes, Counters, Flags, &c.; Three Tents with Poles and Ropes, complete; Seats and Tables;

Used for many years at the PRINCIPAL FAIRS AT CHARLTON, KENT.

The Framework may be seen upon application at the "White Swan," Charlton; and the Canvas, and Service Utensils at the "White Lion," Hackney Wick.

The Canvas covering alone cost 97£ (?) within a year since

A van to carry the tent about from place to place, originally cost 70 guineas may be had with this lot for 20 guineas

Street and Wick Lane. At the auction there were no bids for the White Lion and its running ground but the other properties valued in excess of the considerable sum of £2,500 were nearly all sold on the day.

The White Lion and running ground were sold shortly afterwards by private treaty to Mr W. Parnell who was the proprietor of the Fish and Ring public house in White Horse Lane, Stepney. Parnell wasted no time in re-employing Bill Price as the ground's manager and they officially reopened on 17 May 1869 for the Whitsuntide Sports. The announcement of the opening appeared in flourishing terms:

> As well as pedestrianism there will be all the other old English sports, for which the White Lion, Hackney Wick has been so celebrated. Brass and quadrille bands will be in attendance. Alger's grand Crown and Anchor booth will be erected. There will be dancing on the large platform. The grounds will be illuminated with thousands of variegated lamps. The trees are in full bloom; so old Hackney Wick will again appear in real holiday attire. Trains every seven minutes from Fenchurch Street, Broad Street, and all stations on the North London Railway. Mr. Parnell has great pleasure in announcing that the valuable services of the old and respected manager have been secured, so the whole sports will be under the superintendance of Mr. William Price. Admission, 6d.

Throughout the summer Bill Price put on a popular series of sprint and middle distance handicaps with good entries due to his acknowledged skill as a handicapper. The 'Bookmakers Handicaps' over 100 yards produced particularly strong betting and roped lanes are mentioned for the first time.

Faltering future of the Ten Miles Championship

With William Lang the outright holder of the Ten Miles Challenge Cup and the temporary closure of Hackney Wick it was initially left to others to revive a ten miles championship. In March a race was arranged between Teddy Mills and the up and coming George Hazael at Bow by Messrs Russell and Wearden, which they called the Ten Miles Championship. The race, however, was a farce as Mills who had been beaten twice recently by Hazael over four miles soon realised he had no chance and retired at one third distance. Hazael stopped at four miles reached in 20m.34s.

Mr Peter Waddacor, of the City Grounds, Manchester, then introduced a new Ten Miles Champion Challenge Cup that could be defended by the holder at either Hackney Wick or Manchester and this was competed for

George Hazael, long distance champion

the first time on 15 May 1869. Entries came from Hazael, Sanderson, Fleet, White and Teddy Mills. The fast improving 24-year-old George Hazael, who trained at Hackney Wick under Springhall, proved his recent form was no fluke as he trounced the field in a strong wind, finishing at his leisure in 55m.32½s.

Hazael was ill during August, September and October and resigned the Cup as well as forfeiting a number of matches. However, he kept his eye on the trophy and was fit again by later in the year to race for it at his preferred choice of Hackney Wick on 8 November 1869.

Bill Price was now the landlord of the White Lion as well as manager of the grounds at Hackney Wick and attracted a crowd of 3,000 for this famous event. The handbill for the race is worth quoting verbatim for its wonderful phrasing:

> To be even the 'Holder' of the above trophy, not alone for its worth as a triumph of the Silversmith's Art, nor for its intrinsic value, is it to be cared for; but it represents the highest honour that can be obtained in the curriculum of the 'Fleet of Foot,' for he who wins it has obtained, and justly so, the title of 'Champion Runner of England.' To be in the position to be called upon to defend this proud title, would have been an incentive for even the bravest Knights of olden times of Chivalry to maintain; and he who will be able to engrave his name on its spotless shield, as the final winner,

after twelve months, why then his doings in the pedestrian world, will, not only be handed down to his children's children, but be remembered with pride, by those who follow, compete, or promote the athletic sports of 'Merrie Old England.' The fifteen names in the above list of contestants have never been equalled in the annals of pedestrianism; and never before will Hackney Wick, famous as it has ever been for Champion Races, have such an array of talent to contend. White, who has been observed, 'runs on wheels,' will laugh at the Bicycle scorn. Hazael, (the Champion), who, comet-like, has of late, appeared in the pedestrian hemisphere. Young England and his Brother – why their names are synonymous with speed and endurance. McKinstray, from the 'Land of Heather,' will maintain the country's proud motto – 'Nemo me impune Lacessett.' John Brighton will again astonish the spectators as he has oft done before. The performances of the two Manchester Men (Fleet and Lang) are matters of history. Sam Barker and W. Jones must not be held too cheaply; nor must Old Harry Andrews be despised by any who may 'Strive for Mastery,' but 'pull-foot' and no tarrying by the way will be the order to those who would try to shake them off. Corkey, the springy or 'Bounding Roe' will be again enthusiastically cheered on in his efforts by his legion of friends, and the new blood of the Race for the Championship of England – Green,

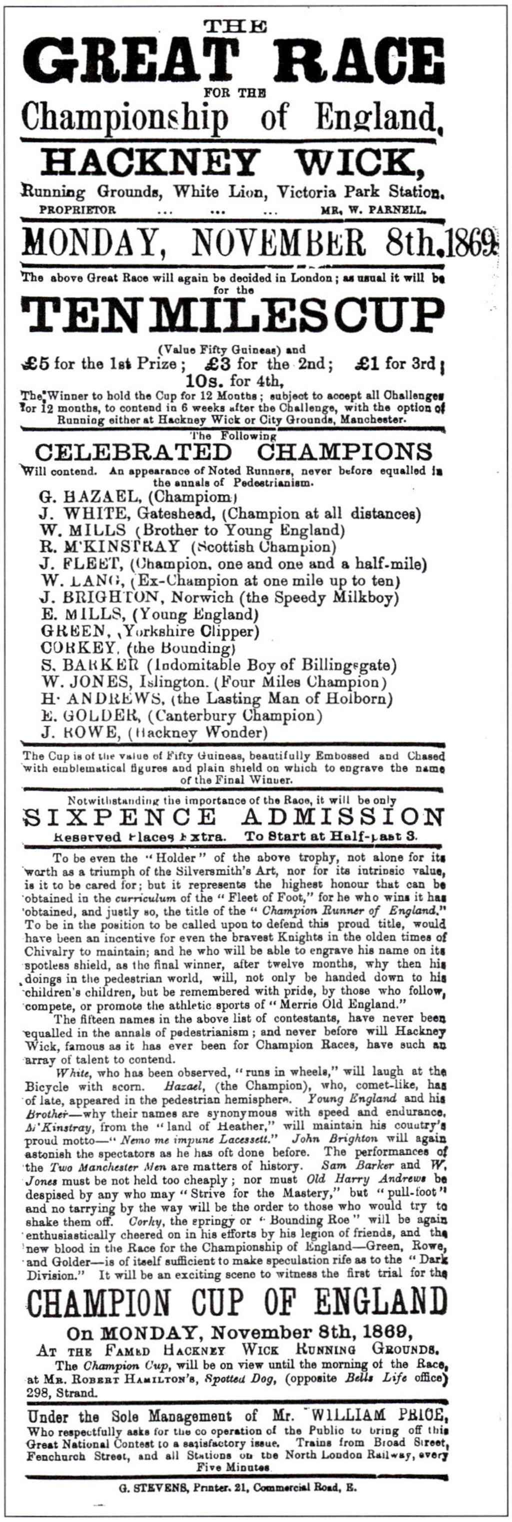

THE
GREAT RACE
FOR THE
Championship of England,
HACKNEY WICK,
Running Grounds, White Lion, Victoria Park Station.
PROPRIETOR ... ... MR. W. PARNELL.

MONDAY, NOVEMBER 8th.1869

The above Great Race will again be decided in London; as usual it will be for the
TEN MILES CUP
(Value Fifty Guineas) and
£5 for the 1st Prize; £3 for the 2nd; £1 for 3rd;
10s. for 4th,
The Winner to hold the Cup for 12 Months; subject to accept all Challenges for 12 months, to contend in 6 weeks after the Challenge, with the option of Running either at Hackney Wick or City Grounds, Manchester.

The Following
CELEBRATED CHAMPIONS
Will contend. An appearance of Noted Runners, never before equalled in the annals of Pedestrianism.

G. HAZAEL, (Champiom)
J. WHITE, Gateshead, (Champion at all distances)
W. MILLS (Brother to Young England)
R. M'KINSTRAY (Scottish Champion)
J. FLEET, (Champion, one and one and a half-mile)
W. LANG, (Ex-Champion at one mile up to ten)
J. BRIGHTON, Norwich (the Speedy Milkboy)
E. MILLS, (Young England)
GREEN, (Yorkshire Clipper)
CORKEY, (the Bounding)
S. BARKER (Indomitable Boy of Billingsgate)
W. JONES, Islington. (Four Miles Champion)
H. ANDREWS, (the Lasting Man of Holborn)
E. GOLDER, (Canterbury Champion)
J. ROWE, (Hackney Wonder)

The Cup is of the value of Fifty Guineas, beautifully Embossed and Chased with emblematical figures and plain shield on which to engrave the name of the Final Winner.

Notwithstanding the importance of the Race, it will be only
SIXPENCE ADMISSION
Reserved Places Extra. To Start at Half-past 3.

To be even the "Holder" of the above trophy, not alone for its worth as a triumph of the Silversmith's Art, nor for its intrinsic value, is it to be cared for; but it represents the highest honour that can be obtained in the *curriculum* of the "Fleet of Foot," for he who wins it has obtained, and justly so, the title of the "*Champion Runner of England.*" To be in the position to be called upon to defend this proud title, would have been an incentive for even the bravest Knights in the olden times of Chivalry to maintain; and he who will be able to engrave his name on its spotless shield, as the final winner, after twelve months, why then his doings in the pedestrian world, will, not only be handed down to his children's children, but be remembered with pride, by those who follow, compete, or promote the athletic sports of "Merrie Old England."

The fifteen names in the above list of contestants, have never been equalled in the annals of pedestrianism; and never before will Hackney Wick, famous as it has ever been for Champion Races, have such an array of talent to contend.

White, who has been observed, "runs in wheels," will laugh at the Bicycle with scorn. *Hazael*, (the Champion), who, comet-like, has of late, appeared in the pedestrian hemisphere. *Young England* and his *Brother*—why their names are synonymous with speed and endurance. *M'Kinstray*, from the "land of Heather," will maintain his country's proud motto—"*Nemo me impune Lacessett.*" *John Brighton* will again astonish the spectators as he has oft done before. The performances of the *Two Manchester Men* are matters of history. *Sam Barker* and *W. Jones* must be not held too cheaply; nor must *Old Harry Andrews* be despised by any who may "Strive for the Mastery," but "pull-foot" and no tarrying by the way will be the order to those who would try to shake them off. *Corky*, the springy or "Bounding Roe" will be again enthusiastically cheered on in his efforts by his legion of friends, and the new blood in the Race for the Championship of England—Green, Rowe, and Golder—is of itself sufficient to make speculation rife as to the "Dark Division." It will be an exciting scene to witness the first trial for the

CHAMPION CUP OF ENGLAND
On MONDAY, November 8th, 1869,
AT THE FAMED HACKNEY WICK RUNNING GROUNDS.

The *Champion Cup*, will be on view until the morning of the Race, at MR. ROBERT HAMILTON'S, *Spotted Dog*, (opposite *Bells Life* office) 298, Strand.

Under the Sole Management of Mr. WILLIAM PRICE,
Who respectfully asks for the co operation of the Public to bring off this Great National Contest to a satisfactory issue. Trains from Broad Street, Fenchurch Street, and all Stations on the North London Railway, every Five Minutes.

G. STEVENS, Printer. 21, Commercial Road, E.

Handbill for the Ten Miles Champion Cup race in November 1869

Rowe, and Golder – is of itself sufficient to make speculation rife as to the 'Dark Division.' It will be an exciting scene to witness the first trial for the CHAMPION CUP OF ENGLAND.

In the race George Hazael, the champion, lined up against ten challengers. Edward Mills, White, Golder, Corkey, William Mills, McKinstray,

GEORGE HAZAEL (1845–?)
George Hazael was born on 22 November 1845 in Commercial Road East, London. Known as 'Handsome George', he first trod the cinder path in 1866, when his first race was a one mile handicap at Hackney Wick on 26 December. By 1867 he was winning handicaps against some of the best in the land, the likes of Sanderson, Fleet, Lang, etc. He came to notice as a pedestrian of some note when on Boxing Day 1868, he beat Mills for £100 and a four miles championship at Bow. In 1869 he beat Edward Mills at Bow to become the Ten Miles Champion and soon went on to become outright holder of the new Ten Miles Champion Cup presented by Peter Warrador of the City Grounds, Manchester. Hazael was predominantly a long distance runner, recording 52m.05s. for 10 miles at Springfield Recreation Ground, Glasgow, on 13 May 1876. He ran two miles in 9m.32s. at Bow in 1870 and 14m.45s. for three miles in 1872. Little was heard of Hazael in 1873 and 1874, but in August 1875 he took up the challenge of a Four Miles Champion Belt held at Hackney Wick and beat McLeavy, Hescott and others. Then he beat McLeavy for a Four Miles Champion Cup in Glasgow. He turned to ultra-distance running in the mid 1870s, beating Achille Bargossi of Italy to set a world record of 1h.57m.27s. for 20 miles at Lillie Bridge on 10 December 1877. Other long distance marks included 50 miles in 6h.14m.47s. and 100 miles in 15h.35m.31s. at the Agricultural Hall, Islington on 21 April 1879. In 1881 he visited the USA and among his races in New York came close to Deerfoot's 12 mile record with a time of 1h.7m.15s. Hazael ran in a number of six-day events in London and New York between 1878 and 1882. His best performance was a world record of 600 miles 220 yards at Madison Square Gardens between 27 February and 4 March 1882. His earnings from these events was considerable and in the last race he won $9,000 in the sweepstake and took $9,380 in gate receipts. He settled for some time in America where he kept a hotel in Brooklyn around 1885 with a small track at the rear. Back in England in 1887, he became landlord of the Stamford Arms, opposite Stamford Bridge Athletic Ground. Sadly he was not a good manager of his money and the *W. G. Athletic Weekly* of 17 September 1904 said: 'seventeen years after he was proclaimed champion long distance runner of the world he was collecting and selling bottles and scrap iron.'

Barker, Jones, Rowe and Brighton. Those who did not accept the invitation were Fleet, Lang, Andrews and Green from Yorkshire. The entry was a veritable who's who of the decade's middle and long distance runners. The race became a battle between William Mills and Hazael. By half distance the excitement was so great that the spectators began to scale the palings and the middle of the enclosure was soon crowded. At one time it was feared the runners would be impeded, but luckily this did not occur. For lap after lap neither of the leaders was able to get away from his antagonist as the others fell by the way. At the end Hazael won by a mere yard in the fast time of 53m.55½s.

Davison against time: A final record achievement at Hackney Wick

In December Bill Price again proved his ability to promote races at Hackney Wick, attracting crowds equal to those in the north of England. Early in the month it was announced that George Davison, the walking champion, would once again attempt to walk against time, 21 miles in three hours in an effort to erase Westhall's long-standing record. Davison could not have picked a more difficult venue at which to undertake such a feat, having to walk 142 laps and 40 yards over a very uneven surface. He had previously failed at Brompton in 1868 on the hottest day of the year, having to retire at 16 miles, leaving the *scyth-bearer* the victor. The date set down for this second attempt was 15 November. But the rain was falling in torrents at the start and continued for two hours, so with the agreement of the backer of time and a consideration, the race was postponed until 6 December. In the interim Davison met his commitment to race Robert Brown of Regents Park over eight miles at Hackney Wick and in steady rain won in a time of 1h.4m.15s. gaining many new friends.

The history of walking 21 miles in three hours started with the attempt of James Smith of Ipswich at Manchester on 25 May 1850 reaching 20 miles in a shade over three hours. Nearly eight years later, at Newmarket on 20 February 1858, Charles Westhall, on a day that proved so windy that a cart with a screen affixed went by his side, walked the distance 'touch and turn' between the 58th and 59th milestones in 2h.59m.01s. Thereafter it became known as the 'Westhall Feat'. A month later William Spooner tried at Manchester but had to give up at 17¾ miles reached in 2h.34m.00s. James Miles tried twice at Garratt Lane Wandsworth; first on 11 August 1862 when he completed 17 miles and then again on 11 September the same year when he lost out by just eight seconds. George Topley was said to have accomplished the feat on Boxing Day 1865, with the last few miles walked in the dark, but the performance was sometimes considered doubtful, particularly by the

GEORGE DAVISON (1844–1885)
George Charles Davison was born in Mitchell Street, St. Lukes, Hoxton on 2 September 1844 and before becoming a professional athlete was a toy-maker. He first came to the attention of the walking fraternity in 1865, trained by Bob Rogers of Chelsea, at Hackney Wick, where he beat William Howes of Haggerston over seven miles in August 1866. Davison beat George Topley and Joe Stockwell in 1867 then established himself as a champion walker with three matches against James Miles at Hackney Wick in 1868 when with stakes raised at every meeting – £50 to £100 to £200 – he dead-heated once and won twice. His greatest feat was breaking Westhall's record for 21 miles when he achieved a time of 2h.53m.54s. at Hackney Wick on 6 December 1869, advised by Bill Price and assisted by his trainer J. Gregory who ran the whole distance with him. After this race he never performed to the same level again and became proprietor of the Hope public house in Hyde Road, Hoxton. Davison was reported to be living in reduced circumstances in 1879 and died of bronchitis in the Shoreditch Infirmary on 27 April 1885.

pedestrian editor of *Bell's Life* with whom Topley never found favour. The most recent attempt had been by Davison in 1868.

Davison came to the line in fine fettle accompanied by Bill Price and J. Gregory, his trainer, who was to run the whole distance with the champion and whose judicious guidance made a great contribution to the success of his principal. Davison stopped only once during the walk, for tea and dry toast at 14 miles and the great feat was accomplished with a new Record Time of 2h.53m.34s., breaking the British Record for seven miles on the way in 54m.10s.

One might venture to say that Hackney Wick was once again the middle and long distance capital of England. There had certainly been no accomplishments elsewhere in the country in 1869 that stood up to the performances of George Hazael and George Davison at the White Lion Grounds. The year finished on Boxing Day when a crowd of between 1,000 and 2,000 were once again able to witness an exciting programme and see some of the best long distance runners of the day when Hazael, McKinstray, William Mills and Coney competed in a Five Mile Champion Sweepstake for £80.

12

1870–1875, Final Decline of Hackney Wick

The last years of Hackney Wick

The opening match of 1870 did not take place until the beginning of February when a crowd of 500 braved awful weather. A full programme included a mile for novices, a two mile walk with Davison off scratch and two heats of a three mile handicap which included all the local runners – Hazael, Golder, Rogers, William Mills, Coney, Rowe and Barker. The finals were held the following Monday. These men met not infrequently at Hackney Wick during the year, contesting distances between one and four miles with Hazael generally proving himself the best. Price continued to put on two programmes a week (Saturday and Monday) drawing reasonable entries and average crowds during the summer and autumn months. Serious competition, however, was coming from Mr Russell's Prince of

WILLIAM JOSEPH STOCKWELL (1844–?)

William Joseph 'Joe' Stockwell, born in Camberwell on 13 January 1844, was considered one of the fairest walkers of his time. In his debut race at Hackney Wick on 8 September 1862 aged 18 he won the Great Exhibition Four Miles Handicap and was immediately recognised as a walker with potential. Because of this performance he found it difficult to find matches but managed to record wins against Allen of Bayswater and George Topley. In his match against Hatley in July 1866, he made up part of his handicap when Hatley set a two miles record and if the newspaper reports had been clearer he could well have been attributed with a faster time. At Bow on 14 February 1870 he virtually earned the title of Champion, by beating George Davison in a six mile race, as, although he had a 30 seconds start, he proved himself the better man. Subsequently he failed to walk 7¾ miles in the hour having walked the first two miles far too fast in 14m.33s. He held the Tom Senn Challenge Cup for four miles by defeating Hurley of Camberwell and in winning a return match at the Star Grounds, Fulham he passed the two mile mark in a best time on record 13m.50s. On 1 June 1874 at Lillie Bridge he was beaten by William Perkins who went through the first mile in a record 6m.23s. and was to become the new short distance champion.

Wales Grounds at Bow only a few miles away which had better facilities, and to a lesser extent Mr Fox's Star Grounds at North End, Fulham, and the grounds at Lillie Bridge. Bow attracted many of the top middle distance runners and walkers and Davison, trained as usual by Gregory at Hackney Wick, walked and lost his last race of any significance there on 14 February 1870. In the match over six miles against Joseph Stockwell with £200 at stake, Davison made no impression on the 30 seconds start of his rival.

Final running of a Ten Miles Cup at Hackney

The most important race staged at Hackney Wick in 1870 was undoubtedly Hazael's defence of his Ten Miles Champion Cup on 18 June, against the challenge of William Mills, whom he had narrowly beaten the previous year. In front of a large crowd of 3,000, Mills again gave a good account of himself, pressing the champion all the way to six miles when Hazael put in a spurt to which Mills had no response.

Hazael won the Cup outright on 17 December at the City Grounds, Manchester, beating the challenge of Fleet and Golder in front of the grounds' largest ever crowd of 10,000.

Appearance of another American Indian

Middle distance pedestrianism was enlivened towards the end of 1870 by the visit from North America of a 24-year-old Iroquois Indian, unknown in England. Known as 'Debeaux', he was brought to this country by the pedestrian entrepreneur Dick Lewis, who lived in Park Street, close to the Hackney Wick grounds. The Indian, real name Daillebout, the son of a celebrated pedestrian of the same name, came from Cannawaga, a village near Montreal in Canada, and had a recent four-mile victory over an ageing Deerfoot to his credit. Initially called 'Redhead' he raced Teddy Mills over a mile at Lillie Bridge at the end of October. Mills gave away 25 yards but could not catch his man who finished in a time of 4m.47s.

Interest was soon aroused and, carefully advised and backed by Dick Lewis, challenges were soon received from McKinstray, Golder, Mills and Hazael. In hard negotiations at Bill Richardson's, Church Street, Shoreditch, articles were drawn up producing matches generally to the Indian's advantage, although £25 aside was all that was staked by the contestants. The initial races all took place at Hackney Wick between 7 November and Boxing Day 1870. In the first match over two miles, Golder allowed the Indian a 50 yards start and soon regretted it. Debeaux won by 130 yards in 9m.23s. In a second match against Teddy Mills over three miles on level terms, Debeaux again proved he was a runner to be reckoned with. Against a runner far past his best, the Indian played the waiting game and came home an easy winner in a respectable time of 14m.53s. watched by a crowd of 2,000.

The final race at Hackney on Boxing Day was against Hazael over five miles in which the English champion was to give 250 yards. The race took place only two days after Debeaux had visited Manchester where he had easily beaten Lang over three miles at the Royal Oak. The Hackney race attracted a crowd of between 2,000 and 3,000 many of whom felt that Hazael's handicap was too great, particularly in view of his recent hard training for the ten mile championship race that had taken place at the City Grounds, Manchester only a few days before. So it proved, with the Indian keeping his unbeaten record winning in a snowstorm by 30 yards.

The Indian's next races were scheduled for Scotland: against McKinstray over three miles at the recently opened Powderhall Grounds, Edinburgh, on 31 December; against Hindle at one mile on the Greenhill Cricket Ground in Paisley on 2 January 1871, then finally a 2,000 yard sweepstake with McKinstray and Hindle at Powderhall on 7 January.

However, Dick Lewis's Indian protégé found little success in Scotland and on level terms at Powderhall against the canny McKinstray he was well beaten. Dick Lewis, disappointed in his runner's performance, immediately postponed his meeting with Hindle until 14 January and wrote to the *Sporting Life* to explain the situation:

> Sir.
>
> Will you oblige by informing the pedestrian world that the Indian (Redhead) will not run any more matches in England. All further challenges to him, therefore, will be useless. The reason is, that after the race with Hazael he said he wanted to go home, and should not train any more. I explained through his interpreter that he had to run in Scotland. Debeaux said he would run, but should not train, and could run better fat and strong. The result was a defeat by McKinstray. The Indian rolling about like a tub could not cover three miles in 15min30sec. and weighed more than 10 stone. I managed to draw the stakes with Hindle at Paisley, as the ground was covered with snow a foot deep. The Indian has to contend against McKinstray and Hindle this day (Saturday, January 7th), but I know he has no chance of winning. I have experienced much trouble with him since I brought him to this country, the great difficulty being his objection to train, and when he ran he wore a guernsey to conceal his condition. What I saw of him in his own country (under an almost tropical heat), when very thin, still compels me to think him a fine runner, had he submitted to a thorough preparation. The Indian leaves Liverpool on Thursday next, January 12th, in the steamship Scandinavian

for Montreal. Believing some explanation was necessary to account for his defeat in Scotland, I have simply stated the truth, and beg to remain yours respectfully.
Richard Lewis, Backer of 'Redhead.'
Edinburgh, January 5th, 1871.

The final 2,000-yard race at Paisley went ahead and though McKinstray failed to appear, Hindle duly won by six yards in 5m.42s. Debeaux was on the next boat home.

Last meetings at Hackney Wick

Meetings at Hackney Wick were few in 1871. The first was held in February with 34 entries for a 440 yards handicap, followed by a Three Miles Challenge Cup offered by Bill Price that appears to have been won by Billy Mills on 27 February. Similar meetings followed in March and April. However, 'old Price' was taking less interest in the running grounds and Dick Lewis organised one of the last Hackney Wick meetings in July. It included a four miles 'champions' race' with Edward Mills, Hazael, Golder, William Mills, Corkey, Joe Mills and Shrubsole competing. It was a good contest and if William Mills' shoe had not burst open after just three miles reached in 15m.27s., injuring his toes, the race would have been fast. In the event Hazael proved an easy winner.

The only other meetings of any significance were held at Easter, Whitsun and Christmas. At Easter, a large crowd of 3,000 watched a full programme including an unfit Hazael beaten over four miles for £50 and a championship by John Fleet of Manchester in a slow 20m.57s. At Whitsun the 'Old Wick' was again well attended but the meeting included no personalities. On Boxing Day it seemed there would be no pedestrianism but then Price arranged a match over the traditional Boxing Day distance of ten miles between Sam Barker and Corkey. Unfortunately the 'capital' crowd were disappointed when Barker failed to appear. However Corkey, not wanting to leave the spectators disgruntled, ran the distance against time in a satisfactory 57 minutes.

The situation at Hackney Wick at the end of the year was summed up by the *Sporting Life* in its summary of the Christmas meetings in London:

> This Christmas time there are abundant attractions in the way of sport all over the country. London comes out strong – stronger than usual – notwithstanding that Hackney Wick has gone the way of the old Cope, the West London Grounds, and the famous resort at Battersea. One cannot much regret this. 'The Wick' was most unsuited for the purposes to which it was applied; and we have always consid-

Poster featuring the race between George Hazael and John Fleet in April 1871

ered it one of the most inscrutable Mysteries of London that such an uneven, hole-and-corner sort of place should have been selected for the decision of some of the most important pedestrian contests ever decided in the metropolis. Its neighbour, the Prince of Wales Ground at Bow, has now the East End to itself, and, admirably as it is conducted, is likely to long continue a favourite resort of London peds. Here on Tuesday next – Boxing Day – those well known clippers Teddy Mills and George Hazael are to run a mile and a half, for £50; and as there is another match, and Mr. Russell's half-mile and two miles walking handicaps, there will be plenty to keep the visitors wide awake during the afternoon. At the Amateur Athletic Club grounds at Lillie Bridge on Tuesday and Wednesday, Mr. Tom Senn offers £50.10s. for running handicaps at 130 yards and four miles, and a walking handicap of two miles; and as the prizes are more liberal than is nowadays usual in the metropolitan district, we anticipate a good attendance of those peds who do not fancy their chances for the richer prizes at Sheffield or the more distant Gateshead. The Star Grounds at Fulham, under the direction of Messrs. Fox and Broad, always a favourite resort, will doubtless have a liberal share of the patronage on the same two days to witness the 115 yards handicap, in which there is every prospect of some good racing.

A benefit for Bill Price

The benefit for William Price was the last meeting at Hackney Wick before it closed. It was held on 26 February 1872 when Price was living at 4 Wilton Terrace, Old Ford Road, Bethnal Green. Although the crowd numbered only 500, the meeting was well supported by pedestrians he had helped and encouraged throughout his time at the White Lion grounds as manager, trainer and landlord. Cups and money prizes were presented for every event. Virtually all the top walkers – Stockwell, Davison, Hatley, Hurley and Howes – were among the ten starters in the two miles walk handicap. In the three miles Hazael, the Mills brothers, Rogers and the new Scottish champion McCleary ran, while the 300 yard handicap was equally well supported. The final event, an 80 yards handicap for veterans, was won by 56-year-old Thompson from James Pudney.

The following month Parnell, proprietor of Hackney Wick, acquired the Prince of Wales Ground at Bow and his interest in pedestrianism and pugilism was transferred to this superior venue with Dick Lewis as manager. However few meetings were held and a golden era of professional middle and long distance running both in the metropolis and the north of England was gradually drawing to a close.

WILLIAM 'BILL' PRICE (1827–1872)
William Price of Mile End, London, was born in 1827. He first raced in 1847 at Leytonstone and in the following years was frequently found in minor events around London, usually in sprints but sometimes up to 440 yards. When Hackney Wick opened he raced there between 1857 and 1859. He was celebrated for training James Pudney from a novice to a champion long distance runner and equally celebrated for being the long time manager of Hackney Wick race-grounds. As a first-class trainer he cared for a group of pedestrians which included Teddy Mills, at various times one, six and ten miles champion; Sam Barker of Billingsgate, a good runner at distances from one mile to ten or fifteen; and Dick Lewis of Clerkenwell, who had a dread of his portrait being taken for reasons well known to sprinters at this time. Others in his stable were William Richards, George Beddow, George Davison, William Hatley, William Howes and Bob Rogers. John Levett, a contemporary of Price said that 'to see the old pedestrian counsellor, as he was called, sit at the table with his boys around him, you might fancy him the happiest man alive. Bill was called a pedestrian, but I think he was a little better with his head than his legs; he has run many races, and it used to be a moderate good thing to back him to run a quarter of a mile, on a fine day, and on a good road, in a minute, and I have seen him accomplish this arduous task. He is a quiet, civil, well-behaved man, and has done much towards the advancement of pedestrianism in London generally. People who know, do say of Price 'that he never speaks but he says something' and I am inclined to coincide in their opinion. He is so fond of Hackney Wick race-grounds that he has actually slept many nights close to it.' Price died at Colney Hatch on 20 November 1872 aged 45, leaving a wife and two children. He was buried in Bow Cemetery.

A nostalgic finale

By 1875 the White Lion was in the hands of Mr J. Elves, a keen supporter of pedestrianism who wished to see the grounds once again used for his favourite sport. He re-opened the running ground under the management of Edward Golder, a good class pedestrian from Canterbury who had run there many times, and was now proprietor of the Cambridge Castle public house in Essex Road, Bethnal Green. The first meeting, on Whit Monday 17 May 1875, included handicaps at 440 yards and a one mile, as well as a two miles walk and one-mile for novices. The following Saturday saw a good attendance for the finals. The new partnership announced a 120 yards handicap to be run in June on a path newly constructed through the middle of the ground. In addition it was

RICHARD 'DICK' LEWIS

Richard, known as Dick, Lewis from Clerkenwell, was a moderate pedestrian sprinter with a consuming passion for the sport. He was in Bill Price's stable of runners at Hackney Wick and also became involved in officiating there. When Deerfoot arrived in England, Lewis became his trainer and was present at his famous race at Fenner's in front of the Prince of Wales. When Bill Price gave up management of the White Lion Grounds at Hackney Wick, Lewis, who was living in Park Street where Baum owned a number of houses, took over from 1868 to 1869 and was instrumental in creating a 130 yard sprint track. In 1870 he brought the American Indian pedestrian Daillebout to England from Montreal and arranged a series of races at Lillie Bridge, Hackney Wick and finally in Scotland, where his protégé failed to live up to his potential so that Lewis had to cancel his last races. In 1872 he managed the Prince of Wales ground in Bow for Mr Parnell, the then owner of the White Lion. Shortly afterwards he became the proprietor of the Maid and Magpie public house in Oxford Street, Stepney, and continued to promote pedestrianism. He staged matches at the Agricultural Hall, Islington, including William Gale's walk of 1,000 miles. In 1878–1879 he rented the Wenlock Baths in Wenlock Street, City Road, North London, and put on a successful winter season of indoor meetings which included running, wrestling and displays of 'scientific boxing by all the leading professors of the present day.' In 1878 he donated a Champion Belt for the 26 hour walk won by William Howes, and around this time was closely involved in the craze for ultra-distance walking.

EDWARD GOLDER (1843–?)

Edward Golder from Canterbury, though residing in Bethnal Green, was born on 1 July 1843. Like so many middle distance pedestrians he commenced his career at Hackney Wick. His first race was at the 'Wick' on 2 June 1862 when he won a silver watch in a 600 yard handicap. After a few wins at Hackney he failed to receive decent handicaps and lost to most of the top runners of the decade at distances up to ten miles. He retired in 1871 but continued to train other pedestrians at Bow including at one time the successful walker Joe Stockwell. In 1875 while proprietor of the Cambridge Castle in Bethnal Green he took on the management of the Hackney Wick Grounds until it was sold for development. He made a brief but unsuccessful comeback in a race at Lillie Bridge in 1876.

advertised the ground 'has a good shower bath' and that Mr Hescott, a local long distance pedestrian would attend every day for both professionals and amateurs.

The *Sporting Life* wrote:

> This once famous sporting rendezvous was well patronised on Saturday last, upon which occasion Teddy Golder's 120 yards handicap was partially decided in most beautiful weather. Although the recently made sprint path somewhat altered the appearance of the old Wick, still the surroundings remained the same, and it is indeed questionable if any of the once shining lights of the pedestrian arena had been present they would have recognised any very marked difference in the famous enclosure wherein so many celebrated exponents of pedestrianism have earned themselves undying reputations. The path was of course rather heavy, which can hardly be wondered at, considering that Golder, despite his utmost exertions, was unable to render it fit by the time appointed; it is, however, only natural to expect that in the hands of such an experienced master everything will be rendered perfect in due course.

And regarding the June meeting commented:

> The fame attached to this once celebrated ground is more closely identified with long distance running than sprinting. This being so, the old Wick naturally looked more like its original self on Saturday last, when E. Golder's One Mile Handicap came on for a decision, amidst most beautiful weather and a good attendance of spectators. The old pagoda, in the vicinity of which runners in times gone by used to display their non-staying capabilities, was used as a dressing room.

Throughout July, 120-yard handicaps remained popular, with local personalities offering prizes. Sprinting had always been open to ringing in various forms and with the sport coming to Hackney Wick the practice unfortunately followed. The *Sporting Life* felt obliged to underline the fact that these tendencies had now been attracted to Hackney Wick where the touts were obtaining entry to the stripping room, 'the result of which is that only one man "tries," and the general public are "fleeced," owing to the "talent" refusing to "lay" the winner, and having no alternative, odds are freely accepted about the "dead-uns"'. Both at Hackney Wick and the Star Grounds great efforts were made to stop the practice. But there is no indication as to whether the respective managements had any success.

The August bank holiday Monday meeting was publicised as the grand

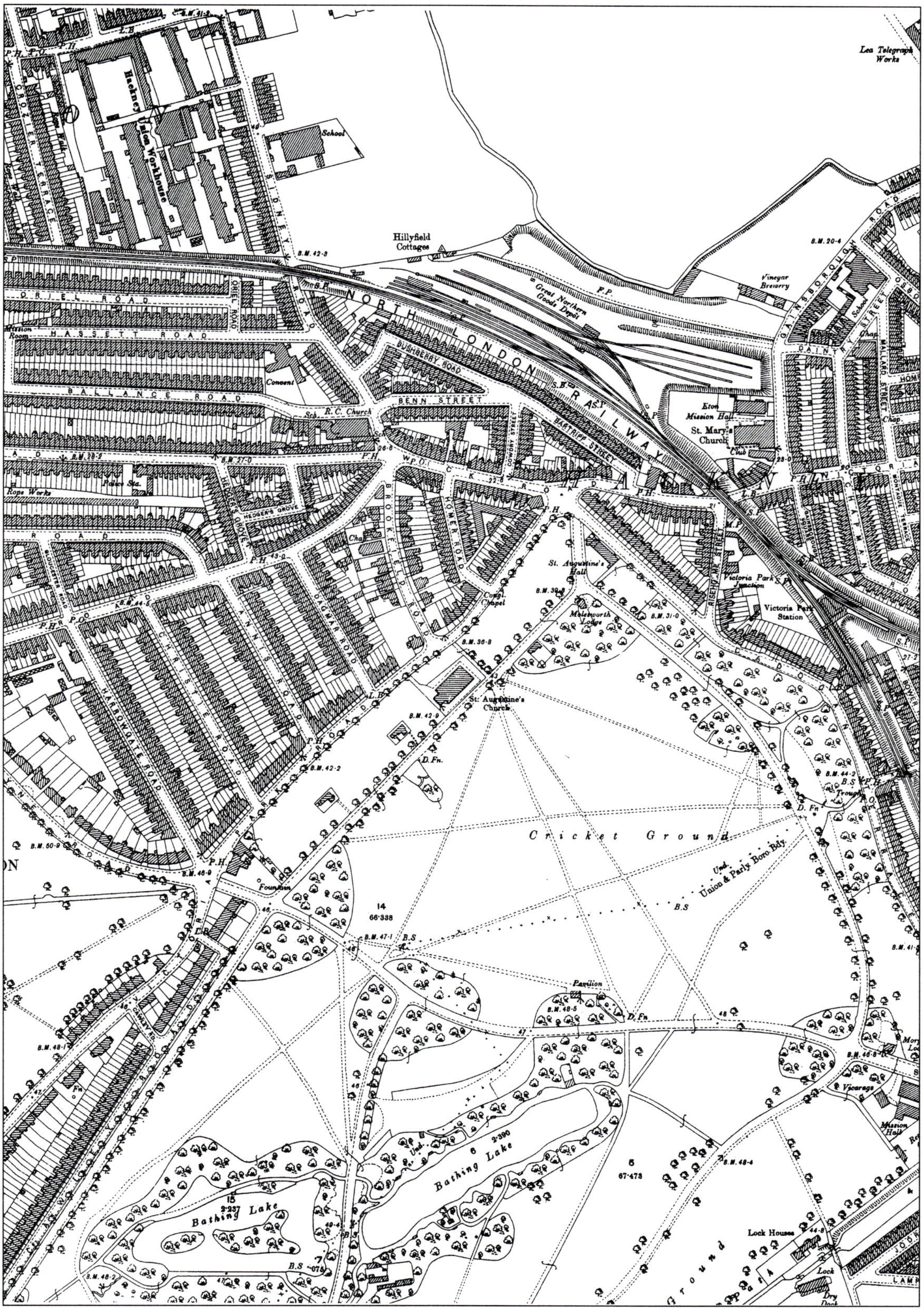

Map with Bartripp Street built over the running grounds at Hackney Wick

revival of Hackney Wick with Mr Elves stating his determination that the ground should once again be second to none for genuine races and valuable prizes. To encourage champions to run there he commissioned a new champion silver belt for a four miles handicap and added an additional £20 in prize money. Eighteen entries were received including James McLeavy, one of a new generation of pedestrians who performed well in the 1870s (scratch), Hazael (50 yards), Hescott, William Mills, Shrubsole and Brighton.

Pedestrian followers in the metropolis were soon buzzing with anticipation and could not help notice serious training was taking place at the various metropolitan grounds. Inquirers at the Star Grounds would have been told 'That's George Hazael (ten mile champion), in training for the Champion Belt at Hackney Wick on August Bank Holiday.' At Bow, they would be told 'That's Hescott, Sammon and Tester – all in for it,' while at the old Wick half a dozen or more, including William Mills were training hard. On the Monday before the race the scratch man, McLeavy, was training at Hackney Wick, having taken up quarters at the Mischief Wine Vaults in Oxford Street, Hackney. Shrubsole and Simpson were at it at Croydon, and everything bode fair for one of the greatest contested races ever seen in London.

This last big race at Hackney Wick attracted an expectant crowd of 3,000. The first mile was run in a nippy 4m.33s. by which time McLeavy had gained little on Hazael who caught Hescott just before half distance. At the finish Hazael won by 120 yards from McLeavy with Hescott a further 10 yards back.

Handicaps remained popular at Hackney Wick throughout August and September 1875. But October saw the last meeting after which commercial considerations took over and the land was sold for development. It was not long before Bartripp Street was built on the site. These days the ground is under a junction of the A12 dual carriageway.

Now there are only the memories ...

13

The Memories

In *THE W.G. ATHLETICS WEEKLY* dated 17 September 1904 under the title 'A FAMOUS OLD RUNNING GROUND' an admirer of some of the old 'uns wrote:

'The finest long distance runner that ever lived, that's what Shrubb is; knocked Sid Thomas' figures into a cocked hat, and licked old Jack White's world's record, which had stood for forty odd years, by over four seconds. There has never been, and there never will be, a runner to touch him.'

When my excitable young friend would let me get in a word, I inquired if he really believed that the runners of today are greatly the superiors to the pedestrians of thirty or forty years ago.

'Better – of course they're better,' was his emphatic reply. 'Look at their times; doesn't that prove it? Was there a man thirty years ago who would do the hundred in level time; or the mile in 4 min.12 secs. Or anything like it; or the quarter in 47 or 48 sec.; or the four miles under 19½ min., or run 11 miles 1,200 odd yards inside the hour? Not a bit of it. Why, the men nowadays know how to run, and they are as far ahead of these old chaps you are talking about as Fry is of George Parr, or Bosanquet of old Fuller Pilch.'

'Well, why is it so?' I asked mildly.

'Why? Why, because they're better men, that's the only reason; there's no actual reason why one man can run faster than another; he can, that's all.'

'Don't you think, then, that better training, better tracks, better conditions have anything to do with it?'

'Nothing to speak of. No, depend upon it, the runners and other athletes of today are far and away better than those of thirty or more years ago.'

* * *

The certainty, the cocksureness of the youngster was amusing – irritating, perhaps, to some people it might have been, but not to me, for I could make allowances for his inexperience and want of knowledge. Better than the men of half a lifetime ago, are they? – these new-fashioned runners who have pacemakers, and handicaps specially framed for them so that their very utmost powers may be called forth; and do not running tracks over which these new records are made give the record-breakers advantages and assistance which such grounds as the Prince of Wales ground, or that at Hackney Wick, or even the fine track at Copenhagen House, never gave to the old-time performers?

* * *

What a many fine races between the best men in England did that odd little running ground attached to the old White Lion Inn at Hackney Wick see? Races for which the gate-money was the actual reward, albeit the public announcements that a silver cup would be the prize of success or that £50 a side had been staked. And the gate money was something considerable too, for the White Lion was the Mecca of the East London sportsmen, and the Hackney Wick ground was one of the most celebrated in the metropolis. It was then a pleasant little spot surrounded by woods and open fields, 'quite out in the country' as the phrase goes, and the spacious stables of the 'Lion' were filled with the nags and traps of those who had driven five, ten perhaps twenty, miles. A shilling a head was the price of admission, and when such men as Deerfoot were running, or Teddy Mills and the 'Gateshead Clipper,' Jack White had a match on, the oblong ground was filled to overflowing.

* * *

And the track! Ye gods! The Shrubbs and Duffeys of today would turn up their noses in disgust and horror if asked to perform on anything similar. Yet there were one or two records made there, for all that; one in particular, that one which led to the mild argument between my youthful acquaintance and myself, that stood over forty years, in spite of the fact that such men as W.G. George and Sid Thomas have existed in the interim. A track, of which seven or eight laps went to the mile, pear-shaped, and with one end higher than the other; a track that seemed to have been prepared by the simple means of chucking down loads of cinders and ashes so as to form a path a few feet wide; a track which no one had taken the trouble to make even approximately level; that, in consequence, was covered with little depressions, in which gathered rain water after a severe downpour, a track undrained, unraked, and as little in conformity with the modern idea of a running track as such could very well be. Yet on this track it was Jack White that ran five miles in 24min. 40sec. and that during the course of a ten-mile run, setting up figures for four miles which remained the professional record for twenty-five years; for five miles, which Shrubb has just beaten; for six miles – 29min.50sec.;

and for seven miles, 34min. 45sec: the two latter being yet the world's records for either amateurs or professionals.

* * *

It was, too, on this wretched apology for a track that Teddy Mills, who old-timers will tell you was the finest ten-miler that ever put on a shoe, made his wonderful run of ten miles unpaced in 53min., 1min. 54½ sec. worse than the figures Watkins set up thirty-five years later; but then Mills did not have the assistance of runners and a cyclist to make the pace as did the other man.

* * *

'Ran like a machine; the prettiest looking runner that ever stepped.' That was Teddy Mills, ex-catsmeat man and pedestrian, who, although he could neither read or write, died worth £87,000, and owner of more than one prosperous licensed house. Whether he was better than Jack White is more than one would undertake to say. Up to three miles Mills was the better man; from four to ten miles White had his rival at his mercy, but beyond ten miles Mills again asserted himself. 'Never began to run until he was nearly beaten,' was the comment of one enthusiastic backer of Teddy Mills; and again, when to all appearances the little crack was done to the world, he would pull himself together and continue like a man just beginning a race. An odd family were the Mills; five brothers, all crack runners, four unable to read or write, and the only one with education, Dick, was the only one who did not ultimately become rich. Dealing in licensed houses was their business; and Charley, the only one, I believe, alive today, is the owner of over a dozen.

* * *

But Mills and White were not the only attractions at Hackney Wick; Martin, the man who ran the troupe of pedestrians, whose Saturday afternoon matches put money into his pocket and that of the proprietor of the White Lion, held a trump card in the person of Bennett, the alleged full-blooded Seneca brave, who was certainly the colour of the genuine Red Indian. He was sometimes got up in the costume of his character, and invariably finished his races with a blood-curdling war whoop, which the enthusiasts at Hackney Wick were ready to swear could have been emitted by none other than a genuine redskin. A marvellous runner was Deerfoot, one of the kind that seems to be made of steel, of unvarying pace, running the last mile of a ten-mile spin at the same rate as the first, and, in spite of the alleged wonderful superiority of the runner today, still the holder of the twelve-mile record of 1hr.2min.2½sec. Sid Thomas, magnificent runner as he was, could get no nearer to it than 40 odd seconds, while the closest any other professional ever reached was 1hr.7min.15sec. by George Hazael.

* * *

Hazael was another of Martin's troupe that performed at Hackney Wick, and such a quartet of long-distance men have probably never been seen on one ground within so short a period. A grand runner was George Hazael, although he was in his prime after Mills, Bennett and White had made their names. How many long-distance records he once held I should not like to say. Some even yet, stand to his name; while George Crossland is the only runner who ever covered a greater distance than twenty miles in two hours, the record set up by Hazael. Like the rest of his kind, Hazael made money by the barrelful when at the height of his fame, and, as did others, spent it as fast as he received it. Seventeen years after he was proclaimed champion long-distance runner of the world, he was earning a precarious living by the collecting and selling of bottles and scrap iron.

* * *

Then there were the short-distance men who travelled over the pear-shaped track on the little ground now covered with rows of houses. Bill Lang, the 'Crowcatcher,' the man who ran a downhill mile at Newmarket in 4min.2sec; a long, lean, ugly sort of runner, standing 5ft. 9in. or so, and as bony as a herring; Albison, of Bowlee, who could run any distance up to a mile, and in 1865, from the 66 yard mark, won a Sheffield Handicap of 215 yards; McKinstray, Richards (the Welshman), John Brighton (the Milk Boy), and one or two more. How many sweepstakes between Lang, Albison, McKinstray and Richards has the old ground seen? How many mile matches between Brighton and Mills? How many times has Hazael, tottering to the track like an octogenarian badly afflicted with corns or rheumatism, or both, astounded those who beheld him for the first time with the length, the vigour, and the ungainliness of his stride when the pistol had sent him on his long journey?

* * *

Many and varied are the scenes memory recalls; the terrifying boniness of Deerfoot, the marvellous action of Mills, the enormous stride of Lang, and the queer contortions of Jack Prowse, the walker – for walking, as well as running, matches took places at the Hackney Wick ground. There were other scenes, too, occasionally, that appealed more perhaps to the patrons of the noble art who frequented the ground than the lovers of pedestrianism pure and simple; as, for instance, when Gus Giovanella and Walter Medlicott, two hundred yards men, who, disagreeing over some particular of a match which had been arranged between them, agreed to settle their difference of opinion with nature's weapons in one corner of the ground, the battle terminating in favour of Giovanella. The latter was a fishmonger in the Mile End Road, and reputed able to do 100 yards in even time.

* * *

Good Friday was a red letter day at the old ground, for it was there that the old Cornwall and Devon Wrestling Society used to hold their great annual wrestling competitions. The wrestling took place on the turf in the centre of the ground, and the bitter rivalry between the men of the 'Delectable Duchy' and the Devonians was quickly awakened when such champions as Menear and Lewis, or Rundle and Tregellas, or Walter Slade commenced to make play. It was a grand sport, robbed of the brutality which disfigured the game as played in its native haunts, for the men were in their stockinged feet, and kicking would have been not only use-less, but dangerous.

* * *

Well, well! The day of such once-celebrated grounds as Hackney Wick and the Copenhagen fields is over, they have disappeared for ever, obliterated by bricks and mortar; but one should not belittle their usefulness or the prowess and performances of the men who appeared there. Doubtless the modern system is better, but I am by no means convinced that the men who played their parts under the disadvantages which appertained to such places are, or were, so greatly inferior, in spite of the weight of argument backed by figures, to the crack wearers of the running shoe today. Conditions and circumstances may have improved, but the men? No! they were as good then as now.

APPENDIX

Articles of Agreement

An example of the type of agreement in general use.

> **ARTICLES OF AGREEMENT**
>
> ARTICLES OF AGREEMENT, entered into this *7th* day of *March, 1863*, between *Edward Mills* and *William Lang* for £*25* a side. *Edward Mills* of *Bethnal Green* agrees to run *William Lang* of *Manchester* over *ten miles* for £*25* a side, on the *7th* day of *May, 1863*. £*5* a side is now in the hands of *William Price*, to be made into £*25* a side on the *30th* day of *April*, and *Thomas Wilson* to be the final stakeholder. The referee to be *James Pudney*. The men to start by mutual consent, and not off in 5 minutes, to go by the first report of a pistol; the referee to appoint a person to fire the pistol, and either man leaving his station before the pistol is fired, to be put back *two yards* each time. The men to be at their stations at *six* o'clock in the *evening*. In the event of any question arising which may not be provided for in these articles, the referee to have full power and authority to decide such question, his decision to be final and conclusive. This official to receive a sum of (usually 5 per cent) for officiating, such sum to be deducted from the winnings by the stakeholder, or in equitable proportions from each stake in event of a draw. No payment to be made if a forfeit take place. The stakeholder shall in any and every case be exonerated from all responsibility upon obeying the direction of the referee. Either party failing to comply with any or all of these articles to forfeit all moneys down.
>
>)
>) Signatures.
>
> Witness.

Training

There is no doubt that the performances of the pedestrians were quite extraordinary and that they could not have achieved the times that they did without a considerable amount of training about which little is recorded. According to Walter Thom in his book *Pedestrianism*, published in 1813, the famed Captain Barclay exercised from twenty to twenty-four miles a day. I have endeavoured to piece together some notes on training from the fragments of information that are available.

I have taken the following works; *British Rural Sports*, 1875 edition (first published in 1856), and *Athletic Sports and Manly Exercises*, 1864 edition both by 'Stonehenge', a pseudonym for J.G. Walsh; *A Few Practical Hints on Training*, 1876 by Harry Andrews and articles from *Sporting Life* entitled 'How to Train' by John Levett in 1861, and tried to put their comments on middle and long distance training into a context that would be understood by the athlete of today. Much of what was written was on the subject of diet, injuries and general well-being (sweating, meat-eating and purging), and has been omitted in this brief resumé.

Running was divided into three headings: sprinting, which generally included all distances up to 400 yards; medium distances, from one quarter to three quarters of a mile inclusive; and lastly, long distances, from one mile upwards.

At the commencement of training for sprints, the pedestrian should run from three to four hundred yards to get the requisite muscles in play.

Of the 'medium distances,' a quarter mile was considered the most difficult; *in fact, no more trying or exhausting race can be named, inasmuch as the pedestrian is obliged to run at top speed throughout, and therefore requires endurance as well as pace.* The pedestrian was advised to begin by running from half to three-quarters of a mile, according to the distance, and afterwards commence by going 300 yards or so at top speed.

The long distance pedestrians (with the notable exception of Deerfoot) were invariably light, wiry, and springy men, and it was suggested that the best distance to commence this class of running was a mile, gradually increasing the length of the day's spin according to the distance to be accomplished in the race. For the longer distances it was suggested that light weights were used by the athlete *providing they had good pluck and wind, as they get over the ground with less exertion to themselves, and consequently do not tire so soon!*

It was advised, however, that the full distance should not be run before the actual contest itself, *as doing so tires the pedestrian and makes him stale.* In no case were specific distances referred to for the long distance runner, although these pedestrians often completed high mileages in training. William Jackson when training for his one-hour record in 1845 occasionally ran as far as 40 miles in a day.

A typical day included an easy walk for half an hour before breakfast, adjudged to empty the small intestines of their last meal, and prepare the stomach for breakfast. It was generally accepted that breakfast should consist of beef or mutton with dry toast and tea without sugar or milk.

However, according to John Levett (an experienced pedestrian and trainer associating with many of the pedestrians of the day) breakfast would be a more flexible meal than was set out in a number of training manuals. *Every one to his own, maybe beef or mutton with dry toast, but also fresh eggs with buttered toast, or poultry and rabbit, accompanied by ale or tea. There would usually also be a large loaf on the table made with the addition of currants, sugar and eggs.*

Although there was much stress on meat in the diet there were some famous pedestrians who, according to Levett, rarely if ever ate meat. The favourite repast of mile champion Siah Albison was boiled currant dumpling, while the record-breaking sprinter George Seward ate pig's head and cabbage washed down with milk!

For an hour after breakfast, that is, until near eleven o'clock, the pedestrian was to amuse himself as he liked best, with billiards, or any other game; but at eleven he was to be ready dressed in his costume which should be of flannel throughout. For shoes he was advised there was nothing like dogskin upper-leathers, and a moderately thick sole for walking, or a much thinner one for running. Mention is also made of a few 'sparrow bill' nails in the sole or heel.

The main training of the day would be from eleven till two, or half-past two. When, according to Walsh, if the distance to be raced fell into the category of long distance it had to be done more than once every day, depending on the distance, at a good speed, and *with all the encouragement and excitement of competition with the trainer*, who would usually act as pace-maker for his athlete.

Levett talks of walking a mile to the training course at Hyde Park, Sheffield, where frequently between 100 and 150 pedestrians and trainers took their 'gallops' during the course of the morning. The athlete would almost always be accompanied by his trainer who would sometimes have a group of up to six or seven athletes under his care. It was considered that no man could train perfectly without the competitive presence of his trainer.

The athletes would walk seven or eight miles around the ground then run as far or farther, generally at the same pace. Others training for shorter distances would walk only a mile or so, and run one mile or even less, while others loitered about and did no work at all to be talked of. But it was the trainer who dictated the regime and if he was experienced he would know his man's capabilities and be able to bring him to the line as fit as those who had done an immense amount of work.

It was suggested that in training for long distances, at least five or six hours a day must be spent in walking and running, changing from one to the other as a relief during the early part of training, gradually going beyond the racing distance every day. If this was outside that which the athlete was deemed to be capable of, he was advised to do only just as much as his trainer thought he could perform without this effect. *Man, however, bears severe work in a wonderful manner; and if the appetite continues good and the sleep is sound, without dreaming or starting, the trainer need not be apprehensive that his man is doing too much.*

The result of such training resulted in even paced running and it was to be some years before this changed even though the advent of Deerfoot initially proved the benefits. Two golden rules to be observed were, never let the athlete *do his utmost until the actual race itself, and give him immediate rest for a few days if he appears jaded, as by this means his spirits will be revived and elasticity of body restored.*

At the end of training the athletes returned home for dinner, which would normally consist of a roast meat meal and a drink of ale. Later in the day another walk was often suggested.

In 1876 the middle and long distance pedestrian, Harry Andrews, wrote a small training manual. He described a typical day in much the same way as previous writers. Rise at no later than half-past six or seven, and after having a cold bath or a good sponging, and a rub down with a rough towel, a walk of one to two miles was recommended before breakfast at eight or half-past. Walking always made up a high proportion of the training mileage of pedestrians.

After resting for half an hour after breakfast a further easy two or three miles was recommended before repairing to the running ground between eleven and twelve o'clock for some practice at the training distance. His advice for middle and long distance runners had by now evolved to a regime recognisable by today's athletes. In training for the half mile, the full distance should be run about three times a week, and on other days varied by doing quarters (400 metres) and practising 100 yards in order to acquire speed. Training for the mile was similar to the half, but the mile was to be run only twice a week or three times if fit enough. When the distance was two, three, four or five miles, it was not to be run more than once a week, running quarters, half-miles and miles in proportion to the racing distance very much in line with today's methods. For the longer distances of six to ten miles his advice is more confusing, in that the distance to be traversed daily was to be between two to four miles. The full distance to be run not more than once a month, although once again walking would have taken up considerable part of training, indeed the time between tea and supper was to be occupied by further walking or strolling.

There are many athletes today who could learn from these early concepts of 150 years ago

STATISTICS

Matches for the champion cups and belts at middle and long distances

10 MILES Champion Cup presented by James Baum, Hackney Wick. July 1859

11.07.1859	CHARLES COOKE wins the first Champion Cup	
17.10.1859	JAMES ROWAN beats Charles Cooke	Cooke d.n.f.
26.12.1859	JAMES ROWAN beats William Jackson	58m.23s.
23.04.1860	JAMES ROWAN beats James Pudney	Pudney d.n.f.
17.09.1860	JOHN WHITE Cup forfeited by James Rowan	
12.01.1861	JAMES PUDNEY, Cup forfeited by John White	
10.06.1861	JAMES PUDNEY wins race for New Champion Cup but does not defend it	55m.28s.
23.09.1861	DEERFOOT beats Edward Mills, John Brighton, John White	54m.20s.
25.11.1861	DEERFOOT beats Sam Barker Deerfoot surrenders Cup	Barker d.n.f.
06.01.1862	JOHN BRIGHTON wins new contest for the Cup John Brighton forfeits Cup	Others d.n.f.
12.05.1862	SAM BARKER beats W. Jones	Jones d.n.f.
14.07.1862	WILLIAM LANG beats Sam Barker	52m.55¾s.
01.09.1862	WILLIAM LANG beats Edward Mills	Mills d.n.f.
13.10.1862	WILLIAM LANG beats Sam Barker	Barker d.n.f.
02.02.1863	WILLIAM LANG beats Edward Mills	52m.36s.
30.03.1863	WILLIAM LANG beats John Brighton	Brighton d.n.f.
00.07.1863	John White challenges for the Cup but finds no backer	
00.08.1863	Edward Mills forfeits his challenge on the death of his father	
00.10.1863	Edward Mills forfeits his challenge as he is unfit	
00.12.1863	JOHN WHITE, Cup forfeited by Willam Lang who is unfit	
08.02.1864	JOHN WHITE beats Edward Mills	Mills d.n.f.
25.04.1864	JOHN WHITE beats James Sanderson John White surrenders Cup	Sanderson d.n.f.
14.04.1865	EDWARD MILLS wins new contest for the Cup	54m.53s.
27.09.1865	Edward Mills retires and surrenders Cup	
26.12.1865	JAMES SANDERSON wins new contest for the Cup	
00.12.1866	JOHN FLEET, Cup forfeited by James Sanderson	

06.05.1867	JOHN FLEET beats William Lang	Lang d.n.f.
15.06.1867	WILLIAM LANG, Cup forfeited by John Fleet	
21.10.1867	WILLIAM LANG beats John Brighton	56m.40s.
17.02.1868	WILLIAM LANG beats John White	53m.50s.
17.03.1868	WILLIAM LANG retires but holds the Cup without challenge and becomes the outright holder.	

10 MILES Championship at the Prince of Wales Ground, Bow (Hackney Wick was closed due to the death of James Baum)

27.03.1869	GEORGE HAZAEL beats Edward Mills	Mills d.n.f.

10 MILES Champion Cup presented by Peter Warrador and Others, City Grounds, Manchester. May 1869, to be competed for at Hackney Wick or Manchester

15.05.1869	GEORGE HAZAEL beats James Sanderson and John Fleet at City Grounds, Manchester	55m.32½s.
07.08.1869	George Hazael surrenders Cup due to ill health	
08.11.1869	GEORGE HAZAEL beats a field of ten runners at Hackney	53m.55½s.
18.06.1870	GEORGE HAZAEL beats William Mills at Hackney	
17.12.1870	GEORGE HAZAEL beats John Fleet and Edward Golder at City Grounds, Manchester to become outright holder	

10 MILES Champion Belt presented by James Baum, Hackney Wick. May 1863 for a match between Deerfoot and the English Champions

11.05.1863	JOHN WHITE wins the Belt outright White also passed 3 miles in 14m.36s. BRITISH RECORD and 6 miles in 29m.50s. BRITISH RECORD	52m.14s.

6 MILES Champion Belt presented by James Baum, Hackney Wick. June 1860

11.06.1860	JOHN BRIGHTON wins the first Champion Belt	31m.30s.
20.08.1860	JOHN WHITE beats John Brighton	31m.57¾s.
25.02.1861	JAMES PUDNEY beats John White	31m.28s.
29.04.1861	JAMES ROWAN beats James Pudney	Pudney d.n.f.
10.06.1861	EDWARD MILLS, Cup forfeited by James Rowan (no backers)	
09.09.1861	EDWARD MILLS beats Deerfoot	32m.31½s.
11.11.1861	EDWARD MILLS beats John Brighton	Brighton d.n.f.
15.09.1862	EDWARD MILLS beats William Lang	31m.11s.

27.10.1862	EDWARD MILLS beats William Lang	30m.46s.
15.12.1862	EDWARD MILLS beats John White	30m.09s.
26.12.1862	EDWARD MILLS beats Deerfoot and becomes outright holder	30m.46½s.

---

5 MILES Champion Belt presented by James Baum, Hackney Wick. August 1863

17.08.1863	WILLIAM LANG wins first Champion Belt	25m.15s.
05.10.1863	WILLIAM LANG beats Edward Mills	Mills d.n.f.
30.11.1863	WILLIAM LANG beats James Sanderson and John White and becomes outright holder	25m.05s.

---

4 MILES Champion Belt presented by John Roberts, West London Cricket Ground, Brompton. May 1860

28.05.1860	JOHN BRIGHTON wins first Champion Belt	
27.08.1860	JOHN WHITE beats John Brighton	20m.1½s.
23.01.1861	WILLIAM LANG, Cup forfeited by John White (ill, no backers)	
00.00.1862	JOHN BRIGHTON, Cup forfeited by William Lang	
03.02.1862	JOHN BRIGHTON beats Sam Barker	20m.25s.
24.03.1862	JOHN BRIGHTON beats W. Jones and becomes outright holder	21m.56s.

---

4 MILES Champion Cup presented by Charles Wilson, Prince of Wales Ground, Bow. August 1863

10.03.1863	EDWARD MILLS wins first Champion Cup	
03.08.1863	HARRY ANDREWS beats Brunel and others	20m.50s.
24.08.1863	WILLIAM LANG beats Harry Andrews	20m.13s.
09.12.1863	JAMES SANDERSON beats William Lang	Lang d.n.f.
08.10.1864	JAMES SANDERSON asks for challengers before becoming outright holder	

ONE MILE Champion Belt presented by Thomas Hayes, Copenhagen Grounds, Manchester. August 1860

11.08.1860	SIAH ALBISON wins first Champion Belt	4m.24½s.
27.10.1860	SIAH ALBISON beats William Lang in BRITISH RECORD	4m.22¼s.
22.12.1860	CHARLES MOWER beats Siah Albison	4m.24s.
23.03.1861	SIAH ALBISON beats Charles Mower	4m.36s.
12.08.1861	SIAH ALBISON beats William Lang	Lang d.n.f.
18.01.1862	SIAH ALBISON beats John White (sprained ankle)	
31.05.1862	SIAH ALBISON beats John White (off 10 yards)	4m.31½s.

25.10.1862	SIAH ALBISON beats Charles Mower and becomes outright holder	4m.38 ½s.

ONE MILE Champion Cup presented by Thomas Warren, Snape Inn Grounds, Audenshawe. December 1862
(The terms of the Cup were somewhat strange in that Albison, as champion, was to be handicapped 20 yards for the first 12 months

06.12.1862	ALFRED DAY wins first Champion Cup	4m.30 ½s.
24.01.1863	PATRICK STAPLETON beats Alfred Day	4m.30¾s.
29.08.1863	WILLIAM LANG beats Patrick Stapleton	Stapleton d.n.f.
20.08.1864	Race for the Cup not reported	

ONE MILE Champion Silver Cup presented by George Martin, Royal Oak Grounds, Manchester. June 1864

25.06.1864	EDWARD MILLS beats William Lang, James Sanderson, Patrick Stapleton, James Nuttall and Siah Albison in BRITISH RECORD	4m.21s.

ONE MILE Champion Gold Cup presented by George Martin, Royal Oak Grounds, Manchester. August 1865

19.08.1865	WILLIAM LANG and WILLIAM RICHARDS dead heat in BRITISH RECORD	4m.17 ¼s.
28.08.1865	WILLIAM LANG beats William Richards in deciding race for the Cup	4m.22s.

ONE MILE Champion Gold Cup presented by John Cooper, Royal Oak Grounds, Manchester. June 1867

01.06.1867	ROBERT McKINSTRAY wins first Champion Cup	4m.30s.
22.07.1867	JOHN FLEET beats Robert McKinstray	4m.26s.
14.09.1867	JOHN FLEET beats William Lang and John Neary and becomes outright holder	4m.28¾s.

ONE MILE AND A QUARTER Champion Cup presented by Mrs Hannah Heathcote, Hyde Park Grounds, Sheffield and James Darley of the Green Dragon, Folgate. January 1862

20.01.1862	SIAH ALBISON wins first Champion Cup	
15.03.1862	WILLIAM LANG beats Siah Albison	5m.58s.
00.03.1862	William Lang forfeits Cup to Albison through illness	
05.05.1862	SIAH ALBISON beats John White	5m.33 ½s.

28.02.1863	JAMES SANDERSON beats Siah Albison, Edward Mills and John White to become outright holder	5m.36¼s.

ONE MILE AND A HALF Champion Cup presented by Mr Boothroyd, Ash Inn Grounds, Stockport. March 1862

08.03.1862	JOHN WHITE wins first Champion Cup	
14.06.1862	JOHN WHITE beats James Sanderson	6m.54s.
06.09.1862	JAMES SANDERSON beats John White In 1862 Mr.Boothroyd lost his licence to stage athletics at Stockport and became proprietor of the Hyde Park Grounds, Sheffield. He insisted that Sanderson defend the Cup at this new venue and Sanderson agreed, after some negotiation, on the condition that if he was the victor he would be able to keep the Cup.	
01.11.1862	JAMES SANDERSON receives a forfeit from Albison	
21.02.1863	JAMES SANDERSON beats Edward Mills and becomes outright holder	

ONE MILE AND A HALF Champion Gold Cup presented by John Cooper, Royal Oak Grounds, Manchester. February 1867

23.02.1867	JOHN FLEET wins first Champion Cup in BRITISH RECORD	6m.50s.
03.08.1867	ROBERT McKINSTRAY beats John Fleet	7m.3½s.
02.11.1867	ROBERT McKINSTRAY beats John Fleet	Fleet d.n.f.
07.03.1868	ROBERT McKINSTRAY beats James Sanderson	7m.4¼s.
23.05.1868	JOHN FLEET beats Robert Mckinstray and William Lang	7m.5¼s.
18.07.1868	JOHN FLEET beats William Lang	7m.3s.
12.12.1868	JOHN FLEET beats Albert Bird	7m.10s.
26.06.1869	JOHN FLEET beats John Neary and becomes outright holder	6m.57s.

---

7 MILES WALK Champion Belt presented by the proprietor of the Strawberry Hotel Grounds, Liverpool. October 1863

05.10.1863	JAMES MILES wins first Champion Belt	
18.01.1864	JAMES MILES beats James Allen in BRITISH RECORD	55m.00s.
24.03.1864	JAMES MILES beats William Hatley	Hatley d.n.f.
11.07.1864	JAMES MILES beats W. Myers	
25.07.1864	JAMES MILES beats James Allen in BRITISH RECORD	54m.30s.

13.02.1865	JAMES MILES beats William Hatley	Hatley d.n.f.
03.04.1865	JAMES MILES versus Henry Smalley; no decision as neither walker had walked fair heel and toe.	
15.05.1865	JAMES MILES beats Henry Smalley	
23.12.1865	WILLIAM SPOONER beats James Miles and the Belt is purchased by the proprietor for £14.	

THE 'WESTHALL FEAT' walking 21 miles in three hours

20.02.1858	CHARLES WESTHALL at Newmarket	2h.59m.01s.
26.12.1865	GEORGE TOPLEY at Brompton	2h.58m.24s.
06.12.1869	GEORGE DAVISON at Hackney Wick	2h.53m.34s.

British Records set at Hackney Wick

3 MILES			
14m.52.00s. (i)	James Rowan	29.04.1861	equals record of William Jackson, 31.05.1852
14m.50.00s. (i)	John White	15.12.1862	
14m.36.00s. (i)	John White	11.05.1863	
5 MILES			
24m.40.00s. (i)	John White	11.05.1863	
6 MILES			
29m.50.00s. (i)	John White	11.05.1863	
ONE HOUR			
11m.775y.	Edward Mills (2)	12.01.1863	
7 MILES WALK			
54m.10.00s.	George Davison	06.12.1869	
ONE HOUR WALK			
7m.1379y.	George Davison	06.12.1869	

All Comers Records set at Hackney Wick

ONE HOUR			
11m.790y.	Louis Bennett (US)	12.01.1863	known as 'Deerfoot'

British Records set elsewhere forming part of this history

HALF MILE			
1m.58.00s	Henry Allen Reed	11.04.1854	Halifax
1m.56.50s.	Robert McKinstray	20.05.1865	Manchester (Royal Oak)
1m.55.75s.	James Nuttall	31.08.1867	Manchester (Copenhagen)

THREE QUARTER MILE

3m.07.00s.	William Richards	30.06.1866	Manchester (Royal Oak)

ONE MILE

4m.28.00s.	Charles Westhall	26.07.1852	Islington (Copenhagen)
4m.28.00s	Thomas Horspool	28.09.1857	Manchester (Copenhagen)
4m.23.00s.	Thomas Horspool	12.07.1858	Manchester (Copenhagen)
4m.22.25s.	Siah Albison	27.10.1860	Manchester (Copenhagen)
4m.21.75s.	William Lang	11.07.1863	Manchester (Royal Oak)
4m.20.50s.	Edward Mills	23.04.1864	Manchester (Royal Oak)
4m.17.25s. (=)	William Lang	19.08.1865	Manchester (Royal Oak)
4m.17.25s. (=)	William Richards	19.08.1865	Manchester (Royal Oak)

2 MILES

9m.38.00s.	James Pudney	06.04.1852	Islington (Copenhagen)
9m.38.00s. (=)	John White	27.08.1860	Brompton
9m.20.00s.	John White	20.04.1861	Manchester (Copenhagen)
9m.11.50s.	William Lang	01.08.1863	Manchester (City)

3 MILES

14m.52.00s. (i)	William Jackson	31.05.1852	Islington (Copenhagen)

6 MILES

30m.04.00s. (i)	William Jackson	31.05.1852	Islington (Copenhagen)

ONE HOUR

11m.00y.	William Jackson	29.03.1852	Islington (Copenhagen)
11m.350y.	John Levett	28.08.1854	Liverpool
11m.370y.	John Brighton (2)	27.10.1862	Brompton
11m.871y.	William Lang	03.04.1863	Brompton

POLE VAULT

10ft. 8in.	Robert Musgrave	00.00.1861	Durham
10ft. 10½in.	Robert Musgrave	00.00.1863	Cockermouth

ONE MILE WALK

6m.23s. (i)	William Perkins	01.06.1874	Lillie Bridge

2 MILES WALK

14m.26s.	William Hatley	23.07.1866	Brompton

7 MILES WALK

57m.30.00s.	Charles Westhall	01.09.1848	Gravesend
57m.04.00s.	William Spooner	16.05.1853	Barking Road (Royal Oak)
55m.00.00s.	James Miles	18.01.1864	Liverpool (Strawberry)
54m.30.00s.	James Miles	25.07.1864	Liverpool (Strawberry)

All Comers Records set elsewhere forming part of this history

10 MILES

51m.26.00s. (i)	Louis Bennett (US)	03.04.1863	Brompton

ONE HOUR

11m.740y.	Louis Bennett (US)	27.10.1862	Brompton
11m.880y.	Louis Bennett (US)	23.02.1863	Brompton
11m.970y.	Louis Bennett (US)	03.04.1863	Brompton

British best performances 1860–1869

880 YARDS – sub 2 minutes

NUTTALL, James	1:55.75	31.08.1867	Manchester (Copenhagen)
FLEET, John	1:56.25e	31.08.1867	Manchester (Copenhagen)
McKINSTRAY, Robert	1:56.50	20.05.1865	Manchester (Royal Oak)
RICHARDS, William	1:57.50e	20.05.1865	Manchester (Royal Oak)
HEYWOOD, John	1:58.00e	20.05.1865	Manchester (Royal Oak)
WHITEHEAD, Harry	1:58.00	28.12.1867	Manchester (City)
ROGERS, Bob	1:58.75	15.06.1868	London (Brompton)
BINNS, P.D.	1:58.80e	15.06.1868	London (Brompton)
HEWITT, Frank	1:59.00	26.06.1869	Manchester (Royal Oak)
FLEET, John	1:59.00	14.08.1869	Sheffield (Hyde Park)
BIRD, Albert	1:59.20e	14.08.1869	Sheffield (Hyde Park)
ALBISON, Siah	1:59.75	23.09.1861	Manchester (Copenhagen)

ONE MILE – sub 4 minutes 30 seconds

LANG, William	4:17.25	19.08.1865	Manchester (Royal Oak)
RICHARDS, William	4:17.25	19.08.1865	Manchester (Royal Oak)
MILLS, Edward	4:20.50	23.04.1864	Manchester (Royal Oak)
MILLS, Edward	4:21.00	25.06.1864	Manchester (Royal Oak)
LANG, William	4:21.25e	25.06.1864	Manchester (Royal Oak)
LANG, William	4:21.75	11.07.1863	Manchester (City)
LANG, William	4:22.00	28.08.1865	Manchester (Royal Oak)
ALBISON, Siah	4:22.25	27.10.1860	Manchester (Copenhagen)
LANG, William	4:22.50e	27.10.1860	Manchester (Copenhagen)
FLEET, John	4:23.50	10.04.1868	Manchester (City)
MOWER, Charles	4:24.00	22.12.1860	Manchester (Copenhagen)
ALBISON, Siah	4:24.50	11.08.1860	Manchester (Copenhagen)
McKINSTRAY, Robert	4:24.50e	19.08.1865	Manchester (Royal Oak)
FLEET, John	4:26.00	22.07.1867	Manchester (Royal Oak)
STAPLETON, Patrick	4:26.00	27.09.1862	Manchester (Copenhagen)
WHITE, John	4:26.50e	11.08.1860	Manchester (Copenhagen)
SANDERSON, James	4:26.75e	11.07.1863	Manchester (City)
STAPLETON, Patrick	4:27.00	28.05.1864	Manchester (Royal Oak)

SANDERSON, James	4:27.25	17.06.1865	Manchester (Royal Oak)
McKINSTRAY, Robert	4:27.50e	10.04.1868	Manchester (City)
WHITE, John	4:28.00i**	20.04.1861	Manchester (Copenhagen)
DAY, Alfred	4:28.50e	27.09.1862	Manchester (Copenhagen)
SANDERSON, James	4:28.50i*	01.08.1863	Manchester (City)
FLEET, John	4:28.75	14.09.1867	Manchester (Royal Oak)
ROGERS, Bob	4:29.00	18.05.1868	London (Brompton)
NUTTALL, James	4:29.40e	18.05.1868	London (Brompton)
BIRD, Albert	4:29.50	22.03.1869	Sheffield (Hyde Park)
NEARY, John	4:29.75e	14.09.1867	Manchester (Royal Oak)

* James Sanderson led at one mile in Lang's record-breaking two mile race
** John White led at one mile in his record-breaking two mile race

TWO MILES – sub 10 minutes

LANG, William	9:11.50	01.08.1863	Manchester (City)
SANDERSON, James	9:12.50e	01.08.1863	Manchester (City)
WHITE, John	9:20.00	20.04.1861	Manchester (Copenhagen)
SANDERSON, James	9:25.00e	20.04.1861	Manchester (Copenhagen)
SANDERSON, James	9:35.50	09.11.1861	Manchester (Copenhagen)
MILLS, Edward	9:37.00	26.12.1864	London (Hackney Wick)
WHITE, John	9:38.00	27.08.1860	London (Brompton)
WHITE, John	9:44.00i***	15.12.1862	London (Hackney Wick)
LANG, William	9:51.00	12.10.1861	Manchester (Copenhagen)
FLEET, John	9:52.00	04.03.1867	London (Hackney Wick)
MILLS, William	9:54.80i*	08.11.1869	London (Hackney Wick)
BRIGHTON, John	9:56.00e	12.10.1861	Manchester (Copenhagen)
McKINSTRAY, Robert	9:57.00	31.03.1866	Manchester (Royal Oak)
HAZAEL, George	9:59.00i**	23.10.1869	London (Bow)

* William Mills led at two miles in a race for the Ten Miles Cup
** George Hazael led at two miles in a Ten Miles Champion Race
*** John White led at two miles in a race for the Six Miles Belt

THREE MILES – sub 15 minutes

LANG, William	14:36.00i**	11.05.1863	London (Hackney Wick)
WHITE, John	14:36.00i**	11.05.1863	London (Hackney Wick)
BRIGHTON, John	14:48.25	16.09.1865	Liverpool (Strawberry Hotel)
WHITE, John	14:50.00i*	15.12.1862	London (Hackney Wick)
ROWAN, James	14:52.00i***	29.04.1861	London (Hackney Wick)
MILLS, Edward	14:52.00ie*	15.12.1862	London (Hackney Wick)

* John White led at three miles in a race for the Six Miles Belt, Mills one yard behind
** John White and William Lang led at three miles in a race for the Ten Miles Belt
*** James Rowan led at three miles in a race for the Six Miles Belt

FOUR MILES – sub 20 minutes 30 seconds

WHITE, John	19:35.00i**	11.05.1863	London (Hackney Wick)
LANG, William	19:35.00i**	11.05.1863	London (Hackney Wick)
WHITE, John	20:01.00i*	15.12.1862	London (Hackney Wick)
MILLS, Edward	20:01.00i*	15.12.1862	London (Hackney Wick)
WHITE, John	20:01.50	27.08.1860	London (Brompton)
LANG, William	20:13.00	24.08.1863	London (Bow)
MILLS, Edward	20:18.00	24.02.1862	London (Hackney Wick)
BRIGHTON, John	20:25.00	03.02.1862	London (Brompton)
McKINSTRAY, Robert	20:28.40i***	27.12.1869	London (Hackney Wick)

* John White and Edward Mills level at four miles in a race for the Six Miles Belt
** John White and William Lang level at four miles in a race for the Ten Miles Belt
*** Robert McKinstray led at four miles in a five miles sweepstake

SIX MILES – sub 31 minutes 30 seconds

WHITE, John	29.50.00i*	11.05.1863	London (Hackney Wick)
LANG, William	29:51.00i*	11.05.1863	London (Hackney Wick)
MILLS, Edward	30.09.00	15.12.1862	London (Hackney Wick)
MILLS, Edward	30.32.00	26.12.1862	London (Hackney Wick)
MILLS, Edward	30:46.00	27.10.1862	London (Hackney Wick)
MILLS, Edward	30:46.50	26.12.1862	London (Hackney Wick)
WHITE, John	30:57.75	20.08.1860	London (Hackney Wick)
MILLS, Edward	31:11.00	15.09.1862	London (Hackney Wick)
SANDERSON, James	31:22.00	13.01.1866	Oldham (Higginshaw)
PUDNEY, James	31:28.00	25.02.1861	London (Hackney Wick)
WHITE, John	31:29.00i**	17.02.1868	London (Hackney Wick)
LANG, William	31:29.50i**	17.02.1868	London (Hackney Wick)
BRIGHTON, John	31:30.00	11.06.1860	London (Hackney Wick)

* John White was just ahead of William Lang at six miles in the race for the Ten Miles Belt
** John White was just ahead of William Lang at six miles in the race for the Ten Miles Cup

TEN MILES – sub 57 minutes

WHITE, John	52:14.00	11.05.1863	London (Hackney Wick)
MILLS, Edward	52:24.00	09.03.1863	London (Hackney Wick)
LANG, William	52:36.00	02.02.1863	London (Hackney Wick)
LANG, William	52:46.00e	02.03.1863	London (Hackney Wick)
LANG, William	52:55.75	14.07.1862	London (Hackney Wick)
LANG, William	53:50.00	17.02.1868	London (Hackney Wick)
HAZAEL, George	53:55.50	08.11.1869	London (Hackney Wick)
MILLS, William	53:57.00e	08.11.1869	London (Hackney Wick)
MILLS, Edward	54:30.00	18.03.1861	London (Hackney Wick)
BRIGHTON, John	54:37.00i*	17.11.1866	Manchester (Royal Oak)
MILLS, Edward	54:53.00	15.04.1865	London (Hackney Wick)

PUDNEY, James	55:28.00	10.06.1861	London (Hackney Wick)
HAZAEL, George	55:32.50	15.05.1869	Manchester (City)
PARK, William	56:19.75	03.10.1868	Glasgow
LANG, William	56:40.00	21.10.1867	London (Hackney Wick)

* John Brighton led at ten miles in a race to run 11 miles in the hour

BIBLIOGRAPHY

Periodicals

Bell's Life in London
Illustrated Sporting and Dramatic News
Illustrated Sporting News
Land and Water
Sporting Life
The 'W.G.' Athletic Weekly

Books

Annals of Thames Hare and Hounds, The, 1968
Athletic Sports and Manly Exercises, 'Stonehenge', 1864
Athletics, H.H. Griffin, 1898
Athletics, Montague Shearman, 1898
British Rural Sports, 'Stonehenge', 1875
Fifty Years of My Life in the World of Sport, Sir John. D. Astall, 1894
Fifty Years of Progress 1880–1930, H.F. Pash (Ed.), 1930
Guide to British Track and Field Literature 1275–1968, The, Peter Lovesey & Tom McNab, 1969
Hackney and Stoke Newington Past, Isobel Watson, 1998
'House' on Sport, The, W.A. Morgan (Ed.), 1898
Kings of Distance, The, Peter Lovesey, 1968
Long Distance Record Book, The, Andy Milroy, 1988
Official Centenary History of the AAA, Peter Lovesey, 1979
Powderhall and Pedestrianism, D.A. Jamieson & W.A.K. Johnston, 1943
Race Walking, Hugh W. Innes, 1909
Runners & Walkers, John Cumming, 1981 (USA)
Spiked Shoe, The, J. Bull, 1959 (Australia)
Statistical History of UK Track & Field Athletics, A, Andrew Huxtable, 1990
Ultra-Marathoning, Tom Osler & Ed Dodd, 1979 (USA)

Other sources

London Borough of Hackney, Archives Department
London Borough of Tower Hamlets, Local History Library

London Borough of Islington, Central Reference Library
London Metropolitan Archives

Acknowledgements

Thanks are due to:

Sebastian Coe for kindly finding time to write the Foreword.

Peter Lovesey, for his enthusiasm for the project, reading and commenting on the manuscript, and allowing me to use much of his extensive research into pedestrianism.

John Goulstone, for allowing me to use much of his extensive research into pedestrianism and spending many hours correcting the manuscript.

Stan Long, for information on the Gateshead pedestrians John White and James Rowan.

John Andrews, for providing extracts from Harry Andrews' book *A Few Practical Hints on Training for Amateurs*, 1876.

Ronald White for allowing me to photograph the Ten Mile Belt. Carol Archer, Kevin Kelly and David Terry for their help in a variety of ways.

Finally, and most importantly, I would like to thank my wife Pam for her support, help and understanding while I devoted so much of the last three years to completing this book.

Author's note

If anyone reading this book can contribute further information on the pedestrians featured or knows of relatives or the whereabouts of any of the trophies, I would be pleased to hear from them at 36 Ravenscourt Grove, Hornchurch, Essex, RM12 6HS.